CW00338254

Judaism:

Basis – Past – Present – Future
Part 1

Judaism:

Basis - Past - Present - Future
Part 1

Manfred Davidmann

Social Organisation Limited

Published by Social Organisation Limited
30-34 New Bridge Street, London, EC4V 6BJ, United Kingdom
Contact: books@socialorganisation.eu
www.socialorganisation.eu

Copyright   ©   Manfred Davidmann 1978-2007

All rights reserved worldwide.

Manfred Davidmann has asserted his moral right to be identified as the author of this book.

Except for brief quotations in a review, this book, or any part thereof, may not be reproduced, stored in or introduced into a retrieval system, or transmitted, in any form or by any means, electronic, mechanical, photocopying, recording or otherwise, without the prior written permission of the copyright owner Estate of Manfred Davidmann (books@socialorganisation.eu).

A major review and analysis by Manfred Davidmann of the essential but little-known social laws and social system of the Pentateuch (Torah) and of the fundamental scientific Social Cause-and-Effect Relationship which applies to all people everywhere at all times, and of Jewish history, finding the causes of subsequent defeat of the people and loss of country. The author provides a fully documented record of previously undiscovered material in the Talmud about Hillel. And he describes the struggles within Judaism which accompanied the birth of Rabbinical Judaism.

Manfred Davidmann provides the required background knowledge of the essential core of Jewish belief and practice for drawing the only possible conclusion that the procedure called 'Prosbul' is contrary to the laws and intent of the Torah. He then annuls the Prosbul.

He shows that there are two separate root causes of antisemitism which one would normally not consider. And he proves that the right to the land in which one lives, that is the strength and success of a people, depends on how people behave towards each other.

Published by Social Organisation Limited in 2018

ISBN 978-0-85192-060-3

Printed and bound by Witley Press Ltd
24-26 Greevegate, Hunstanton, Norfolk, PE36 6AD, United Kingdom

Cover design by Dr. Angelika Schaumberg

CONTENTS

"It is the social laws of the Torah which in effect state that all are equal, that no person may exploit another or oppress so as to exploit. All have the right to be free and independent masters of their own fate and there has to be a system of social security which guarantees not just freedom from need but also protection against loss of material and spiritual independence. In effect, oppression can be and has to be resisted, struggled against and opposed."

"What we have in the Torah is a comprehensive and fair social system. So why are the social laws and the social system of the Torah not being applied under present-day conditions?"

Manfred Davidmann

In accordance with Manfred Davidmann's will and wishes his works are published in form of books.

Manfred Davidmann is the author of this book's content (Chapter 2 to Chapter 6).

These chapters were selected from Manfred Davidmann's publications on the solhaam.org website, considering as well the author's notes about this book's content and title.

Following the author's wording and style, the description on page 4, 'Contents', 'Overview' (Chapter 1) and the text for the cover's back page have been added in order to complete the book for publication. Additions to the author's original text are stated and marked *.

In loving memory of Manfred Davidmann who taught people worldwide to live by the social laws and social system of the Pentateuch which underlie Judaism, Christianity, Islam and Democracy.

Dr. Angelika Schaumberg, Social Organisation Limited, 2018

Chapter 1

Overview

2 FREEDOM NOW, FREEDOM FOR EVER

2.1 Struggle for Freedom: The Social Cause-and-Effect Relationship

Manfred Davidmann begins by outlining the social and economic environment in which we live, the problems of today, and then discusses uses and misuses of religion in such circumstances. He then outlines the meaning and significance of Judaism, of the essential but little-known social and economic laws of behaviour, sketched within the environment in which we live and work.

The relevant social laws and the social system of the Torah are described and explained as a self-contained and complete system which prevents people being exploited through need if they fall on hard times and which prevents ownership being concentrated in the hands of a few. The system enables people to live good and satisfying lives in a just and fair society which guarantees freedom and equality. The laws of redemption, for example, are shown to be leasehold laws designed to maintain an equal and fair distribution of income and wealth among the population as a whole. Biblical law underlies all freedom.

Most of the problems now threatening the survival of humankind are caused by the selfish interests of those who are attempting to organise and run society for their own gain. On the other hand are those who resist and struggle on behalf of the interests and benefit of the community at large.

The two sides encourage and spread the kind of behaviour which enables them to gain and keep their own type of society: dictatorship and exploitation on the one hand, freedom and good life on the other.

Hence it is vitally important to know what kind of behaviour serves what kind of ends. If we wish to gain freedom and remain free then we need to know which kind of behaviour gives us strength, enables us to co-operate with each other, helps us to raise the quality of life for all, helps us to lead good and satisfying lives.

It is this which makes the Social Cause-and-Effect Relationship so important. It is stated in the Torah as a fundamental scientific law which applies to all people at all times no matter where they live or what they believe in or what their state of development.

The prophets knew and understood the Social Cause-and-Effect Relationship and how it operates when they predicted what would happen as a result of the way people behave.

Knowledge and understanding of the Social Cause-and-Effect Relationship give us an understanding of how what happens depends on people's behaviour, and a greater understanding of what determines the pattern of events.

Manfred Davidmann details the Social Cause-and-Effect Relationship in biblical language as well as in plain English, detailing the consequences of either following the laws or else of ignoring them.

The legislation shows how people can protect themselves against losing their freedom and how to gain even greater freedom. It opens the door to freedom, to a good life and to government which looks after the interests of its people.

Within Jewish law is described the next step ahead towards complete freedom. The strength of individuals and of countries, and even more so the survival of humankind under present conditions, depend on the application of these Torah laws.

2.2 History Speaks: Monarchy, Exile and Maccabees

This is a review and analysis of Jewish history, more particularly of what is known about King Solomon's reign and that of the Maccabean dynasty, finding the causes of the defeat of the people and loss of country.

Manfred Davidmann looks at the social conditions and the trend of events in relation to the type and style of government.

Also discussed are the warnings of the prophets in relation to the Social Cause-and-Effect Relationship.

Much has been written about King Solomon and his glorious reign, his wisdom and his riches. But Jewish Scriptures and other ancient sources look at his reign from the point of view of the people over whom he ruled and tell a different story. Oppression increased during Solomon's reign and some of the country had already been lost by the time he died.

A similar pattern of events can be seen under the Maccabean (Hasmonean) dynasty, given here in considerable detail.

Manfred Davidmann succeeds in opening our eyes to what actually happened, a matter of biblical archaeology. Jewish history shows that each time the country was lost, it was lost in accordance with the Social Cause-and-Effect Relationship.

The prophets warned rulers, establishment and people in advance about their behaviour. But the prophets were not listened to. And loss of country, expulsion and persecution occurred as predicted by the prophets in accordance with the Social Cause-and-Effect Relationship.

We see a consistent pattern which is paralleled by current events and trends. But it is possible and utterly important to learn the lessons of the past. We do not have to repeat the same mistakes.

2.3 At the Time of Jesus, This is What Actually Happened in Israel: The Truth about Hillel and his Times

Here Manfred Davidmann records a breathtaking journey of discovery through events which shaped today's world and today's problems. This is factual and conclusive, a documented statement of what Jewish writers then recorded about what had happened at about the time of Jesus to Jewish belief and practice, an exercise in biblical archaeology.

Fascinating is Manfred Davidmann's fully documented record of previously undiscovered material in the Talmud about Hillel and his time. It is eye-opening to discover the truth about Hillel, about his origin and background, about his political beliefs, about the decisive struggle going on within Judaism at that time.

Torah law provides and ensures equality, independence, freedom from oppression and exploitation, and a good life of high quality. The Jewish establishment argued against such laws so as to expose the people to exploitation through need. The resulting struggle changed Judaism, determined the fate of the Jewish people and gave rise to Christianity.

Manfred Davidmann includes a clear, concise and factual summary statement outlining what the Talmud is and how it came to be written, describing its relative authority and that of its components.

Included also is a similar statement about the Halachah (code of Jewish rabbinical law). Manfred Davidmann shows how Torah, Talmud and Halachah are related to each other and states their relative scope and authority.

Also recorded at the time were extremely relevant statements about what a future generation would have to do to reverse the pattern of events and to establish a good life of high quality for all.

2.4 One Law for All: Freedom Now, Freedom for Ever

Manfred Davidmann here uncovers the innermost secrets of the Talmud, secrets which were buried and hidden there and whose existence had been forgotten for close to 2,000 years until Manfred Davidmann published his work.

This is again a fully documented record of previously undiscovered material in the Talmud, about the decisive struggle then going on within Judaism.

The central theme which emerges is again that Torah law provides and ensures equality, independence, freedom from oppression and exploitation, and a good life of high quality. The Jewish establishment argued against such laws so as to expose the people to exploitation through need.

The resulting struggle changed Judaism, determined the fate of the Jewish people and gave rise to Christianity and it is this struggle which is exposed here to the light of day.

Manfred Davidmann's work is factual and conclusive, a documented statement of what Jewish writers then recorded about what had happened at about the time of Jesus to Jewish belief and practice, an exercise in biblical archaeology.

The Talmud contains key social and historical information carefully written by those who decided to record what was happening to Jewish belief and practice in the time just preceding and during the origin and formation of Christianity. It is these records which later evolved into the Talmud.

Here Manfred Davidmann brings us into contact with the work and mind processes of those who 2,000 years ago exerted their combined mental powers to record how and why their country and freedom had been lost and how and why religious belief and practice changed fundamentally.

These are important records and they took steps to ensure that what they recorded would not be changed or obliterated, distorted or misrepresented. They did so to enable a future generation to reverse the trend of events and move towards a good life of high quality for all.

You can see here how the Talmud refers in one detailed example to early Christians and their beliefs. You can see codes used by the early writers of the Talmud to ensure that later generations could not distort or misrepresent the message which was really there. And you can see how they linked relevant stories and arguments in the same way as was used contemporaneously by Christian gospel writers.

We see a religious establishment which to an increasing extent supported the secular establishment line and weakened the application of basic Jewish law.

There are two sides, two policies. 'Power and wealth for a few at the expense of the many' on the one side, 'Freedom, independence and a good life for all' on the other.

So controversies arose about the meaning of Jewish law, about how and whether certain Torah laws should be observed.

They argued in religious terms about social and political policies. You can see here, for example, how the Talmud records

> That wealth and fund-raising were more important to Beth Hillel than learning and wisdom

> The bitter feelings of ordinary people about what establishment scholars were doing to Torah and people

> That Beth Hillel lost the argument that the law followed them. The argument clearly and without any doubt concludes that the law follows Beth Shammai.

In the Talmud are also recorded earlier decisions which applied Torah law to everyday matters which had not been written down before to this extent. The Talmud is thus also a record of what previously was oral law.

But some scholars attempted to provide their own statements with an authority they did not otherwise have. They did so by claiming that they were stating laws given verbally to Moses about 1,500 years earlier which had been handed down verbally over this period without having been written down.

You can see here how this practice was scathingly condemned in the Talmud.

Also recorded at the time were statements about what a future generation would have to do to reverse the pattern of events so as to establish a good life of high quality for all.

One of these, that about R Johanan b. Zakkai and his disciples, is here shown to state that the Torah is to be taught to all who are unaware of its social laws and social system. The observance of these is to be re-established.

There is a striking similarity between events then and today.

Success and strength of a community depend on observing the social laws and social system. So Manfred Davidmann states that observance of the social laws and social system of the Torah needs to be re-established under present conditions (see Policies for a Better Future)

3   Jewish Belief and Practice

Here Manfred Davidmann provides the required background knowledge of the essential core of Jewish belief and practice and for drawing the only possible conclusion: The procedure called 'Prosbul' is invalid. So he annuls it in part 7. This decision will have far-reaching effects on what Jewish people believe and practice.

In part 1, Rab Judah's story is used to illustrate Maimonides' ruling that most of what is taught at present as valid 'oral law' is in fact invalid. The term 'oral law' here refers to Talmudic laws supposedly given at Sinai to Moses but not written down.

Part 2 describes the conflict at the time of Solomon between the Jewish establishment and the social laws of the Torah.

In part 3, Manfred Davidmann explains the social Cause-and-Effect relationship. The Torah states the social Cause-and-Effect relationship, clearly defining this as a fundamental scientific law which applies to all people everywhere at all times. The consequences of not following the social laws and the social system of the Torah are disastrous and unavoidable until behaviour changes.

Parts 4 and 5 clearly state the relative importance and authority of the Torah, the Talmud ('oral' law) and the Halachah (rabbinical decisions). You will find here short concise statements in plain and meaningful language, describing what Talmud and Halachah are, and what you would want to know about them and about their relative authority and significance.

In part 6 the Torah's essential social laws and its social system are outlined. These protect people against oppression and exploitation and they are stated in the Torah as human rights. They are outlined with respect to (a) wealth and (b) social security.

In Part 7, Manfred Davidmann proves that the Prosbul is contrary to the laws and the intent of the Torah, and that Hillel had no authority for making such a ruling. Manfred Davidmann then annuls the Prosbul.

At the core of the Torah are its social laws and its social system. The Cause-and-Effect relationship clearly shows that they have to be followed to ensure a good life of high quality for individuals and to ensure the survival of humankind on this planet under present conditions.

The events of history confirm the operation of the Cause-and-Effect relationship and people need to be made aware of the Torah's social laws and social system and of the need to follow them.

4 Causes of Antisemitism

Here Manfred Davidmann shows that there are two separate root causes of antisemitism, and these he describes clearly.

These two distinct causes one would normally not consider in relation to antisemitism. But one can quickly see that what is usually talked about or considered in relation to antisemitism are only side-effects and symptoms.

The conclusion is that while one of the causes is of international concern and can be remedied by increasing peoples' awareness, the other is under the control of the Jewish people and can be remedied from within.

5   The Right to the Land of Israel

Manfred Davidmann proves that the right to the land in which one lives, that is the strength and success of a people, depends on how people behave towards each other. And this applies to all.

The author shows that the history of the Jewish people provides a clear and convincing example.

Jewish people have been attacked and persecuted over 3,400 years because the Torah states the behaviour which gives strength, which provides a good life of high quality, which ensures independence and freedom from oppression and exploitation.

Jewish people survived because this knowledge about behaviour is essential for the survival of human ways of living on this planet. Now in Israel for the third time they should be establishing a way of living together based on equality, freedom and independence, a good life of high quality for each one, providing an example to be followed by other people.

The Torah clearly states that all must be free and equal, that no one may oppress or exploit another. Manfred Davidmann points out that the Torah records as a scientific law that the consequences of one's behaviour are inescapable. But Jews twice lost their country, were driven out of Israel, because they were unaware of the inevitability with which their own establishment was causing their downfall.

The same process is taking place today. The people are weakening to the point where expulsion and later persecution already appear possible and almost likely. The only way to change the pattern of events and reverse the trend is to change behaviour. The Jewish people need to ensure that the social laws and social system of the Torah are applied, and this means putting pressure on the secular and religious establishment to do so. It is the people who need to put pressure on their establishment to achieve this.

Manfred Davidmann points out that nowadays a new factor has entered into the equation. The impact of technology, of

20

increasing speed of transport and communication, the accelerating speed of change, make it essential and urgent that the social laws and social system of the Torah be followed and applied. Otherwise the planet will become uninhabitable for human beings.

6   About the Author

Chapter 2

FREEDOM NOW, FREEDOM FOR EVER

Overview

This series of four reports together cover * the social laws and social system of the Pentateuch (Torah) and the fundamental scientific 'Social Cause-and-Effect Relationship' which it describes.

The essential but little-known core social laws and social system of the Pentateuch underlie all freedom and liberty.

See chapter 2.1: **'Struggle for Freedom: The Social Cause-and-Effect Relationship'**

Much is known about King Solomon's reign and about the fundamental changes which took place during the Maccabean dynasty to Jewish belief and practice, social conditions and government. Oppression increased both during Solomon's reign and under the Maccabean (Hasmonean) dynasty. Scriptures and other ancient sources look at events from the point of view of the people over whom they ruled. History shows that each time the country was lost, it was lost in accordance with the Social Cause-and-Effect Relationship.

See chapter 2.2: **'History Speaks: Monarchy, Exile and Maccabees'**

The Social Cause-and-Effect Relationship had been described in detail, stating how people's behaviour determined the course of events. The prophets knew and understood the Relationship and so were able to predict what would happen as a result of the way people behaved. They warned rulers, establishment and people in advance about the effects of their behaviour. Loss of country, expulsion and persecution occurred as predicted by the prophets, in accordance with the Relationship.

See chapter 2.1: **'Struggle for Freedom: The Social Cause-and-Effect Relationship'**
and chapter 2.2: **'History Speaks: Monarchy, Exile and Maccabees'**

The social laws of the Pentateuch (Torah) underlie equality, independence, freedom from oppression and exploitation, and a good life of high quality. But at the time of the Maccabean dynasty, the Jewish establishment argued against such laws so as to expose the people to exploitation through need. The resulting decisive internal struggle changed Judaism, determined the fate of the Jewish people and gave rise to Christianity, shaped today's world and today's problems.

What happened at about the time of Jesus to Jewish belief and practice was recorded in the contemporary early part of the Talmud which describes both the struggle and its outcome.

> See chapter 2.3: **'At the Time of Jesus, This is What Actually Happened in Israel: The Truth about Hillel and his Times'** which is factual, conclusive and fully documented, including much previously undiscovered material from the Talmud.
>
> It includes a clear and concise summary statement outlining what the Talmud is and how it came to be written, describing its relative authority and that of its components. Included also is a similar statement about the Halachah (code of Jewish rabbinical law). Torah, Talmud and Halachah are related to each other and their relative scope and authority is outlined and defined.

They argued in religious terms about social and political policies. You can see how the Talmud records the bitter feelings of ordinary people about what establishment scholars were doing to Torah (Pentateuch) and people. And when some scholars attempted to provide their own statements with an authority they did not have, the practice was scathingly condemned in the Talmud.

You can see how the Talmud refers in one detailed example to early Christians and their beliefs, and codes used by the early writers of the Talmud to ensure that later generations could not distort or misrepresent the message which was really there. And relevant stories and arguments were linked in the same way as was used contemporaneously by Christian gospel writers.

> See chapter 2.4: **'One Law for All: Freedom Now, Freedom for Ever'**. This is a fully documented conclusive record of previously undiscovered material about the decisive struggle then going on within Judaism.

This struggle was about position, influence and control over communities, about changing benevolent rules of behaviour so that people could be oppressed and exploited. It changed Judaism, determined the fate of the Jewish people and gave rise to Christianity and it is this struggle which is exposed here to the light of day.

---

* Changed by editor to: "This series of four reports together cover…"
  (Was: On the solhaam.org website in Volume 1 to 4 which are here
  chapter 2.1 to 2.4, under the subtitle 'Overview':
  "This report is one of a series of four which together cover…")

Struggle for Freedom:
The Social Cause-and-Effect Relationship

Introduction and Summary
The Struggle for Freedom
    From Dictatorship to Democracy
    Struggle within Democracy
    Impact of Behaviour
        Our Troubled Times
Jewish Religion
    Religion
    Jewish Religion
    Biblical Law Underlies all Freedom
    Today's Battle for Freedom
Biblical Law
    Ten Commandments
    To Every Family its Home, Land and Income
    Ownership of Land, of the Means for Independence
    Forms of Service and Conditions of Employment
    Weekly Day of Rest (Sabbath)
    Year of Release (Shemittah)
    Year of Freedom (Yovel)
    Social Relations
    Government
Social Cause-and-Effect Relationship: From Oppression to Freedom, From Exploitation to Good Life
    In the Torah
    Predictions of the Prophets
    In History
Appendices
    1 Forms of Service and Conditions of Employment
    2 Year of Release (Shemittah)
    3 Stranger who is a Settler
    4 Cause-and-Effect Relationship in the Torah

Introduction and Summary

Manfred Davidmann begins by outlining the social and economic environment in which we live, the problems of today, and then discusses uses and misuses of religion in such circumstances. He then outlines the meaning and significance of Judaism, of the essential but little-known social and economic laws of behaviour, sketched within the environment in which we live and work.

The relevant social laws and the social system of the Torah are described and explained as a self-contained and complete system which prevents people being exploited through need if they fall on hard times and which prevents ownership being concentrated in the hands of a few. The system enables people to live good and satisfying lives in a just and fair society which guarantees freedom and equality. The laws of redemption, for example, are shown to be leasehold laws designed to maintain an equal and fair distribution of income and wealth among the population as a whole. Biblical law underlies all freedom.

Most of the problems now threatening the survival of humankind are caused by the selfish interests of those who are attempting to organise and run society for their own gain. On the other hand are those who resist and struggle on behalf of the interests and benefit of the community at large.

The two sides encourage and spread the kind of behaviour which enables them to gain and keep their own type of society: dictatorship and exploitation on the one hand, freedom and good life on the other.

Hence it is vitally important to know what kind of behaviour serves what kind of ends. If we wish to gain freedom and remain free then we need to know which kind of behaviour gives us strength, enables us to co-operate with each other, helps us to raise the quality of life for all, helps us to lead good and satisfying lives.

It is this which makes the Social Cause-and-Effect Relationship so important. It is stated in the Torah as a fundamental scientific law which applies to all people at all times no matter where they live or what they believe in or what their state of development.

The prophets knew and understood the Social Cause-and-Effect Relationship and how it operates when they predicted what would happen as a result of the way people behave.

Knowledge and understanding of the Social Cause-and-Effect Relationship give us an understanding of how what happens depends on people's behaviour, and a greater understanding of what determines the pattern of events.

Manfred Davidmann details the Social Cause-and-Effect Relationship in biblical language as well as in plain English, detailing the consequences of either following the laws or else of ignoring them.

The legislation shows how people can protect themselves against losing their freedom and how to gain even greater freedom. It opens the door to freedom, to a good life and to government which looks after the interests of its people.

Within Jewish law is described the next step ahead towards complete freedom. The strength of individuals and of countries, and even more so the survival of humankind under present conditions, depend on the application of these Torah laws.

The Struggle for Freedom

What people like and what they aim at {7} is to provide for and to satisfy the basic needs for
> shelter, warmth, clothing, food, affection and belonging (within family), friendly and trustful co-operation and companionship, housing, education, good health and good medical services, security against internal and external threats, employment and satisfying work at increasing levels of skill and usefulness and thus of pay, the highest possible standard of living and constructive satisfying leisure activities.

In other words, people wish to live and behave towards each other in a way in which each serves the community which in turn provides for and looks after its members.

They are opposed in this by those who wish to exploit others. Hence the aims of a community have to be achieved by means of struggle, at the level of the human mind and then at the level of events. This is a struggle both for men's minds and for a good life here on earth. It is a struggle which has gone on since one man tried to enslave another.

From Dictatorship to Democracy

Under dictatorship the freedom of the individual is brutally repressed, the individual is at the mercy of state and employer, is told what to do and how to live. The 'state' attempts to destroy that which enables the individual to resist by attempting to weaken and destroy opposing religious beliefs and the strength of the family unit.

Revolutions are successful only when they succeed in replacing an oppressing dictatorship or government by one providing greater personal freedom, such as is obtained by moving away from dictatorship towards democracy. It is in democracies that people have more individual freedom than under dictatorships of the left or of the right, and it is in democracies that people have a far higher standard of living than under dictatorships.

Struggle within Democracy

Successful struggle against dictatorship leads to a democratic form of government and in western democracies there is a large measure of individual freedom, a high standard of living, and the opportunity to struggle and battle freely towards a better life and greater happiness for their citizens. The point of balance has been shifted away from dictatorship towards greater freedom and a better life but the intense struggle taking place within democracies is the same struggle between on the one side those who wish to exploit and oppress, and on the other those who wish to gain, preserve and strengthen freedom.

Correspondingly, there are two ways {6} in which democracies can move, namely on the one side back towards dictatorship and on the other forwards towards a better, more secure and happier life, towards greater freedom from oppression and exploitation, towards a more satisfying life, towards a more egalitarian society.

Those who wish to oppress and exploit use money and the power this provides as a means for doing so. Western democracies are still materialistic societies, money counts and people work for money and material wealth, sometimes regardless of the costs to others or to the community. He who pays the piper calls the tune and the dictates of those who run society, the dictates of those few in whose hands wealth, patronage and power is concentrated, then often seem more important to those whom they employ than the welfare and happiness of the population.

Most of the problems now threatening the survival of humanity are due to this conflict between the selfish interest of those who are attempting to organise and run society for their own personal gain on the one hand,

28

and the interests and benefit of the community at large on the other. There are many examples of which but a few are the man-made Minamata disease {1}, and the cases discussed by Heilbronner {2} and Carson {3}.

The two sides encourage and spread the kind of behaviour which enables them to gain and keep their own type of society: dictatorship and exploitation on the one hand, freedom and good life on the other. Hence it is vitally important to know what kind of behaviour serves what kind of ends.

Impact of Behaviour

It is a well-known fact that the way in which people behave determines their own life and freedom, and the strength and thus freedom of their people as a whole.

Behaviour of a particular kind strengthens individuals, strengthens their ability to resist oppression and exploitation. Basic is that people behave in a way which enables them to trust and assist each other, that men and women co-operate with each other in a way which will protect and strengthen both, behaving in a way which ensures that all benefit from gains made.

The younger generation has much to gain from the past experience of their parents, has much to gain from their parents' knowledge of tried and proved beliefs and values. Clearly it is one's parents who have the short and long-term interest of the child and teenager at heart, regardless of other considerations. The family is the basic unit of society and it looks after the interests of all its members, as individuals as well as collectively. This gives great strength to each member of the family in the struggle for daily bread, security and happiness.

It is those who wish to weaken democracy and freedom who condone and thus permit and encourage behaviour which separates people and turns them against each other. They also stress material considerations because religious values emphasize that people are all-important.

Here is an example. Causing Jews to disregard the teachings of the Jewish religion encouraged them to turn against each other and live off each other instead of co-operating towards achieving a good life for all.

Another example is promiscuous behaviour. People who behave promiscuously have sexual relations before marriage, or after marriage with a person other than their spouse. Promiscuity turns men against women and robs both of the support of their family.

So you see how important behaviour is and we will now explore this in more detail.

29

Our Troubled Times

Oppression through Need

In Egypt there were years of famine but Pharaoh had much grain in his stores. In return for food the people handed over all the money they had, then their horses and farm animals, finally selling themselves to Pharaoh into slavery and selling all their land. The people were then moved from their cities from one end of the land to the other, to drive home to them that they were slaves, that they had to obey regardless of the consequences, that they and the land belonged to their master - Pharaoh. But he had fed his priests so that they had no need to sell either themselves or their land and they glorified Pharaoh in the eyes of the people. From then on the people, Pharaoh's slaves, belonged to him totally and had to pay Pharaoh each year one-fifth of all they produced.

We have not made much progress since then. Much the same situation exists today, much the same techniques are used today to oppress and enslave, in varying degrees in different countries.

For example, the Khmer Rouge in Cambodia took a generous and fine people, drove them away from their towns and homes into the countryside into utter starvation and dependence at great loss of life, thus subjecting and enslaving them. In the USSR the land and all other productive capital belonged to the state, the establishment's communist party controlling the people for its rulers. People had no individual freedom. Job and livelihood depended on following the dictates of the state. The people were effectively enslaved, had to do as they were told, were subjected to vicious inhuman treatment if they protested.

'He who pays the piper calls the tune' applies equally in a democracy as in a dictatorship, applies to political parties no matter whether of right or left. It illustrates what happens when power is concentrated in the hands of a few who run a country. Their influence is extended through wealth and patronage. Those who dispense patronage are those who control jobs, are those who through controlling employment in effect control the means of livelihood and of survival. When these few wish to exploit their people they, and their establishment which depends on them for patronage and income, attempt on the one side to persuade and compel the people to obey and on the other to weaken them so that they become less able to resist oppression. In democracies, freedom and good life are under attack.

Brutality of Man to Man

The consequences of regarding religious values and norms as irrelevant and of thus allowing oneself to be divided against one's fellow, that is the consequences of antisocial behaviour, are very clear. People begin to behave in ways which harm other people, and begin to pursue their own selfish interests. Apathy and neglect towards others result, followed by disregard of community and personal property and by cruelty and viciousness towards others.

There is increasing wanton antisocial behaviour such as vandalism and mugging. There is a loss of internal security, both from loss of property and from attack against the person. The quality of life is lowered even further by those who pursue personal gain regardless of its cost to other people.

Viciousness and brutality of people towards each other, disregard of the value of the individual and of life itself, are not normal behaviour. People who behave in this way become isolated and divided against each other. People who behave in this way do not gain, as in reality they are working for the personal power and wealth of their own brutalised leadership.

Promiscuity

Those who understand its effects know {4} that sex performs the enormously important function of creating a special single deep emotional relationship between two people which gives them the strength to overcome life's problems, to form a strong family unit which serves and protects all its members. The depth of such a relationship between husband and wife can be appreciated as one sees them both battling on together successfully regardless of how tough the struggle.

In all countries where sex education has been introduced the same corruptive pattern of social change has been observed {5}: sexual experimentation starts and promiscuity increases. Promiscuity leads to increasing sexual dissatisfaction, to the weakening of family life and marriage bonds and to sexual excesses. The substitute satisfactions of smoking, drinking, and drug-taking increase and there is a lowering of the age of those involved. There is an upsurge in wanton destructive aggression in the community and a rise in aggressive juvenile delinquency. There is increasing concern over the harm done on young children by the practices and by the lack of concern and commitment of their parents, and concern has already been expressed over increasing male impotence. These effects are now obvious to any intelligent reader of the informed press.

It is well known that those who engage in sexual relations outside marriage find themselves looking in vain for the affection which is missing to an ever greater extent from their relationships, become less and less able to commit themselves to the other person, mean ever less to each other. Increasing divorce rates, the resultant delinquency of children, the completely casual and inhuman ways some parents treat each other and their children, are almost the direct outcome of pre-marital and adulterous, that is promiscuous, sexual relations.

History shows that free societies which allow themselves to become 'permissive' (promiscuous) weaken themselves to the point where their civilisation destroys itself, or is destroyed by outsiders. Those who wish to weaken democracy condone and/or encourage 'permissiveness'. On the other hand, those who restrict sex to within marriage gain creativity and increase their strength. {4}

The family is the basic unit of society. Its strength depends on the ability of the partners to commit themselves to each other and that means on those who restrict sexual relations to within marriage. Men and women who do so practice a form of self-control which enables them to form a deep and lasting relationship, which in turn lays the basis for happy and contented family life for themselves and their children. The relationship between them is based on mutual trust and respect arising from the sure knowledge that they are in a vital exclusive relationship to each other, that they are working and co-operating with each other for the common good of themselves and their children.

Those Responsible

The media are at present being used to persuade and condition people into thinking that religion is irrelevant, that antisocial behaviour will not have unpleasant consequences. However, the cost to the community of the kind of negative and antisocial behaviour outlined in the sections above, of the lowering of the quality of life, of loss of freedom for the individual, and of loss of satisfaction from the work we do, is enormous. {8}

To answer the question: "Who encourages antisocial behaviour?" we need to ask: "Who benefits from antisocial behaviour?"

It is those who have power through controlling patronage, money and wealth who benefit from antisocial behaviour and who are thus responsible for permitting and encouraging the different forms of antisocial behaviour we have discussed.

Jewish Religion

Religion

Religions teach what is good and should be done, what is bad and should not be done.

However, there are movements and so-called religions which condition and brainwash their members into working so as to enrich the founders or the establishment, or which brainwash members into obediently working for and serving the leadership in unquestioning obedience.

Also one has to appreciate that when it suits their purpose those who run countries will encourage and use religion. Such a 'religion' may be used as a tranquilliser to prevent the population from complaining about being downtrodden and exploited, when the message the religion spells out is 'never mind a hard life now, reward will come in the next life'. Religion may be used in an attempt to give aim and purpose and thus strength to a people who are falling apart. Another example is when a religion is used at a time of war as a kind of stimulating driving force with 'god' helping the side one happens to be on. Or religion may be misused to divide people against each other, for example when religion is used as a way of persuading some people into attacking those who believe in freedom, into attacking those who are on the side of the people as a whole.

The Jewish religion, however, is quite different and does not readily lend itself to such misuses.

The whole record of the exodus from Egypt shows that slave societies can be defeated from within. This is of tremendous importance to those who are oppressed but the Torah (that is the five books of Moses) goes much further. The lessons are driven home: Freedom and good life can be and were gained and then can be and were defended as well as strengthened.

The legislation clearly shows how people can protect themselves against losing the freedom they have gained and how to gain even greater freedom. This is of the greatest importance to democracy, as it shows how to keep and strengthen freedom and good life for its people.

Within Jewish law is described the next step ahead towards complete freedom. Jewish law contains the key which opens the door to freedom, to a good life and to government which looks after the interests of its people.

Jewish Religion

The Torah describes the one successful uprising by an enslaved people against their slave drivers, against the enslaving rulers and their establishment, against the oppressing state.

The exodus from Egypt some 3,300 years ago was probably the first, if not the only, really successful uprising. Events which took place were recorded at the time and have been preserved unaltered to this day. It is a fully documented record of the way in which freedom was gained, of the kind of behaviour which is necessary so as to keep and strengthen freedom, a guide to a social order which serves people and not their masters.

The Torah provides a factual statement of the steps that were taken and that have to be taken if freedom is to be gained, kept and strengthened. The Law goes even further. It lays down a social order and structure to enable the people to be governed by and for the people, with safeguards designed to prevent the few from grasping power so as to oppress the many.

The Torah using religious language lays down a way of behaviour and community organisation which is essential for the survival and strengthening of human dignity, values and freedom. The Jewish people undertook the obligation to follow this way of behaviour as a way of life and as a matter of law.

In Jewish law people are important and matter. The law is a guide which directs people into behaviour which gives increasing trust and co-operation, which gives increasing strength. Its prohibitions enable society to protect itself. On the one hand ability, effort and work for the community are rewarded while on the other hand differentials are limited. Those who experience difficulties are treated with respect and helped to achieve a good life. Those who behave according to the law know that their behaviour will not hurt or harm other people.

The Jewish religion emphasises social responsibility, emphasises that man is responsible for man. It emphasises accountability for inhuman behaviour and thus emphasises justice. It emphasises family ties. The consequences of behaving in accordance with the law, or of breaking it, while spelt out in the Torah in religious terms are fully paralleled by historical facts and backed by present-day statistics.

Judaism provides for people a way of life which is good and just, satisfying and rewarding, in which people help and support each other. Judaism is a way of life, its teachings are laws which need to be adhered to as they protect the community, as they ensure its survival, and as behaviour in accordance with these laws underlies all individual and social freedom.

The law is intended to be applied to help and protect people in a good and just way. When it is applied as intended then the law and those who interpret it and apply it are respected by the people.

Biblical Law Underlies all Freedom

Jewish law and the family give strength to resist. Jewish law teaches that people are more important than the inhuman or antisocial dictates of an oppressive management or of an oppressive state machine, that people must not be forced into obedience through exploiting their needs for example by threat of hardship through dismissal.

People are more important than money and power. This means that patronage, money and wealth must not be used to oppress and exploit. Jewish law maintains that everyone has a right to work and should be helped to work at the highest level he is capable of reaching and that he should be rewarded accordingly.

Outstanding is that Jews have been attacked and persecuted for such beliefs ever since the patriarchs gained the knowledge that there was only one God, who cared for people and who expected them to behave kindly towards each other. The Torah, the five books of Moses, has been handed down generation by generation in unaltered form. It is a comprehensive blueprint for a just and fair society and government, aimed at giving people the good and satisfying life they have a right to expect. Behaviour according to Jewish law underlies all freedom and because of this Jewish law survived every attempt to destroy it.

The point has been put rather beautifully {1} in a rabbinical saying:
> When at the end of time Almighty God sends complete redemption, he will turn to the persecuted people and say "My children, I am astonished to see how you have been able to support so much waiting for this day". They will reply "Lord, if it had not been for your Torah, we would have perished among nations a long time ago".

Today's Battle for Freedom

Jewish history shows that in the past the Jewish people have been betrayed again and again, by non-observant leaderships no matter whether right or left and by orthodox leaderships who weakened the application of Jewish law so as to be able to oppress the people in order to exploit them. It was those who did not follow the law who in the past grasped power and then weakened and defeated Judaism and the hope for achieving freedom and a good life for the Jewish people and thus in due course for the rest of humanity.

35

It is equally certain that the same battle is being fought today and it is just as certain that on the one hand is the opportunity to gain freedom while on the other hand our defeat can only result in mankind rapidly destroying itself.

Biblical Law

Ten Commandments

The Ten Commandments are so important and are so well known because it is behaviour in accordance with these laws which is the basis for people trusting each other and so for people co-operating and working well with each other. They are listed both in biblical language and in plain English in Appendix 5.

When Moses brought the tables of the law he brought 'freedom upon the tables'. It is the Ten Commandments as a whole which underlie freedom, independence and strength to oppose and resist oppression. Wherever there is any spiritual and material freedom today it exists because people followed these laws (rules) of behaviour and it exists to the extent to which they do so. In other words, following the provisions of the law results in freedom and ensures it, ensures strength and security.

The statement that there is one God and one God alone who delivered us from slavery in Egypt means that only these laws, only this code of behaviour, enables you to gain freedom and stay free.

If you follow advice given by those who want you to behave differently then you are in fact praying to another god, no matter whether this so-called 'god' attempts to influence you through the attitudes and opinions of your external enemies or through opinions and practices being spread internally.

The rules of behaviour of the Ten Commandments are based on a knowledge of what goes on in peoples' minds, of the inner workings of communities and societies, and of democratic and authoritarian organisation. To free ourselves from mental conditioning and brainwashing we have to follow the Ten Commandments and apply the social laws and the social system of the Torah.

To Every Family its Home, Land and Income

God promised the Hebrews the land of Canaan (Erez Israel), the Torah clearly laying down its borders {1}.

36

Having counted the people of Israel of age twenty upward by their fathers' houses (by family) {2}, the land was divided among them accordingly, each family receiving land in proportion to the size of the family {3}. Some tribes had already received their allocated lands and were thus excluded from this distribution {4}. The land was shared out by drawing lots {3}.

All the land was to be allocated to Hebrews. With the exception of the Levites {5} every family had its own plot of land, the land having been shared out fairly. The means of production and of creating wealth had been shared out fairly among the population with each family independently controlling its own share. Each family had its own home and land, its own independent source of income.

Each family has the right to work the land and to its produce as long as a number of specific requirements are met. This right is hereditary and passes to one's heirs {6}, but laws prevent the division of land from becoming unfair, prevent the accumulation of land in the hands of a few, prevent land passing from tribe to tribe.

Land for example does not pass from tribe to tribe on marriage. While daughters inherit land from their father when there are no sons, they then have to marry into their father's tribe {7}. The widow of a childless marriage is protected, the laws of levirate marriage also having the effect of preventing land leaving the tribe and of preventing land accumulating in the hands of one branch of the family.

As time passes some people gain wealth and power, others fall into poverty and need, and one has to restore the equal, fair and appropriate distribution of basic productive wealth. This is done in a number of different ways. Jews may not oppress or enslave Jews. Those falling on hard times are supported and helped to regain their independence. One may not treat an employee harshly and every seventh day is to be Sabbath, a day of rest for those who are employed as well as for those who employ.

Every seventh year is a year of rest in which all the produce of the land is freely shared out among all at no cost.

In every fiftieth year servants are released from their labours and return to their hereditary properties as free men, returning to their land and means of livelihood as free people free of all debt. In this way land is not allowed to accumulate in the hands of a few who could use it to oppress and exploit others.

Again and again in the course of history has property been concentrated in the hands of a few and the mass of the people been prevented from enjoying the benefits of productive property such as land, prevented from sharing the benefits of property and a good life. As a consequence the greatest states fell to pieces internally and were destroyed because they found no way of preventing this internal decay and resultant destruction {8}, because they found no way of limiting the concentration of wealth in the hands of a few, of ensuring that the mass of the people could benefit from the productive wealth and income of the community.

The Torah battles against unfairness, injustice and oppression and has the answer to this problem of the concentration of ownership in the hands of a few. Its laws are just and it warns against preferring the rich or favouring the poor. It legislates against the concentration of ownership and corrupting power in the hands of a few by three main laws, namely the laws of Sabbath (rest), Shemittah (release), and of Yovel (freedom).

When ignored, the resulting and increasing oppression of the people was twice followed by the destruction of the temple and exile. The importance of these laws is stressed in the Torah again and again. They are so important that they appear to determine to a considerable extent the strength of the people and stay in the country.

To see and understand the importance of these laws one needs to be aware of the social system of the Torah and the sections which follow discuss ownership of land, forms of service and conditions of employment, the laws of rest (sabbath), release (shemittah) and freedom (yovel).

Ownership of Land, of the Means for Independence

The productive capital (land) was shared out among the Hebrew tribes and then among the people, family by family, in proportion to numbers. Only Hebrews can own land and land is a hereditary possession. The owner may 'sell' the land to another Hebrew or to a non-Hebrew, but is only transferring {9} the use of the land for a limited period, which cannot be longer than to the next Year of Freedom (yovel year) since the original owner or his heirs return to their land every Yovel year.

Selling land in this way amounts to leasing it to a tenant, the lease terminating at the Year of Freedom. The land itself cannot be transferred permanently, cannot be sold.

That only the use of the land is transferred and not ownership is underlined {10} by the owner's right of 'redemption': He and his relatives for him have the duty and right at any time to terminate the lease by paying back to the tenant an amount corresponding to the unexpired part of the lease.

This section of the Torah then clearly states that land cannot be sold permanently, defines leasehold giving the maximum length of the lease and defines the owner's right of terminating the lease to regain possession while protecting the tenant from financial loss.

Only when the hereditary owner is in severe need should he lease his land to someone else.

The laws relating to the ownership of land deal with the means for generating wealth and are detailed. They are important because it is through accumulated wealth that power accumulates to exploit others, and to oppress so as to exploit others.

This is what Hirsch {11} says:

> '... striking is the effect which the automatic reversion in the Yovel (year of freedom) of all landed property to the original owners or their heirs, must have in the prevention of complete permanent poverty of some families by the side of overpowering accumulation of property in the hands of a few.

> ... every fiftieth year the whole land reverts to its original division, and the richest goes back to the original acres of his heritage, and the poorest is given back the acres of his.

> The cheaper the buyer of a property has bought it the less can he be sure of being able to keep it, the easier will it be for the seller to afford the sum necessary for its redemption, or for his relative to decide to redeem it. If a rich man really would like to have the field for as long as possible, he would have to be careful not to bargain for the very lowest price, as it is only a high price which would render redemption difficult.'

The basis for any system of ownership is the law of the land. In some countries state ownership of means of production is the law and individuals may not own private productive property while in other countries private ownership of productive property is the legal norm.

State ownership and control of the means of production leads to direct control, oppression and exploitation of the people. In the USSR all land and capital were owned by the state. A revolution which results in state ownership merely replaces one set of oppressors by another.

In countries in which the means of production are owned privately, their accumulation in the hands of a few leads to the oppression and exploitation of the working people. In Britain, for example, the laws of leasehold perpetuate and favour the concentration of ownership of land in the hands of a privileged few.

The Torah states that the land belongs to God, that the Hebrew who 'owns' the land is God's tenant {12}. Hence he may continue to use the land as long as he keeps the conditions of the agreement. So the Torah clearly states that the Hebrews who dwell in the country may treat the land as their property only as long as the law is followed, as long as they observe God's laws. This corresponds precisely to how ownership is defined in other countries.

Land was the means of production which provided independent income and security. Jewish law (that is God's laws) lays down how the land, the means of production, is to be shared out among and owned by the population and how ownership is to be controlled so that productive wealth cannot accumulate in the hands of a few. Jewish laws of leasehold maintain a fair distribution of wealth among the population.

Forms of Service and Conditions of Employment

Masters, Slaves and Servants

Slavery is utter degradation and oppression, denying to the enslaved the consideration due to them as fellow human beings, denying to the enslaved their basic human rights. At the time of the liberation from slavery in Egypt about 3,300 years ago the enslavement of one human being by another was common practice.

The master in effect owns and controls the slave's body through what he can force the slave to do by means of the law of the land and by force of economic necessity. The children of slaves belong to the master who can use them as he wishes.

Human beings were enslaved by force of circumstances beyond their control, by the need to survive, their masters entitled to treat them like unfeeling property. Slaves were without hope for release for themselves, for their children or for future generations.

Jewish law laid down 3,300 years ago that no Jew may enslave another and severely limited the extent to which a person could be oppressed in employment.

There are really only three forms of service between Hebrews, namely 'Hired' servant, 'Bond' servant, and 'Lifebond' servant. This is illustrated by Figure 1. The hired servant is hired as and when required, the bond servant serves for up to but not more than six years while the lifebond servant serves his master for life. Forms of service between Hebrews and strangers are discussed in Appendix 1.

Hired Servant

A hired servant (sochir) was hired {13} as and when required.

One must not oppress a hired servant who is poor and needy, whether he be Hebrew or stranger {14}. He had to be paid promptly, one could not delay paying him {15}, and when hired by the day and when poor and needy he has to be paid the same day.

He hired himself out and served until the Year of Freedom (yovel) when he and his children return to his hereditary possession, once again becoming independent farmers {16}.

In similar position would appear to be a present-day farm labourer, factory worker and office employee, anyone who is hired by an employer by the day, week or month, anyone who is being paid according to time spent or work done.

Figure 1

FORMS OF SERVICE AMONG HEBREWS (2)

Stranger Employer (E.g. tenant)		Hebrew Employer (Such as landowner or tenant)	
Redeemable Lifebond (1) Servant (Hebrew)	Lifebond (1) Servant	Bond (1) Servant	Hired Servant
Hebrew 'sold' to a stranger serves 'for life' unless redeemed	Serves for life	Serves for six years	Hired as and when required

Notes (1) Bond is 'service contract'
(2) There are no Hebrew slaves
(3) All are freed in Year of Freedom

Bond Servant

The bond servant (eved) works {17} for a period of up to six years and is freed in the seventh {18}. He is also freed in the Year of Freedom (yovel year) if this occurs before the six years are up.

The text {18} indicates that a bond servant is a Hebrew who hired himself out against payment in advance. He was not to be pressed into such service as a consequence of his poverty and need {19}. However, a thief when unable to make restitution could be hired out by a court {20}.

The Torah states {21} that he has served 'to the double of the hire of a hired servant' for 'six years' and there is considerable doubt about the meaning of this sentence.

However, restitution for theft meant paying double the value of that which had been stolen and the thief may have been hired out into service for a period corresponding to this.

'Double of the hire of a hired servant' could also mean that the bond servant serves that much longer to allow for accommodation, food and presumably clothing which may have been provided by the master during the period of service, and for the capital given to the bond servant at the end of his service period.

It was not permitted to rule one's servants ruthlessly nor to illtreat them (see also Appendix 1). It would appear that he received no wages for his work while employed but was a member of his master's household and enjoyed the day of rest (the sabbath) and other Jewish holidays.

The bond servant could not be redeemed, could not free himself from his contract of service. He is freed in the seventh year without having to pay anything to his master {22}. On the contrary, he must be well provided for when he leaves {23}, being provided by his master with the means for earning an independent living so that he can have a fresh start.

Very similar would be a present-day contract of employment for a specific number of years which provides also for the payment of a lump sum to the employee at the end of the period of service.

Lifebond Servant

A lifebond servant (eved olam) {24} is a bond servant who decides to serve for life.

A bond servant was allowed at the end of his period of service to choose bond service for life by clearly stating that he wished to serve 'for ever'.

The procedure involved (see also Appendix 1) seems to indicate clearly that freedom was much to be preferred.

Protection by the Law

Hebrews were freed by God and must not be enslaved {25}. Freedom is so utterly important that the death penalty was imposed on him who steals another and on the Hebrew who steals any Hebrew to enslave him {26, 27}. Hebrews must not be sold as slaves {25}.

Hebrews must not be treated harshly no matter what the form of service {28}. Indeed a bond servant who has run away from his master must not be turned over to his master but is to live in a place he shall choose and which he likes best and must not be wronged {29}.

Slaves and slavery are replaced by servants and service. Hebrews must not exploit or be exploited, must treat each other with consideration. Those falling on harsh times are protected by the law while serving others and are helped back to independence and freedom.

We now see a social system in which the productive land is shared out among the people who are in this way provided with the means for independence and a good life. Independence is protected by the laws of ownership relating to land and those working for others are protected by laws which uphold independence and counter oppression.

In the following sections on Sabbath (weekly day of rest), Shemittah (year of release) and Yovel (year of freedom) we will see how the law further improves the life of the people, provides even greater protection. The weekly day of rest, the Sabbath, has spread and benefits almost all the civilised world. The Year of Release (shemittah) and the Year of Freedom (yovel) provide for the kind of good life and protection not yet achieved in the democratic countries.

Weekly Day of Rest (Sabbath)

Every seventh day is a day of rest for all. It is called the Sabbath and the basic law 'You shall not labour on the Sabbath' is repeated {30, 31} several times in the Torah. The Jewish people have spread the idea of the Sabbath throughout the world. Almost all of mankind now benefits from a weekly day of rest.

Work stops on the Sabbath in order to let those who labour have a regular day of rest. On this day the servant is as free as the master, the worker is as free as the employer. All are equal on this day.

The law is so important that it is clearly stated in the Decalogue (Ten Commandments) {31} being the only holy day singled out in this way. Here its importance is further underlined by the clear statement that Israel is to keep the Sabbath so that those who work can rest because this is the command of God who liberated Israel from Egyptian bondage. The prophets stressed again and again the importance of keeping these laws, the dire consequences of disregarding them.

This is what Dayan Grunfeld says {32} about the Sabbath:

> Sabbath lays the foundation for the brotherhood of man. It is 'a weekly-recurring divine protest against slavery and oppression. Lifting up his kiddush-cup on Friday night, the Jew links the creation of the world with man's freedom, so declaring slavery and oppression deadly sins against the very foundation of the universe. Can one be surprised that tyrants of all times would not permit Israel to celebrate the Sabbath?'

Or that those who wish to oppress their people using modern means of persuasion attempt to brainwash Jews into relaxing sabbath observance.

The Sabbath {32} is a unique experience. There is the happy companionship of family and friends and the enjoyment of good food. There are table-songs in praise of God and the Sabbath, and there is the study of the Torah. All combine to refresh the body, to relax nervous tension and to refresh the mind, to bring one closer to the essence of all being and life and to equip one better for the task of living.

Year of Release (Shemittah)

Every seventh year is a Year of Release (shemittah year). The name comes from Shanath haShemittah (year of the release). There are three main provisions:

Release from work. One is not allowed to cultivate the land or trade its produce. People are released from work. Available food is shared, is freely available at no cost.

Release from debt. Unpaid debts are cancelled at the end of the year.

Learning the law. The Torah was read to the people at Succoth so that they could learn the law so as to observe it.

Observance of the Year of Release (shemittah) laws is so fundamental and important that scripture as well as the Jewish sages have described their neglect as one of the causes of Israel's loss of Erez Israel and of Israel's dispersion among the nations.

Release from Work

The Year of Release is a year of rest {33}. Working the land is prohibited. The land must rest and is left fallow. By 'land' is meant fields, vineyards and oliveyards. Ploughing, sowing and pruning are not permitted.

No one works the land and people live from what grows by itself. This belongs to those who need it who take only what they need.

The individual farmer may in the Year of Release only reap as much as he needs for his own household, in small quantities covering the needs of three meals. Produce is not harvested and what has been reaped must not be stored away. The reason is that the produce of the Year of Release must be common property and available to all for the common good, so that the poor can eat.

Cassuto {34} considers that every Hebrew is intended to work for only six consecutive years, and that after this period he shall be freed in the seventh year from the yoke of hard toil. The whole year is to be observed as a year of rest agriculturally and Rashi comments {35} that others have an equal right to its produce with the owner. The produce are to be ownerless and available to all, so that the poor may eat and what the poor leave is to be left for animals.

The owner may eat his own produce but only as long as some of the produce he is eating still remains in the field for the animals. That is as long as some of the produce is also available to all, is also available to the poor.

As soon as each kind of produce ceases to be available in the open for animals, no one may store that kind of produce in his house. This means that stored produce has to be shared with all.

Dayan Grunfeld {36} points out that observance is a considerable financial sacrifice for farmers.

Release from Debt

The needy borrower has fallen into a state of social dependence on the lender {37} and the Year of Release (shemittah) was intended to prevent this. The word 'shemit' means 'to escape from your hand'. The lender 'held the borrower in his hand', had power over him. After the Year of Release the lender may no longer demand the debt and has allowed the borrower to escape from his hand.

Unpaid debts are cancelled {38} at the end of the Year of Release {39}. This does not apply to unpaid wages or credit for day by day purchases but means that a lender is legally prevented from collecting {8} all debts which have not been repaid by the end of the Year of Release. The effect of the cancellation on post-dated loans and on pledges is discussed in Appendix 2.

In any case one may not press for payment {40} and no creditor would seem to have the right to press for payment of a debt during the seventh year.

Hirsch {41} says that if the borrower insists on repaying then the lender may accept it since it is not the tendency of the Torah to release those who can pay from paying and this means that those who can pay should pay.

Only money lent to Hebrews is released during the Year of Release. Rashi {42} considers that it is a positive command to ensure repayment of debts by non-Hebrews, presumably because they themselves do not release debts and do not adhere to other benevolent Jewish laws such as those which forbid charging interest on loans and enforcing repayment.

One needs to release all debts without quibble or question or precondition or doubt or difficulty, without trying to dodge or avoid or modify the release of those whom one has in one's power because of their indebtedness.

Release from Ignorance (learning the law)

It is laid down that at the end of every Year of Release during Succoth (Tabernacles) the law written by Moses is to be read {43} before all Israel.

This is to be done so that all hear, learn, respect and observe all the words of the law, so that knowledge and observance are passed on to future generations as long as Jewish people live in the land of Erez Israel.

Release from Want Every Seventh Year

The Year of Release applied to present-day working conditions, say a sabbatical year and release from debt every seventh year for all, could have an impact as great as the Sabbath has on the dignity of individuals and on the quality of life itself.

This is discussed in more detail in later sections.

Year of Freedom (Yovel)

The Year of Freedom (yovel year) is the year after seven release cycles (shemittahs) each of which is seven years long. This means that the Year of Freedom is the fiftieth year after seven times seven which is forty-nine years.

The laws of the Year of Freedom have the following effects {44}:

> **Freedom is restored** to those who lost it, is to be restored to those who are serving others. The people are thus freed to return to their families and to their land.

> **Land is returned** to the hereditary owners, or to their heirs. The source of wealth, the productive land, is once again shared out among the people.

> **Year of rest.** It is a year of rest from working the land, it appears to be a year of rest from work for others. Just as in the Year of Release, farm work may not be carried out and the produce of the land is to be made freely available to all free of charge.

This is how Dr. Jacobus {8} describes the effect of the provisions of the Year of Freedom:

> 'At the end of the fifty years of the Yovel period some people have amassed a fortune of land, some have lost theirs, some have had to sell themselves into slavery and at the end of the period the land reverts back to its original owners, the slaves regain their freedom. Freedom and ownership revert back to the original fair distribution.'

It was the shofar sounding on Yom Kippur which restored freedom to servants and restored property.

Restoring Freedom

Jewish law clearly states that Hebrews are not to be enslaved; it lays down {45} humane forms of service and humane conditions of employment.

In addition, those who are forced by need and circumstances to hire themselves out for long periods are assured of being freed in the Year of Freedom.

Freedom is restored by the Year of Freedom to those who serve.

Returning to One's Land

We saw {46} that land was shared out fairly among the Hebrew tribes and families. However, as time passes some sink into need and lease their land to others. The livelihood of those who serve depends on being employed by the more fortunate, on whom they depend for survival. There are then those who are able to accumulate land and thus productive wealth, who in this way are able to control and exploit the lives of others.

We also saw {47} that the land could be used by the owner or his heirs on condition that it was never sold. If in need he could lease it to another but the lease had to terminate at the next Year of Freedom.

In the Year of Freedom the leases terminate, the land is returned to its hereditary owner. In this way permanent inequality is prevented and the original distribution of land restored at regular intervals.

Freedom

A freed servant who is unable to find paid work would soon be forced by need to re-enter the kind of service from which he had just been freed.

The Year of Freedom not only frees people but returns to them their hereditary share of the productive land, of the means for independence and good life.

The initial distribution of land, which was fair, is maintained. The laws of the Year of Freedom have the effect of preventing land from accumulating in the hands of a few, of preventing the concentration of power and wealth in the hands of a few, of preventing the few from oppressing, exploiting and economically enslaving the many.

These laws of Sabbath, Shemittah and Yovel deal with the core of inequality and oppression and needless to say many arguments have been put forward for not observing them.

Corresponding legislation under present conditions would have to measure a country's population and its productive resources and wealth. It would then have to share them out fairly among the population, in a way which allowed each family full control of its share.

The national wealth and capital would have to be re-assessed and redivided at regular intervals.

Such legislation {48}, effectively applied, would indeed eliminate much if not most conflict from within the community and later sections will show that the laws are valid and relevant today and discuss their application under present conditions.

Social Relations

Helping Those in Need

If a Hebrew sinks into poverty and his means fail {49} then he needs to be supported. Instead of being forced by his need into lower-grade service he is to live as 'stranger and settler'. This means (see Appendix 3 'Stranger who is a Settler') that he is to be treated like a tenant who has paid in advance for the use of the land he farms, whose lease expires at the next Year of Freedom and who works independently on his own account.

He may have had to hand the use of his own land over to someone else so as to be able to live, perhaps to support his family. It is possible that while working a piece of land as a tenant he paid an annual rent for the use of the land, perhaps paying it from its produce.

As long as he works a piece of land and farms it as a tenant he may in this way regain his financial strength and redeem his own property in due course.

In other words, he is to be helped to keep and regain his independence.

He is to be treated like a tenant but in addition he is to be supported to an even greater extent: he must not be charged interest nor may one profit from supplying him {50}.

If he continues to sink into poverty in spite of assistance and aid, becoming unable to support himself and his family, then he is forced by need to serve others.

His need must not be used to exploit him. He is to be employed {51} as a hired servant and must not be treated harshly. He returns to his hereditary possession in the Year of Freedom thus regaining his independence.

We have seen some of the ways in which the law protects and helps any Hebrew to overcome difficulties without being oppressed or enslaved, until in the end he regains his original standing and possessions. The same would seem to apply to today's independent shopkeepers, business men, accountants, garage mechanics, electricians, farmers and so on. As the same laws apply today it should be possible to make available {48} aid towards getting established as independent owner, aid towards growth and expansion, and aid towards overcoming difficult periods, in much the same way. The application of the law under present circumstances to those in need of protection and help is discussed in more detail later on. {48}

Providing and Lending Money

One may help those who need it by giving charity or by providing a loan. To assist a poor brother is not optional but obligatory {52}, one is merely doing one's duty in giving loans {53}.

While one should give as much charity as one can, an average amount is 10% of one's income.

Interest-free loans are to be provided {54} to those who need them. Hebrews must not charge each other interest nor pay interest to each other.

When lending money to those who need it one may not press for repayment, particularly so when one knows that the borrower is unable to pay.

One may charge interest when lending to a foreigner {55} and foreigners have to repay their debts, presumably because they are not Hebrews and thus do not adhere to benevolent Jewish law.

One factor which affects the application of laws such as these under present conditions is inflation.

Selling and Buying

Jewish law insists that the customer has rights in that he is protected against being sold faulty goods and against dishonesty on the side of the seller. One has to be honest in one's dealings. Faults in goods should be pointed out before sale. The law insists on fair weights and measures.

The seller is under obligation not to exploit his customers. One may not oppress by profiteering in selling. The law controls profit margins. The net profit is limited to not more than one-sixth.

The task of religion, according to Samuel and according to Rav, was to bring to the market places God's message of righteousness. Rav founded and headed the academy in Sura while Samuel was head of that in Neharde'a, both in Babylon, about 210 CE. Both condemned hoarders of food, usurers, manipulators of fraudulent weights, and profiteers. Samuel warned against selfish disregard of the common good for one's own enrichment.

The poor are to be protected from exploitation in the field of religious practice as otherwise religious observance might be affected. The aim is to protect the people from being exploited by means of excessive prices.

When merchants overcharged {39} for the perfect myrtle twigs which are required for the Succoth festival, Samuel told them to sell perfect myrtle twigs for Succoth at the normal price or else he would decide and proclaim that even broken myrtle twigs would be valid for the ceremony.

Another example from these cases is that a Jewish court of Justice is obliged to appoint inspectors to prevent profiteering, especially in foodstuffs, and to punish severely those convicted of transgression. Price-fixing committees were eventually authorised to be established in every city to curb profiteering and had the authority to punish those who acted against their rules.

Local fishmongers decided to increase their profits as they knew that Jews were anxious to buy fish for the Pesach festival even though prices were high. The local rabbi decided (about 1650) to break 'the iron ring of monopoly by declaring all fish prohibited for a period of two months' including the Pesach festival. This undoubtedly 'taught a powerful lesson to the fish interests'. The rabbi said that 'his major concern was not so much with the rich who would buy the fish no matter how expensive but with the poor who, because of high prices, would be prevented from celebrating the holiday and relaxing for its duration from the burdens and tensions of the workaday week'.

In this section on trading, and in the next on employing, we are merely scratching the surface of relevant Jewish law. It is a body of legislation which has been built up over thousands of years and which insists that the customer has rights, that employees may not be oppressed.

Employer and Employee

Jewish law places the employer under obligation not to oppress his employees. One needs to provide the highest possible standard of living for those whom one employs without in any way tying them, that is without binding them economically or in any other way.

One needs to pay good wages and pay promptly. Jewish law protects the employee by insisting on clearly defined pay preferably agreed in advance {56} and on prompt payment of wages. The employer should pay enough to keep the employee and his family and this presumably is pay earned by one member of the family for one job.

The employee also accepts certain ways of behaviour as being both just and good. For example, an employer's property is inviolate, theft and misappropriation of any kind being completely against the law.

In Jewish law the satisfying of basic needs is the responsibility of the community and this includes work and pay. Strikes are regarded as being in the public interest if the men are exploited.

Some rabbis have interpreted Jewish law in a way which maintained full employment, protecting the community against mass unemployment. For example, when a rabbi prohibited the use during passover of matzos produced by machine {39}, he insisted on his opinion being accepted by 'all living in the sphere of his influence'. The reason was that a great number of Jewish families in his district derived their livelihood from home made matzos. These would have suffered if machine production had been approved. The rabbi appreciated the benefits of the industrial revolution but as the poor Jews in his community could not have obtained other work he acted to protect the community.

Government

There are laws which define a system of administration but here we are looking at laws which govern the behaviour and limit the power of the top executives and of the establishment.

A ruler may not amass servants and may not oppress the people for his own benefit, neither may he amass wealth nor may he behave promiscuously.

In other words, he may not put himself above others by grasping power, may not satisfy personal desires at the expense of others.

Rulers have to be Hebrews and what any ruler or the establishment may do is clearly limited by these laws.

Positive laws tell what has to be done so as to create a strong and just society and a good way of life. But the laws discussed here are negative laws which state what must not be done and such laws protect the people from harm, weakness, oppression and exploitation.

Social Cause-and-Effect Relationship: From Oppression to Freedom, From Exploitation to Good Life

Vast power to control our environment is at our beck and call. During the short interval of only about eighty years we have learned to travel by car, to fly, explore space and land on the moon. We communicate with each other within seconds all around the planet by sound and sight, have learned to harness the power of the atom and are attempting to control the power of the sun itself. Computers help us to store and retrieve the ever increasing flood of data, enable us to carry out intricate calculations in the twinkling of an eye which previously would have taken months to do. We have made enormous progress in technology and science. A good and satisfying life for all can be ours here and now.

The same period has also seen the concentration camps of Europe, the damage done by thalidomide and that by mercury in the Bay of Minamata, what has been done to the Cambodians, the misuse of psychiatry in Russia and the misuse of power within some American corporations. Our increasing technological and scientific skills are so far unmatched by similar progress in human relations, in our knowledge about why people behave as they do, about how people should behave towards each other, about what needs to be done and can be done to help people co-operate with each other.

The increasing problems which threaten our environment are eloquent witness to our lack of progress in the field of human relationships. These problems, increasing in frequency as well as in sheer size and in number of people affected by them, are in the end caused by people, caused by the way people treat each other, by the way people co-operate with each other. We see the daily increasing cost.

Daily it is becoming more essential for people to co-operate with each other for the common good. People are becoming more and more aware of this.

Daily more and more people speak up and get together and make their opinions felt, becoming more and more aware of basic causes. They co-operate and struggle successfully towards better life and greater freedom.

The key to this is behaviour, the way in which people behave towards each other. It is only now that we are beginning to understand why people do what they do and why they behave as they do. We now know some qualitative cause-and-effect relationships between what people do and the effects of their actions on themselves and on others.

If we wish to become free and remain free then we need to know which kind of behaviour gives us strength, enables us to co-operate with each other, helps us to raise the quality of life for all, helps us to lead good and satisfying lives.

Indeed this is the reason we are looking at the Social Cause-and-Effect Relationship, illustrating this from 3,000 years of continuous Jewish history.

In the Torah

It seems to me that it was not possible to describe the cause-and-effect relationship between social behaviour of individuals and of people, and the resulting freedom or oppression and conflict, three thousand years ago in a way which could have been understood by those then reading the Torah. Hence it was stated to the people in a way which could be understood so as to enable them to follow the law and thus benefit from knowledge of the effect of their behaviour, even if they did not understand at the time the basis of and the reason for the legislation.

There is no mistaking the clear knowledge of the relationship and the deep concern for people which the text indicates: it clearly states the consequences arising from opposite kinds of behaviour and lays down behaviour as a norm which strengthens and protects the individual and the community.

Relatively few scientific papers are able to report their findings in such comprehensive manner, are able to describe and illustrate a complete relationship from beginning to end, clearly stating the extent to which it applies.

Appendix 4 lists some relevant passages from the Torah in plain English as well as in the Torah's religious language. It will be seen that they clearly describe the relationship and the range over which it applies. The relationship itself is clearly illustrated by examples covering the range of effects from one end of the scale to the other.

History and recent social statistics clearly show that behaviour which is contrary to the law lowers the quality of life, increases internal stress and conflict to the point of social disruption and military weakness. Those who behave according to the law have good and satisfying lives, gain social and military strength. {1}

Predictions of the Prophets

The warnings of the prophets are discussed in 'History Speaks' {3} and their role is discussed in 'One Law for All' {4}. Here we are looking at their predictions in relation to the Social Cause-and-Effect Relationship.

The prophets foretold what would happen as a result of how people were behaving if people continued to behave as they did. They foretold that Israel would be lost if people continued to behave as they did.

A scientist predicts what would happen in the future as a result of some experiment if the experimental conditions are maintained. The

54

prediction, if based on knowledge of proved scientific laws, will be valid.

To someone who has no knowledge or understanding of science and its laws, the scientist's prediction will appear to be a 'prophesy', a foretelling of what will happen as if by divine inspiration.

And so the predictions of the prophets were divinely inspired prophesies to those unaware of the knowledge which the prophets had.

What the prophets said were predictions based on knowledge and understanding of the Cause-and-Effect Relationship in the Torah. This is stated as a fundamental scientific law (See Appendix 4) which applies to all at all times. To understand this relationship means to understand the inevitability of events predicted by them.

The Cause-and-Effect Relationship is just as valid today as then, and it applies to all at all times, no matter where they live or what they believe in or their state of development.

Knowledge and understanding of the Cause-and-Effect Relationship and of how it operates is what the prophets had when they predicted what would happen as a result of the way people behave.

Knowledge and understanding of the Cause-and-Effect Relationship and of how it operates gives us similar understanding to that which the prophets had, of how what happens depends on how people behave, and enables us to understand today's events and what determines the pattern of events.

In History

When talking about results of 'behaviour', what is meant is not just the behaviour of individual persons but also the behaviour of people as a whole. It includes the behaviour of the people, of their leadership, of their religious dignitaries, of their kings and rulers. 'Behaviour' then includes the crime (evil) of allowing their secular and religious leadership to corrupt them, to mislead and oppress them.

The lessons from the past are there for all to see. There is no need to keep repeating the same mistakes. The events speak for themselves.

History clearly and convincingly illustrates the working of the relationship through successive periods of exile and return to Erez Israel. History shows that behaviour determines events in the way described by the Social Cause-and-Effect Relationship.

The relationship applies to all people and not only to the Jews. However, it is the Jews who retained their belief as a way of life during periods of exile and adversity and who were thus able to survive, return to Erez Israel and regain freedom.

In the next few sections (chapter 2.2 'History Speaks: Monarchy, Exile and Maccabees') I will be looking at case histories drawn from Jewish history to illustrate the social relationship in operation, showing the remarkable way in which behaviour and consequences correlate with each other. We will understand how freedom gained was later lost and see what has to be done so as to move towards greater freedom and better life.

Appendix 1

FORMS OF SERVICE AND CONDITIONS OF EMPLOYMENT

Masters, Slaves and Servants

In addition to the forms of service between Hebrews there is the Hebrew who has been bought by a stranger and there is the stranger who has been sold to a Hebrew.

The Hebrew who has been bought by a stranger has to serve for life but has the right to be freed, to be redeemed. The stranger who has been sold to a Hebrew has been bought from slave-owning slave-selling strangers.

The various relationships are illustrated by Figure 2.

Bond Servant

A slave's master owns the slave like a piece of property and also owns the slave's children. The master could give the bond servant a non-Hebrew female slave as a wife but retained ownership and was allowed to keep both the wife and any children when freeing the bond servant. But the master has no property rights over the bond servant. The bond servant is not a slave and has to be freed at the end of his period of service {1}.

Lifebond Servant

A lifebond servant who wishes to serve 'for ever' has to have his ear bored through {2}. The act of boring through his ear apparently expresses a dislike of choosing servitude {3} and serving 'for ever' has been taken {4} to mean 'until the Yovel (year of freedom)'.

Hebrew Bought by Stranger

A Hebrew could be 'bought' by a foreigner who was not a Hebrew.

The Hebrew servant (sochir) {5} who has been forced by dire need {6} to hire himself out for life to a stranger has the right to be redeemed. He can be freed by himself or by Hebrew relatives. If not redeemed then he is freed with his children in the Year of Freedom (yovel year) {7}.

Whatever has been paid to him is regarded as if it had been paid in advance for hiring him year by year, from the year of start of service to the stranger to the end of the period, the end of the period being the Year of Freedom (yovel year). Hence he is freed by repaying an amount corresponding to the unexpired years of service, corresponding to the years of service paid for in advance which will now not be worked {8}.

The stranger was not allowed to treat him harshly, he had to be treated as if he were a servant hired year by year {9}.

Stranger Sold to Hebrew

There seems to be no Hebrew word for slave, the word 'eved' meaning servant or worker. A slave is described {10} as a servant who is bought and sold (mimkeret eved).

Hebrews must not be enslaved {10} but Hebrews could buy slaves from slave-owning slave-selling strangers. The slave was bought for life and both he and his children were his master's property.

The home of a Hebrew was to them a home of freedom. There he was protected by law against mishandling {11}.

A slave owned by a Hebrew could convert to Judaism. Successful conversion and observance seem to have meant freedom after a period which could not exceed six years.

Figure 2

FORMS OF SERVICE

Between Hebrews and Strangers.		Among Hebrews (2)		
Hebrew Employer (Such as landowner or tenant)	**Stranger Employer** (E.g. tenant)	**Hebrew Employer** (Such as landowner or tenant)		
Slave (stranger)	Redeemable Lifebond (1) Servant (Hebrew)	Lifebond (1) Servant	Bond (1) Servant	Hired Servant
Stranger bought by Hebrew from slave-owning slave-selling strangers	Hebrew 'sold' to a stranger serves 'for life' unless redeemed	Serves for life	Serves for six years	Hired as and when required

Notes (1) Bond is 'service contract'
(2) There are no Hebrew slaves
(3) All are freed in Year of Freedom

Appendix 2

YEAR OF RELEASE (SHEMITTAH)

Post-dated Loans

Loans which are due to be repaid on a date after the Year of Release are said by Hirsch to form an exception because the lender only becomes 'a lender' from the day he can demand repayment so that this type of loan is not released. The conclusion is drawn from this that if the date of repayment of a loan is after the Year of Release then the loan is not released by the Year of Release.

However, the lender becomes 'lender' and the borrower becomes 'borrower' the moment the money is transferred from lender to borrower. There would have been no need to stress that loans should be made even when Year of Release approaches {1} if it had been the intention to allow debts to be carried through the Year of Release by fixing a later date of repayment.

Dayan Grunfeld {2} states that the Torah attaches such importance to this law that it warns the one who refrains from lending because of a fear that the loan might not be repaid because of the Year of Release, warning him by using the particularly severe expression "an act of Beliya'al", an act of treachery, for this kind of behaviour.

Pledges

Pledges are an old institution and the Torah warns against oppressing the poor through taking as pledges the basic necessities for living {3}.

A 'pledge' is a security {5} for the 'obligation to repay a loan'. The pledge is taken only as a security {6} which means it is taken not as a payment but only to ensure payment. Presumably the pledge becomes the property of the lender if the loan is not repaid {8}.

If the lender holds a pledge in his hands for the loan then some say that the release does not apply {6, 9}.

However, when a pledge is not a payment but is kept by the lender only to ensure payment, then it clearly follows that when the debt is cancelled the pledge has to be returned to the borrower since cancelling a debt takes the place of repaying it.

Appendix 3

STRANGER WHO IS A SETTLER

We saw that Hebrews who dwell in the country may work the land and use it as long as the law is followed. While the entitlement to work and use the land is a hereditary possession which passes to one's heirs, the land cannot be sold.

What can be sold (leased) is the entitlement to work and use the land for a period not exceeding that to the next Year of Freedom when the lease must expire and when the hereditary owner returns to his land.

The land is owned only by Hebrews but can be leased to another Hebrew or to a stranger.

Strangers (ger) live in the country more or less permanently and some of these may settle and work the land. The stranger who is working the land, that is the 'stranger who is a settler' (ger toshav), cannot own land. Hence he is a tenant whose lease expires at the next Year of Freedom.

Having paid in advance for the use of the land to the end of the lease he presumably works independently on his own account.

Hebrews could lease land to other Hebrews and it was thus possible for Hebrew landowners to increase their landholding very considerably until the next Year of Freedom.

However, the Hebrew who rents land so as to use it, like the stranger who is a settler, is a tenant whose lease expires at the next Year of Freedom.

The term 'stranger who is a settler' {1} should thus be interpreted as meaning 'stranger who is a tenant whose lease expires at the next Year of Freedom'.

Appendix 4

CAUSE-AND-EFFECT RELATIONSHIP IN THE TORAH

The Relationship Underlies All Freedom

Plain English	Religious Language
This is the voice of freedom. I proved this by freeing you.	I am the Lord your God, who brought you ... out of the house of bondage. {1}
What is being given to you in the Torah is the pattern of behaviour which underlies all freedom.	And the tables were the work of God, and the writing was the writing of God, freedom upon the tables. {2}
If you want freedom and a good life then there is no other way.	You shall have no other Gods before Me. {3}

Introduction to Relationship

Plain English

You are unable (at your present stage of knowledge and development) to understand the Cause-and-Effect Relationship. However, the information given here enables you to see what will happen as a result of your behaviour.

Even if you do not see how that which happens results from your behaviour, the consequences of your behaviour are certain to occur and will be as stated.

Religious Language

The secret things belong to the Lord our God; but the things that are revealed belong to us and to our children for ever, that we may do all the words of this law. {4}

I call heaven and earth to witness against you this day ... {5} (See also explanatory note in Bibliography, ref. 6)

Outline of Relationship

Plain English

The quality of your life can range from freedom and a good secure life at one end of the scale to oppression and enslavement at the other end.

Where you will be on this scale depends on the way you behave towards each other, that is on the extent to which you follow the law.

Allow yourself to be persuaded into contrary behaviour and you will be oppressed and enslaved. Follow the law and you will be free and have a good life.

Religious Language

See, I have set before you this day life and good, and death and evil, ... {7}
... I have set before you life and death, the blessing and the curse; ... {8}

But if your heart turn away, and you will not hear, ... you shall surely perish; ... choose life, that you may live, ... {9}

Extent to Which It Applies

The relationship applies:

Plain English	Religious Language
(1) to all without exception	... your heads, your tribes, your elders, and your officers, even all the men of Israel, your little ones, your wives, and your stranger that is in the midst of your camp, from the hewer of your wood to the drawer of your water; {10}
(2) at all times, to the present as well as to the future	... with him that stands here with us this day ... and also with him that is not here with us this day {11}
(3) here and now, wherever you may happen to be	... it is not too hard for you, neither is it far off. ... It is not in heaven ... neither is it beyond the sea ... {12}
(4) to your mind (thoughts) and to your emotions (feelings)	(It) is very close to you, in your mouth and in your heart, that you may do it. {12}

THE RELATIONSHIP

Plain English	Religious Language	
	Results of Observing the Law	**Results of Disregarding the Law**
The actual results of behaviour both ways are listed and described, clearly and powerfully illustrating intermediate	Blessed shall you be in the city, and blessed shall you be in the field. {13} Blessed shall be the fruit of your body, and the fruit of your land, and the fruit of your cattle, the	Cursed shall you be in the city, and cursed shall you be in the field. {14} Cursed shall be the fruit of your body, and the fruit of your land, the increase of your

62

stages between the two ends of the scale.

increase of your kine and the young of your flock. {15}

The Lord will cause your enemies that rise up against you to be smitten before you; they shall come out against you one way, and shall flee before you seven ways. {17}

And the lord will make you over-abundant for good, in the fruit of your body, and in the fruit of your cattle, and in the fruit of your land, in the land which the Lord swore to your fathers to give you. {19}

...you shall lend to many nations, but you shall not borrow. {22}

And the Lord will make you the head, and not the tail; and you shall be above only, and you shall not be below; if you shall hearken to the commandments of the Lord your God, which I

kine, and the young of your flock. {16}

The Lord will cause you to be smitten before your enemies; you shall go out one way against them, and shall flee seven ways before them; and you shall be a horror to all the kingdoms of the earth. {18}

The fruit of your land, and all your labours, shall a nation which you do not know eat up; and you shall be only oppressed and crushed away; {20}

The Lord will bring you, and your king whom you will set over you, to a nation you have not known, you nor your fathers; and there shall you serve other gods, wood and stone. {21}

The stranger that is in your midst shall mount up above you higher and higher; and you shall come down lower and lower. {24}

He shall lend to you, and you shall not lend to him; he shall be the head and you shall be the tail. {25}

63

command you this day, to
observe and to do them;
{23}

Plain English	Religious Language	
	Results of Observing the Law	**Results of Disregarding the Law**
The process is reversible.		The Lord will bring a nation against you from far {26}
Increasingly disregarding the law results in greater suffering and oppression.		... and he shall eat the fruit of your cattle, and the fruit of your ground, until you be destroyed {27}
		... and he shall besiege you in all your gates throughout all your land {28}
		... and you shall be plucked from off the land {29}
		And the Lord shall scatter you among all peoples, {30}
		And your life shall hang in doubt before you; and you shall fear night and day and shall have no assurance of your life {31}

64

Plain English	Religious Language	
	Results of Observing the Law	**Results of Disregarding the Law**
Increasingly behaving according to the law results in greater freedom and a better life.	... when ... you bethink yourself among the nations, {32}	
	and ... hearken to all that I command you {33}	
	(then) the Lord your God will bring you into the land which your fathers possessed, and you shall possess it; {34}	
	And the Lord your God will put all these curses upon your enemies, and on them that hate you, that persecuted you {35}	
	And the Lord your God will make you over-abundant in all the work of your hand, in the fruit of your body, and in the fruit of your cattle, and in the fruit of your land, for good; {36}	
	if you keep His commandments and His statutes which are written in this book of the law; if you turn to the Lord your God with all your heart, and with all your soul. {37}	

Appendix 5

TEN COMMANDMENTS {1}

RELIGIOUS LANGUAGE	PLAIN ENGLISH
1	
I am the Lord your God, who brought you ... out of the house of bondage.	This is the voice of freedom. I proved this by freeing you from enslavement.
And the tables were the work of God, and the writing was the writing of God, freedom upon the tables {1}.	What is being given to you is the pattern of behaviour which underlies all freedom.
You shall have no other gods before Me.	If you want freedom and a good life then there is no other way.
2	
You shall not make for yourself a graven image, even any manner of likeness, of anything that is in heaven above, or that is in the earth beneath, or that is in the waters under the earth.	You shall not bow down to or serve any other kind of god or image or likeness of anything whatsoever.
You shall not bow down to them, nor serve them.	
For I the Lord your God am a jealous God, visiting the iniquity of the fathers upon the children, and upon the third and upon the fourth generation of them that hate Me, but showing mercy to the thousandth generation of those who love Me and keep My commandments.	Those who respect and serve other gods, respect or serve oppressing, exploiting or enslaving beliefs or ideologies, they hate me and they and their children will suffer the consequences even on the fourth generations.
	But those who love Me and keep My commandments are shown mercy to the thousandth generation.

You shall not take the name of the Lord your God in vain; for the Lord will not hold him guiltless who takes his name in vain.

3

You shall not use God's name to lend authority to a statement which it would not otherwise have or to a false or misleading statement.

4

Observe the sabbath day, to keep it holy, as the Lord your God commanded you. Six days shall you labour, and do all your work;

Observe the sabbath day, the seventh day which is a day of rest from work for all,

but the seventh day is a sabbath to the Lord your God: in it you shall not do any manner of work - you, nor your son, nor your daughter, nor your man-servant, nor your maid-servant, nor your ox, nor your ass, nor any of your cattle, nor the stranger who is within your gates;

on which all are equal and rest,

that your man-servant and your maid-servant may rest as well as you.

on which your servants rest just as you do.

And you shall remember that you were a servant in the land of Egypt, and the Lord your God brought you out from there by a mighty hand and by an outstretched arm; therefore the Lord your God commanded you to keep the sabbath day.

You shall remember that it was God who freed you from most brutal service by a mighty hand and by an outstretched arm.

Therefore God commanded you to keep the sabbath day.

5

Honour your father and your mother, as the Lord your God commanded you; that your days may be long, and that it may go well with you, on the land which the Lord your God gives you.

Honour your father and your mother and willingly accept God's commands and the tradition, knowledge and life experience of your parents so that you will progress and advance in understanding and in life and so that you will have long and secure lives of high quality in the land God will give you.

6

You shall not murder.

7

You shall not commit adultery.

8

You shall not steal.

9

You shall not bear false witness against your neighbour.

10

You shall not covet your neighbour's wife; neither shall you desire your neighbour's house, his field, or his man-servant, or his maid-servant, his ox, or his ass, or any thing that is your neighbour's.

Bibliography

The Struggle for Freedom

{1}   The Horror of Pollution: This Water has Maimed a
       Generation, Sunday Times
       Magazine, 1973 November 18.

{2}   In the Name of Profit, R. L. Heilbronner, Doubleday,
       New York.

{3}   Silent Spring, Rachel Carson, 1962.

{4}   If You Want a Future, Read On ..., David Baram

{5}   Louise W. Eickoff, Consultant Psychiatrist, Guardian,
       1970 September 12

{6}   In 'Management and Leadership: Local, National,
       Multinational (Global), Principles and Practice'
       Manfred Davidmann
       ISBN 978-0-85192-057-3
       see chapter 2: 'Style of Management and Leadership'

{7}   In 'The Human Mind and How it Works:
       Group Minds in Action: How the Human Group Mind
       Shapes the Quality of Our Life and Living'
       Manfred Davidmann
       ISBN 978-0-85192-055-9
       see chapter 9: 'The Will to Work: What People Struggle
       to Achieve'

{8}   In 'Messianic Struggle: The Worldwide Struggle for a
       Good and Secure Life for All, Here and Now'
       Manfred Davidmann
       ISBN 978-0-85192-059-7
       see chapter 2: 'Social Responsibility, Profits and
       Social Accountability'

Jewish Religion

{1}   Manoscritti Biblici Ebraici, Roberto Bonfil, Adei-Wizo,
       Milano, 1966

Biblical Law

{1}   Bamidbar **34**, 1-12

{2}   Ibid **26**, 1-63

{3}   Ibid **26**, 52-56; **33**, 53-54

{4}   Ibid **34**, 13-15

{5}   Of the tribe of Levi

{6}   Bamidbar **34**, 2, 13; **36**, 2

{7}   Ibid **36**, 1-13

{8}   Der Gottesstaat, Dr Abraham Jacobus, Berlin 1923 and 1927

{9}   Lev **25**, 13-16

{10}   Lev **25**, 23-28

{11}   The Pentateuch, Translation and Commentary by S. R. Hirsch. Translated by Dr Isaac Levy, 2nd Edtn, 1971, Judaica Press. (Lev (Vol 2) p.763-)

{12}   Lev **25**, 23

{13}   Lev **25**, 40-43

{14}   Deut **24**, 14

{15}   Deut **24**, 15; Lev **19**, 13

{16}   Lev **25**, 40-41

{17}   Exod **21**, 2; Deut **15**, 12-15, 18

{18}   Exod **21**, 2; Deut **15**, 12

{19}   Lev **25**, 39, 42

{20}   Exod **22**, 2

{21}   Deut **15**, 18

{22}   Exod **21**, 2; Deut **15**, 12

{23}   Deut **15**, 13-15

{24}   Exod **21**, 5-6; Deut **15**, 16-17

{25}   Lev **25**, 42

{26}   Exod **21**, 16

{27}   Deut **24**, 7

{28}   Lev **25**, 43

{29} Deut **23**, 16-17

{30} Exod **23**, 12; **34**, 21

{31} Exod **20**, 8-11; Deut **5**, 12-15

{32} The Sabbath, Dr I. Grunfeld, Feldheim, 1972

{33} Exod **23**, 10-11; Lev **25**, 1-7

{34} A Commentary on the Book of Exodus, V. Cassuto
(Translated by I. Abrahams),
Magnes Press, 1974 (1951)

{35} The Pentateuch and Rashi's Commentary,
R. Abraham b. Isaiah and R. Benjamin
Sharfman, S. S. & R. Publishing Co. Inc., 1950

{36} The Jewish Dietary Laws, Dr I. Grunfeld,
Soncino Press, 1972

{37} The Pentateuch, Translation and Commentary by
S.R. Hirsch. 2nd Edtn, 1971,
Judaica Press

{38} Deut **15**, 1-11

{39} Human Relations in Jewish Law, Leo Jung,
Jewish Education Press, Board of Jewish
Education Inc, 1967

{40} Exod **22**, 24

{41} Hirsch {11} quoting Gittin 37b

{42} Rashi {35} on Deut **15**, 3

{43} Deut **31**, 10-13

{44} Lev **25**, 8-13, 20-22, 39-42, 47, 54-55

{45} See 'Masters, Slaves and Servants' (p.32)

{46} See 'To Every Family its Home, Land and Income' (p.28)

{47} See 'Ownership of Land, of the Means for Independence
(p.30)

{48} In 'Judaism: Basis - Past - Present - Future, Part 2'
Manfred Davidmann
ISBN 978-0-85192-061-0
see chapter 7: 'The Way Ahead: Policies for a
Better Future'

{49} Lev **25**, 35

{50}   Lev **25**, 36-37

{51}   Lev **25**, 39-43

{52}   Exod **22**, 24. Rashi {35}

{53}   Exod **22**, 24. Hirsch {37}

{54}   Exod **22**, 24-26; Lev **25**, 36-37; Deut **23**, 20-21

{55}   Deut **23**, 21

{56}   Ahavath Chesed (Kindness as Required by God), Chafetz Chaim, Feldheim, 1967

Social Cause-and-Effect Relationship

{1}   'If You Want a Future, Read On ...', David Baram

{2}   See Appendix 4

{3}   In chapter 2.2: 'History Speaks: Monarchy, Exile and Maccabees'
See 'Monarchy Followed by Two Kingdoms - Warnings of the Prophets'
Manfred Davidmann

{4}   In chapter 2.4: 'One Law for All: Freedom Now, Freedom for Ever'
See 'Tell the People - Role of the Prophets'
Manfred Davidmann

Appendix 1

{1}   Exod **21**, 4

{2}   Exod **21**, 6; Deut **15**, 17

{3}   Rashi on Exod **21**, 6

{4}   Rashi on Exod **21**, 6; Deut **15**, 17

{5}   Lev **25**, 47-55

{6}   Lev **25**, 47

{7}   Lev **25**, 54

{8}   Lev **25**, 48-52

{9}   Lev **25**, 53

{10}   Lev **25**, 42

{11}   Exod **12**, 44; Commentary by S.R. Hirsch

Appendix 2

{1}   Deut **15**, 9

{2}   The Jewish Dietary Laws, Dr I. Grunfeld, Soncino, 1972

{3}   Exod **22**, 25-26; Deut **24**, 6, 10-13, 17

{4}   The Pentateuch, Translation and Commentary by S. R. Hirsch. 2nd Edtn, 1971, Judaica Press

{5}   Hirsch {4} on Deut **15**, 6

{6}   Hirsch {4} on Exod **22**, 26

{7}   The Pentateuch and Rashi's Commentary, R. Abraham b. Isaiah and R. Benjamin Sharfman, S. S. & R. Publishing Co. Inc., 1950

{8}   Rashi {7} on Exod **22**, 25

{9}   Hirsch {4} on Deut **15**, 3 quoting Baba Metzia 48b

Appendix 3

{1}   Lev **25**, 23, 35, 47

Appendix 4

{1}   Exod **20**, 2

{2}   Exod **32**, 16

{3}   Exod **20**, 3

{4}   Deut **29**, 28

{5}   Deut **30**, 19

{6}   'I call heaven and earth to witness against you this day ...'. Witnesses in Jewish law are directly concerned with punishing the culprit. Heaven and earth will enforce the relationship both ways which is equivalent to saying that we have here a direct cause-and-effect relationship, that the consequences of given types of behaviour will be as stated.

{7}   Deut **30**, 15

{8}   Deut **30**, 19

{9}   Deut **30**, 17-19

{10}   Deut **29**, 9-10

{11}   Deut **29**, 14

{12}   Deut **30**, 11-14

{13}   Deut **28**, 3

{14}   Ibid, 16

{15}   Ibid, 4

{16}   Ibid, 18

{17}   Ibid, 7

{18}   Ibid, 25

{19}   Ibid, 11

{20}   Ibid, 33

{21}   Ibid, 36

{22}   Ibid, 12

{23}   Ibid, 13

{24}   Ibid, 43

{25}   Ibid, 44

{26}   Ibid, 49

{27}   Ibid, 51

{28}   Ibid, 52

{29}   Ibid, 63

{30}   Deut **28**, 64

{31}   Ibid, 66

{32}   Deut **30**, 1

{33}   Ibid, 2

{34}   Ibid, 5

{35}   Ibid, 7

{36}   Ibid, 9

{37}   Ibid, 10

Appendix 5

{1}   Deut **5**, 6-18; Exod **20**, 2-14

History Speaks: Monarchy, Exile and Maccabees

Summary

This is a review and analysis of Jewish history, more particularly of what is known about King Solomon's reign and that of the Maccabean dynasty, finding the causes of the defeat of the people and loss of country.

Manfred Davidmann looks at the social conditions and the trend of events in relation to the type and style of government.

Also discussed are the warnings of the prophets in relation to the Social Cause-and-Effect Relationship.

Much has been written about King Solomon and his glorious reign, his wisdom and his riches. But Jewish Scriptures and other ancient sources look at his reign from the point of view of the people over whom he ruled and tell a different story. Oppression increased during Solomon's reign and some of the country had already been lost by the time he died.

A similar pattern of events can be seen under the Maccabean (Hasmonean) dynasty, given here in considerable detail.

Manfred Davidmann succeeds in opening our eyes to what actually happened, a matter of biblical archaeology. Jewish history shows that each time the country was lost, it was lost in accordance with the Social Cause-and-Effect Relationship.

The prophets warned rulers, establishment and people in advance about their behaviour. But the prophets were not listened to. And loss of country, expulsion and persecution occurred as predicted by the prophets in accordance with the Social Cause-and-Effect Relationship.

We see a consistent pattern which is paralleled by current events and trends. But it is possible and utterly important to learn the lessons of the past. We do not have to repeat the same mistakes.

Monarchy Followed by Two Kingdoms (First Temple period)

The successful struggle for liberation under the leadership of Moses was followed by the conquest of Canaan under Joshua. It was incomplete and for the next 200 years the tribes struggled against their neighbours, at times led by so-called Judges.

The period under the Judges was followed by a period of roughly 100 years under the 'Monarchy'. Samuel reluctantly agreed to Saul becoming King. Saul was followed by David who in turn was succeeded by his son Solomon. At the time of king Solomon's death the country split up into two kingdoms called Judah and Israel (Samaria). Israel fell about 200 years later and Judah fell roughly another 130 years later with the destruction of Jerusalem and the first Temple.

King Solomon, greatly praised, of such wonderful wisdom, of great power, wealth and horses, having many wives. But his reign was immediately followed by the kingdom splitting into two kingdoms which fought each other, which largely disregarded Jewish law until both kingdoms were destroyed and the people exiled to Babylon.

On the surface it seems unlikely that the reign of one so great should have contained within itself the causes of subsequent weakness and destruction. But it did and we need to understand what happened to avoid history repeating itself, to avoid making the same mistakes again, to avoid weakness and destruction.

What then was it that caused the decline and destruction?

Period under King Saul and King David

We know that Samuel reluctantly appointed Saul in God's name. The tribes were loosely knit together and while perhaps able to hold their own and defend themselves, had been unable to complete the conquest of the country. Saul apparently struggled to set up a single command and to impose his authority. But he followed his own judgement rather than subject himself to God's will. Hence Samuel appointed David while Saul was still alive.

Shortly after king Saul's death, David was able to unite the tribes under his rule and defeat the Philistines and other foreign tribes and complete the conquest of the country.

Initially it was those who were in distress, in debt or discontented who joined David who became captain over them {1}.

But David ruled for 40 years and became rich and powerful. He had properties throughout the land {2} and took concubines and wives {3}. There was a 'levy', apparently a form of conscription for military service, or for royal service such as working on royal properties, or for both {4}. He also numbered the population for his own purposes and against God's will, almost certainly for the purposes of recruiting and taxation {5}. The census was apparently disliked. It met with opposition and was thus incomplete.

The popular leader of those who were oppressed and in need became powerful. He started to use the people and consequently met with some opposition.

King Solomon's Rule

Much has been written about Solomon and his glorious reign, his wisdom and his riches. But Jewish scripture and other ancient sources look at his reign from the point of view of the people over whom he ruled and tell another and completely different story.

Solomon continued the process David had started. Under his reign the country seemed secure from external attack but the king's power over the people increased. Scripture and other writings tell what actually happened in many different ways. You will see that it is plainly told, consistent and to the point.

Conscription

'Raising a levy' seems to mean getting together people to labour for the king, this being compulsory (forced) labour. Adoniram was in charge of the levy {6}, Jeroboam was in charge {7} over the levy of the house of Joseph.

'King Solomon raised a levy {8} out of all Israel; and the levy was 30,000 men, under Adoniram. And he sent them to Lebanon, …'. They spent one month out of every three in Lebanon, 10,000 each month, in turn.

In addition Solomon had 70,000 who 'bore burdens' and had 80,000 who were 'hewers in the mountains' besides 3,300 chief officers who ruled over the people that did the work. This is further amplified {9} by an 'account of the levy which king Solomon raised; …'. The levy consisted of all strangers living in the land, a 'levy of bondservants …'.

'But of the children of Israel did Solomon make no bondservants; but they were {9} the men of war, and his servants, and his princes, and his captains, and the rulers of his chariots and of his horsemen'. There were 550 chief officers who ruled over the people that did the work.

This clearly mentions <1> that Hebrews served Solomon as soldiers and officers and also as servants, supervisors and administrators. The numbers must have been considerable.

Horsemen, Horses and Chariots; Taxation and the Tribe of Judah

Solomon had 12 'officers' over all Israel who were responsible for providing what provisions the king needed for himself and for his household, each in turn providing for one month in each year {11}.

He had 40,000 'stalls of horses' for his chariots and 12,000 horsemen {12} <2> and 'they let nothing be lacking', also providing swift horses and barley and straw for the horses.

He had 12,000 horsemen as well as 1,400 chariots, located {13} in 'chariot cities' as well as with the king in Jerusalem.

They provided for the king and the needs of his 'household'. Presumably they also provided for the upkeep and arming of the horsemen and their officers, collecting all this from the people of Israel.

The tribe of Judah is pointedly omitted from the list {14} of those being taxed. The name of the officer in overall charge is also pointedly omitted {15}.

David and Solomon were of the tribe of Judah. The king's tribe was the king's establishment. It seems that his tribe was exempted from paying the tax but was in charge of collecting it, presumably enforcing its collection and probably also enforcing conscription. Hence it is mentioned separately and before the people {16}.

Income and Wealth

The king had a very great annual income {17} in addition to that from the merchants, the traffic of the traders, the kings of the mingled people, the governors of the country. Some of this, if not all of it, must have come from the people of the country either directly or indirectly.

The amount of this additional income is given as 666 talents of gold each year <3>.

He made 200 targets of gold and 300 shields of gold but all of these together amounted to no more than 55 talents of gold <4>. Compared with the wealth of gold being stored, his annual income is vast. It amounts to 2 million shekels <5> and could have bought all his 12,000 horses.

The population of the country at the time of Solomon has been estimated as about 1,800,000 {18}.

He obtained the vast sum of 2 million shekels annually from an unspecified source. This amounts to at least 1 shekel per person and correspondingly more per family.

He could have collected such a vast sum each year only by taxing the people. To pay a tax of something like 5 shekels each year is likely to have been a heavy burden.

His wealth is described as having been very great indeed {19}. 'All king Solomon's drinking vessels were of gold, and all the vessels of the house of the forest of Lebanon (Solomon's palace) were of pure gold; none were of silver'. And we are told that {20} every man brought his present, 'a rate year by year'.

It seems to me that the figures confirm the thought. We are being told that he obtained his wealth by taxing the people, that this was paid as an annual tax and that this was a heavy burden on the people.

We saw that Solomon had formed a force of 12,000 horsemen and officers who provided him and his 'household' with provisions {12}. It seems that under the control of the tribe of Judah they collected the provisions from the people.

But later {22} the king with the help of this force 'made silver to be in Jerusalem as stones'.

This force did not just provide provisions for his household, but also collected and probably enforced both the tax and the compulsory labour service.

Other Gods

The Hebrews were told by God that there were people with whom they must not have any contacts as otherwise these people would turn Israel's heart towards their beliefs.

We are told {23} that king Solomon loved many foreign women from these people, that his foreign wives turned away his heart after other gods, that he built places of worship for all his foreign wives {24}.

We are also told {25} that his heart was turned towards their beliefs and it seems that he is here being accused of following some of their practices. Some of these foreign gods are mentioned by name and it may be that he is being accused of the particular practices of these religions. We know only little about the rites and practices of these people but it seems that he is being accused of promiscuous and incestuous behaviour, of allowing the children of the people to be influenced by foreign beliefs and practices, of turning their allegiance towards the beliefs of those who oppressed their people.

If he had adhered to the laws of the Torah then he would not have been able to oppress the people. In other words, he ignored basic Jewish law and weakened its application so as to weaken resistance to oppression, so as to oppress the people.

Wives and Concubines

Solomon {25} had '700 wives, princesses and 300 concubines'.

Solomon is most unlikely to have had 700 wives and 300 concubines. I have seen it stated that his marriages were politically motivated but then how many countries and tribes surrounded Israel or were known? Very few.

We have already seen that all foreigners who lived in the country were put to forced labour. So perhaps most of these women were slaves? Or are we being told indirectly (as with the amount collected by tax) that most of these were Hebrew girls?

Pharaoh's Daughter

After Solomon had eliminated those who might have disputed his rule he 'became allied to Pharaoh king of Egypt by marriage' and brought Pharaoh's daughter to Jerusalem until he had built the Temple and a palace for himself {26}. He also built a house for Pharaoh's daughter {27}.

It seems that what is being said here is that Solomon had learned Pharaoh's ways, that he began to oppress the people. He started to oppress them just as soon as he was unopposed and had undisputed authority.

Temple and Palace

King Solomon built the first Temple {28} and he also built a palace for himself {29}. It took seven years to build the Temple and after that it took thirteen years to build Solomon's palace. Figure 1 compares the dimensions of the two and it can be seen that the porch alone of Solomon's palace occupied more groundspace (1,500 sq cubits) than the combined Temple and Temple porch (1,400 sq cubits). Looked at another way, Solomon's palace occupied over four times the groundspace which the Temple occupied.

Figure 1

FIRST TEMPLE AND SOLOMON'S PALACE

	Temple	Solomon's Palace
Main Building		
Length (cubits)	60	100
Breadth (cubits)	20	50
Height (cubits)	30	30
Porch		
Length (cubits)	20	50
Breadth (cubits)	10	30
Groundspace		
Main building (sq. cubits)	1200	5000
Porch (sq. cubits)	200	1500
Total Groundspace	1400	6500
Time to build (years)	7	13

Solomon held a feast to celebrate the completion of the Temple {30} <6> which lasted two times seven days but he sent the people away on the eighth day.

So who was it who feasted during the second seven-day period after the people had been sent home?

We are also told {31} that 'when he had built the Temple and completed it, he arranged a seven-days' dedication, and then he further celebrated the seven days of the festival. <7> Thus they forgot to observe the Day of Atonement, and were distressed.'

Who was it who forgot about the Day of Atonement, about Yom Kippur?

Solomon's palace was much bigger than the Temple and this indicates the relative importance of the two in Solomon's mind. Particularly so when one remembers that the Temple served all the people.

The point is being made that it was Solomon and his establishment who feasted after the Temple had been completed and after the people had been sent home. It was Solomon and his establishment who forgot about that most solemn occasion, namely Yom Kippur. They ignored the social legislation, the basic constitution which guaranteed freedom and independence, because they were running the country for their own benefit.

We are also told {32} that there were two celebrations after Solomon had built the Temple and taken the daughter of Pharaoh to wife: 'the one in rejoicing for the erection of the Temple, the other in rejoicing for the daughter of Pharaoh'. Said God: 'Whose (rejoicing) shall I accept, of these or of the others?' At that moment it entered His mind to destroy Jerusalem.

Presumably the question was whether the constitution, the Torah, was being applied in the land or whether the people were being oppressed, that is whether it was the people or the establishment which were stronger, which were rejoicing. Solomon and his establishment were the stronger, laughed louder, and hence the automatically following consequence of the destruction of the system, that is of the country and of its oppressing establishment and of its people.

Scripture

Scripture tells us in religious language that Solomon had a choice, namely to follow the law or not, that is either to lead or to rule. He was warned about the inevitable consequences described by the cause-and-effect relationship.

We are told {33} about the feasting at the completion of the Temple. This is immediately followed by a warning to Solomon that he can either follow the law when Israel will be successful for ever, but that if he or his children turn away from following God then will Israel be cast out of the land and punished terribly.

Scripture then tells us what Solomon did and {34} the resulting anger of God.

We read that God will punish Solomon by taking the kingdom away from his dynasty, out of the hand of his son {34}. Foreign opponents began to be 'raised' against him. Of three opponents {35} of Solomon, two found refuge in Egypt where they were hospitably received while the other reigned in Damascus.

We see that scripture tells us how he behaved, that he went against the law and that this started the processes which destroyed the oppressive authoritarian system.

Later Ancient Interpretations

What Solomon did and what happened as a direct result is told in many different ways. Here are a few examples.

The Midrash tells us {36} that Solomon left his palace and travelled without being recognised. He visited the synagogues, academies, and the houses of the eminent men of Israel, saying {37} 'I, Koheleth, have been king'. Then they smote him with a rod, and set before him a dish of grits. He wept and exclaimed, 'This was my portion from all my labour' {38}.

This story clearly tells how unpopular the king was. But it also clearly tells why they treated him in this way. The particular sentence which is quoted reads as follows:

> And whatsoever my eyes desired I kept not from them; I withheld not my heart from any joy, for my heart had joy of all my labour; and this was my portion from all my labour.

In other words, he did whatever he wanted to do regardless of the law and the last sentence has Solomon acknowledging in sorrow that the treatment he received was the result of what he had done.

The gemara in the Talmud {39} tells that the doors of the sanctuary of the completed Temple would not open to receive the Ark no matter what prayers Solomon uttered. It was only {40} when he asked God to remember the good deeds of his father 'David your servant' that the doors opened to admit the Ark.

The story is told {41} that when the Torah, the law, accused Solomon before God of having broken the kingship laws that God replied "As you live, Solomon and a hundred of his kind shall be annihilated before a single one of your letters shall be obliterated.

Solomon's Wisdom

There is one last point about Solomon. He is said to have been very wise.

Just how 'wise' is a ruler who betrays and destroys his people and thus the foundation on which his home is built?

All we now know about Solomon makes one strongly suspect that the stories about his 'wisdom' may well have the reverse meaning of that commonly read into them. Scripture would not state that it is wise to betray God and oppress the people.

Take the well-known story about the two women, the king being asked to decide which of the two was the baby's mother. Does the judgement

{42} say clearly to whom the child is to be given? The verdict could refer to either one of the two women. The whole story could have quite a different meaning.

Solomon's Reign

Solomon died after he had reigned for forty years and Rehoboam his son took over {43}.

The whole record of Solomon's reign which I have given here shows a ruler who is more concerned with personal wealth and power than with leading the people towards a better life.

We are told that he broke the 'kingship' laws, the laws of government which protect the people. It is these laws which are discussed in the next section.

Laws of Kingship (government)

The Torah {44} leaves little doubt about what a ruler in Israel must not do:

>He must not 'multiply horses to himself'.

>He must not 'cause the people to return to Egypt, to the end that he should multiply horses'. This means that he must not amass servants to himself and that he must not cause the people to be oppressed and enslaved for his own benefit.

>He must not 'multiply wives to himself' so that his heart is not turned away.

>He must not 'greatly multiply to himself silver and gold'.

>He must read this law 'all the days of his life', 'that he may learn to fear the Lord his God, to keep all the words of this law and these statutes, to do them; that his heart be not lifted up above his brethren, and that he turn not aside from the commandment, to the right hand, or to the left; to the end that he may prolong his days in his kingdom, he and his children, in the midst of Israel.'

The king must be 'from among your brethren', may not be a foreigner who is not a brother. This suggests to me that he has to be a fellow Jew, that is one who observes the law and its intent and who aims to see it applied. He must follow the law and abide by it every day.

The Torah states that the king should copy out these few sentences and that he should read them regularly so as never to forget them. It seems to me that the king soon ignored the laws of the Torah which clearly states that he should not oppress the people so as to increase his own possessions and power, that he should not put himself above the people and so enrich himself. The Torah warns against him oppressing people so as to multiply his power (horses), it prohibits his taking a large number of wives and the amassing of silver and gold.

Positive laws point the way ahead towards greater strength and freedom, negative laws (prohibitions) protect people from the anti-social behaviour of others, safeguard the people's strength and freedom.

Hence the laws quoted here protect people and safeguard their strength and freedom.

While at this point the Torah does not define the kind of rule or administration one should have, what rulers and their establishment may do is clearly limited by these laws. They may not grasp power, may not oppress the people, may not behave promiscuously, may not enrich themselves.

The Two Kingdoms

Solomon died and his son Rehoboam reigned in his place. Before he could be installed, however, the people sent to Egypt for Jeroboam and all went and spoke to Rehoboam saying {45} 'Your father made our yoke grievous; now therefore make you the grievous service of your father, and his heavy yoke which he put upon us, lighter and we will serve you'.

Rehoboam asked the old men who had advised his father Solomon and they said 'If you will be a servant to this people this day, and will serve them, and answer them, and speak good words to them, then they will be your servants for ever.'

Rehoboam also asked the young men of his own age and they advised him to oppress the people even more severely than his father had done.

So Rehoboam answered the people roughly and said 'My father made your yoke heavy, I will add to your yoke; my father punished you with whips, but I will punish you with scorpions'.

Israel then rebelled against the descendants of David, and installed Jeroboam king over all Israel. However, the tribe of Judah followed the descendants of David. In this way Solomon's kingdom split up into two separate kingdoms, namely Judah and Israel (Samaria).

Oppression increased during Solomon's reign and once again it was the internal conflicts which broke up the country and so destroyed it. The lesson is driven home very clearly by the advice given to Solomon's son Rehoboam by the elders as compared with the advice he received from his younger and more impetuous contemporaries who had been persuaded to follow other gods, that is who had been turned against God and the people. The point is very clearly made that the choice was his. Just as Solomon was given a choice and judged according to the way in which he behaved, so here Solomon's son is given a choice by the people of Israel and decided to opt for strict rule instead of leadership, decided to increase their burdens. The result was that they rebelled and gained independence.

Rehoboam sent Adoram who was in charge of the forced labour but he was stoned by 'all Israel' so that he died.

Rehoboam then assembled the house of Judah and the tribe of Benjamin in Jerusalem so as to fight against the house of Israel to bring the kingdom back to Rehoboam {46}. They were told by a 'man of God' not to fight against the house of Israel 'for this thing is of Me' and they did not fight.

In this way the kingdom of Solomon was split into two separate countries.

Jeroboam ruled over Israel and made two calves of gold, saying that these were the gods which brought Israel out of the land of Egypt, the people being persuaded to worship them, priests being appointed who were not of the house of Levi. He even changed the times for the festivals.

With these changes the new ruler moved even further away from Jewish law and its application, changing the religion so as to strengthen his grip on the people, so as to increase his personal power over them by separating the two parts of the Jewish people even further so that the people would not return to Jerusalem, so that the people of 'Israel' would not join the people of 'Judah'.

The application of the Torah, the basic constitution which protects the people, had been abrogated and the people were worse off than before, had even less protection against the ruler and his establishment, against the misuse of his power.

Social Conditions at the Time

This is what Ze'ev Falk {62} says:
> ... Transfers of land were made without any limitation based on the rules of the Jubilee (Yovel) and of redemption. Under the monarchy it became possible to acquire large estates and to have them cultivated by slaves and hired workers. Poor farmers were often forced to mortgage their holdings, to sell them and even to suffer their own or their children's enslavement. By the time of the first prophets, real as well as personal property changed

hands frequently and capital was concentrated in the hands of a few.

Omri, king of Israel, ruled about fifty years after Solomon's death. At that time {47} there grew up a wealthy class

> with luxurious standards of personal comfort and little regard for the basic rights of others. The process of dispossessing people from their land was hastened in defiance of Jewish tradition by pitiless administration of the laws of debt. Large estates were accumulating, worked by slave labour. Official religion tended to be more and more formalised, concentrating its attention on the execution of ceremonial, to the exclusion of all that was ritual. Justice was frequently corrupt, and at its best, rigid.

It seems that interest was charged and that farmers fell into debt, that the ownership of land and houses passed into the hands of a few people and that the poor were oppressed and forced into severe forms of bondage.

Warnings of the Prophets

A few quotations from the sayings of the prophets show clearly that the prophets were very much aware of the consequences of what was taking place. They pointed out what was bound to happen if the rulers, their establishment and perhaps also the people continued to behave as they were doing and events proved them right. We would now say that intuitively or consciously they were aware of the social relationships, that they were aware of the social consequences of different types of behaviour.

The prophets, motivated by a deeply seated sense of social responsibility and urgency, by love of God, Torah and people, continued with increasing frequency and increasing urgency to warn of the inevitable consequences unless rulers and establishment changed their ways, pointing out that all the people would suffer horribly unless behaviour changed. They were bitterly opposed by the rulers and establishment of the day and struggled for God and people while alone and unsupported. They were not listened to, the rulers and their establishments continued to corrupt and oppress the people until both kingdoms were destroyed and the people most viciously dispersed.

So now let us look at the kind of behaviour the prophets warned against as it was that kind of behaviour which was weakening the people and thus the country. For example at the time of Elisha we read {48} about the widow whose two children are to be taken away to be bondmen by the creditor (money lender or person to whom the money is owed) and see that money could pay the debt and thus protect the children {49}.

Amos, Hosea, Isaiah and Micah warned about the coming destruction in the period preceding the fall of Israel. They accused the rulers and their establishment of the kind of practices which need to be corrected if Israel and Judah are to survive.

Amos, for example, says {50} that they 'sell the righteous for silver, and the needy for a pair of shoes', that a man and his father 'go unto the same maid'. He accuses them of oppression, that they 'know not to do right', that they oppress the poor, crush the needy, tell their establishment to 'bring, that we may feast'. He further accuses them, saying that they trample on the poor and that they take from him 'exactions' of wheat. It is clear {51} that he is addressing himself to, and attacking, the rulers of the country. Later on {52} he addresses those who would 'swallow the needy, and destroy the poor of the land', who make 'the ephah small and the shekel great' (that is who give less and charge more), those who cheat so as to 'buy the poor for silver, and the needy for a pair of shoes, and sell the refuse of the corn'.

He warns {53} about the coming destruction of Judah and Jerusalem because Judah has rejected the law of the Lord. He warns Israel {54} about the disaster that was going to overtake it. Events proved him right. He shows his understanding of the relationship between cause and effect by telling them that defeat is certain as they will not have the moral or physical strength to fight or to escape. He refers to and discusses {55} the 'day of the Lord'. He is clearly referring not so much to a day of redemption as to a day of retribution against the oppressor, making the point that there will be no escape and that it would be better to change their ways before disaster overtakes them, here plainly referring to the disaster which will strike Israel and Judah. Perhaps he is stating that the hope of all mankind for justice and freedom is no empty dream, that justice takes its course, that the law is such that oppressors are punished in the end.

Hosea {56} makes the point that there is no truth, no mercy, no knowledge of God in the land, that there is lying, killing and stealing, that there is prostitution (harlotry) and adultery. He compares the princes of Judah to those who 'removed the landmark'.

Isaiah {57} also points to those who join house to house and field to field, thus increasing their own estate. He refers {58} to people either being sold, or having sold themselves, to creditors.

Micah {59} points out that those who want fields take them, that those who want houses take them away; that they 'oppress a man and his house, even a man and his heritage'. He accuses {60} the 'heads of the house of Jacob' and the 'rulers of the house of Israel' of abhorring justice, of perverting all equity, that they 'build up Zion with blood and

Jerusalem with iniquity', that their heads 'judge for reward' and that the priests 'teach for hire'.

We see that the prophets warned about the consequences of delinquency, crime, sexual permissiveness and corruption. They warned about land being concentrated in the hands of a few, of Jew exploiting and oppressing Jew, of people being oppressed and enslaved through debt and through need.

So far I have covered in outline some of the knowledge which we have from the warnings of the prophets about the behaviour of the Hebrew rulers and their establishment, a story of increasing oppression and exploitation of the people, of increasing disregard of basic Torah law, with consequences which were very clear to the prophets who warned and who appear to have had a clear understanding of the inevitability with which the law acts, of the inevitability with which the behaviour of the establishment caused the effects which destroyed their people and thus the rulers and their establishment themselves.

The Monarchy and the Two Kingdoms

At the beginning of this period the tribes are scattered and on their own, each more or less fighting its own battles and looking after its own interests. We see freedom, people following the law and behaving in a way which guarantees freedom and a good life. We see the tribes coming together under a single central rule with combined forces. Military success went hand in hand with bringing the tribes together in one united country, resulted in the opposing foreign tribes being defeated, resulted in a country and a people which were united and powerful. Then we see those who rule using their power for their own benefit and to impose their rule. We see the emergence of those who grasp power and rule and then weaken the law so as to rule more forcefully, so as to oppress, so as to exploit the people. This led inevitably to internal confrontation and conflict which divided the country.

The Year of Release (shemittah) and Year of Freedom (yovel) laws safeguard the people from oppression and exploitation. It was from the time that laws such as these, as well as some of those relating to behaviour, were beginning to be disregarded that the Jewish people moved away from equality and co-operation, towards oppression by a few and consequent conflict. In this way they moved away from religious observance, humane behaviour and freedom, moved towards oppression, internal stress and conflict.

The prophets based their statements on a deep understanding of Jewish law and of the consequences of antisocial behaviour. They acted for the people and for freedom. They knew that Jewish law underlies all freedom, understood the inevitable disastrous consequences of behaviour contrary to the law and warned accordingly.

The story of the two kingdoms is not just one of the rulers and their establishment oppressing their own people in each of the two countries, but also one of two kingdoms struggling with each other. It is a story of a divided people weakening each other by fighting each other, sinking into behaviour which was harming them, weakening them to the point of destruction.

It seems to me that during the period of the monarchy and of the two kingdoms there was a continuous struggle between the forces which supported God, Judaism and the people, and those forces which supported central rule, the establishment and oppression of the people. It was the rulers who generally acted contrary to Jewish law and the Jewish religion seems to have been belittled, opposed and in some ways negated by them.

Outstanding is that the warnings of the prophets were ignored, that the establishment of the day ignored the writing on the wall. They did not act then, they did not act at other times. In so doing they did not just oppress their people, what they were doing was to destroy their people and to destroy themselves as well.

During the period of the monarchy, that is during the period of Saul, David and Solomon, we see central military authority being more effective in an emergency and see the military leader subsequently taking over the administration, taking over the government. This is followed by increasing centralisation of power and the formation of an establishment (secular and religious) which serves the source of power and is used to oppress the people. The military are used to give and obey orders but the skills involved are completely different from those expected from an effective manager. In general, while authoritarian organisations are effective in an emergency they are generally ineffective and wasteful at other times. What we see is increasing centralisation of power, increasing corruption and oppression, increasing enslavement of the people with consequent social stress and subsequent destruction.

Return from Exile and Maccabean Dynasty

Return from Exile

The two kingdoms were destroyed. The country was desolate. Most of those Jews who survived in the country had been taken to captivity in Babylon.

The details are obscure but what we do know is that the Persians took over Babylon. Cyrus, King of Persia, called for the rebuilding of a Jewish community and of the Temple in Jerusalem. He asked the Jewish community in exile to support the expedition financially while he himself contributed the Temple treasures which the Babylonians had carried off to Babylon when the first Temple was destroyed some 50 years earlier.

It took about 100 years for the Temple to be rebuilt and for the walls of Jerusalem to be reconstructed. We have a pretty good idea about how an enlightened administrator, called Nehemiah, struggled to overcome the oppressive practices of the Jewish establishment and about the struggle for re-establishing the application of Jewish law in the daily lives of the country's inhabitants, of re-establishing the observance of the law of Moses.

People were poor, times were hard and once again many had to mortgage their land to the Jewish rich. When in need they not only had to hand over their fields but had to give their children to serve others, had to sell their children as slaves, were forced to lose their own freedom.

Nehemiah argued with the nobles and the rulers and in a moving speech {61} succeeded in persuading them to return the fields, vineyards, oliveyards, houses, the 'hundred pieces of silver', the corn, wine and oil that had been exacted from the people. Marrying out (intermarriage) was denounced, the law clearly stating that it was prohibited. They agreed to stop charging interest on loans and the practice of bondage for debt was abolished. Nehemiah also ensured that the Sabbath was observed and they also instituted the Year of Release (shemittah year).

About 60 years later Alexander the Great conquered the country which became part of his empire. When he died about 10 years later his generals fought with each other for the succession. Ptolemy I took over in Egypt and conquered Israel, with Seleucus I opposing Ptolemy from what is now Syria. About 125 years after the death of Alexander the country passed to the Seleucids (198 BCE).

Maccabean Dynasty (The Hasmoneans)

Uprising

We know little about life in Israel during the period of about 300 years between the time of the return from Babylon and the time of the taking over of the country by the Seleucids. We do know that religious observance was so important that they would not even defend themselves when attacked on the Sabbath (the weekly day of rest) so as not to desecrate it.

The Seleucid rulers started a process of hellenisation. Among the Jewish leadership were those who served the Seleucid rulers by offering greater annual taxes for the sake of obtaining personal power. They collected them from the people. At the same time they weakened and opposed the influence of the Jewish religion so as to weaken the people. It was of course the people who suffered and who became more and more discontented.

The Seleucids robbed the Temple of its wealth and destroyed the walls of Jerusalem. They then attempted to hellenise the country by brutal force. Those who observed the Jewish laws and customs were bitterly persecuted, pagan worship and practices were introduced into the Temple and they destroyed written records (scrolls) of the law whenever they could find them. The high priest Menelaus continued in office but served Jupiter.

Mattathias (a priest) rebelled against pagan worship. The people could stand no more and led first by Mattathias and then by his son Judah Maccabee they rebelled against the imposed vicious rule of the Seleucids.

First Generation: Liberating the Country, Centralising Power

Judah Maccabee was one of the five sons of Mattathias and for a period of 30 years the brothers led the people against the oppressing invader.

Judah Maccabee was followed by Jonathan who in turn was followed by Simeon. The leadership of the three brothers covers a period of 30 years during which much of the country was freed.

Jonathan was appointed high priest about 8 years after taking over the leadership. Simeon was confirmed by the 'Great Assembly' as high priest, ethnarch (ruler) and commander of the Jewish people. Simeon's positions were to be hereditary.

It seems that the family was united and that the brother who was ruling at the time had the full support of the other brothers. What is known is that whenever the brother who was ruling at the time was either killed in battle or assassinated by the enemy, that one of the other brothers simply stepped into his place and provided the required leadership. In this way they struggled successfully.

Appointing Jonathan as high priest transferred religious authority and power to a secular leader. When the Great Assembly confirmed Simeon's position, a few years after he had assumed the leadership, they confirmed that religious and secular as well as military authority and power had been vested in one person and were to be hereditary.

What had happened was that able military and secular leadership absorbed religious authority and power. That this concentration of all authority and power in the hands of one person was to be permanent and later to be transferred to his descendants is an indication that the establishment of the day was already concerned with consolidating its own position.

I think that combining all power in the hands of a single ruler is against the spirit and intent of Jewish law as religious authority which should serve God and the people, which should indicate direction and provide drive, may then too readily be misused to serve the establishment of the day instead of God and the people.

Second Generation: Power Centred on Ruler, Start of Discontent

Simeon was succeeded by John Hyrcanus I who ruled 30 years. He was very successful in consolidating gains which had been made and in expanding the area under his control. His conquests included the whole of Edom and he forcibly converted the Edomites to Judaism. Under his leadership the country gained what probably amounted to complete independence.

But the struggle was not just between the Jewish people and the Seleucid rule but also between the Jewish people and their own ruler. What we know is that during his reign opposition against the combination of religious and secular power, against the dominating role of the hereditary ruler and his establishment in all aspects of life, began to be felt.

It was a struggle against those rich and 'high born' who were in sympathy with and actively supported hellenic ideas and practices, it being the mass of the population who would not relinquish their beliefs, who could not and would not relax religious observance.

It seems that under the reign of John Hyrcanus I the opposing factions became known as pharisees and sadducees.

Third Generation: Country Consolidated, Conflict Between Royal Brothers, Increased Conflict Between Opposing Factions

John Hyrcanus I was succeeded for about a year by his eldest son Judah Aristobulus I.

The indications are that he supported hellenic ideas and it was either he, or his brother Alexander Yannai who succeeded him, who first adopted the title of 'king'.

When Judah Aristobulus died his brother Alexander Yannai married the widow (as required by Jewish law) and ruled Judea for just under 30 years. He succeeded in expanding the area under his control which covered much if not all of the area settled originally by the tribes.

When Alexander Yannai died the leadership passed to his wife, Salome Alexandra.

The indications are that Aristobulus I placed his personal power above family and that he attempted to impose his personal authority by eliminating opposition from his mother and brothers.

During Alexander Yannai's reign the conflict between opposing factions deepened. It seems that he was ruthless and that secular and religious power were concentrated in his hands to a previously unknown extent.

Queen Salome Alexandra ruled for about nine years. She had two sons. The older son was Hyrcanus II, the younger son was Aristobulus II.

We saw that Alexander Yannai died and that his wife Salome Alexandra succeeded to the throne. By that time both secular and religious power and authority were centred on the person of the ruler and this was of course strictly against the spirit and intent of the original Hasmonean revolt, against the spirit and intent of the Torah.

It seems that Queen Salome Alexandra attempted to halt and reverse the trend of centralisation of power and consequent oppression and exploitation of the people, attempting to move the government towards greater observance of the Torah and its social legislation. The elder son, namely Hyrcanus II, was high priest and considered the heir to the throne. The younger brother, namely Aristobulus II, was the military commander. In this way the power to rule and oppress was less important than the authority of the ruler who was high priest and would thus be expected to place greater importance on the meaning and intent of the Torah rather than on exploiting the people for his own benefit.

Figure 2

MACCABEAN DYNASTY

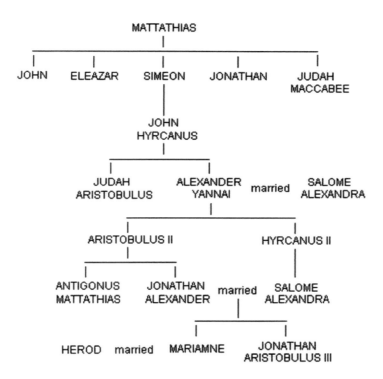

It seems that civil war broke out while the Queen was still alive and that the younger brother who was the military commander (Aristobulus II) was able to defeat his elder brother who was high priest and heir to the throne (Hyrcanus II).

Fourth and Fifth Generation:

(a) Civil War by Aristobulus Against Hyrcanus

When Queen Salome Alexandra died the younger brother (Aristobulus II) proclaimed himself king and high priest. The elder brother (Hyrcanus II) surrendered his power to the younger brother as he had been defeated in battle. The younger brother (Aristobulus II) ruled for about four years.

Hyrcanus then obtained the support of the Nabateans by promising to hand over to them some parts of Judea. He defeated Aristobulus and besieged him in Jerusalem.

But by this time the Romans had arrived in Syria which had become a Roman province. The Roman commander (Scaurus), apparently favouring Aristobulus in return for a large sum of money, told the Nabateans to withdraw from Jerusalem and this they did.

Shortly afterwards a new Roman commander, namely Pompey, took over the command. The dispute between the brothers was taken to him and it seems that he favoured Hyrcanus. Aristobulus surrendered to Pompey but managed to get away. The Roman army advanced on Jerusalem and while Hyrcanus' followers opened the gate of the city to the Romans, it took the Romans three months to take the Temple Mount. It seems that thousands of its defenders were killed.

This was virtually the end of independence for the country as they were now subservient to the Roman governor of Syria. Judea was very much reduced in size and its rulers were not allowed to call themselves kings. Once again the Jews were obliged to pay taxes to a foreign government.

(b) Antipater and Herod

What had happened was that the two brothers, struggling against each other for the sake of personal power, had involved foreign powers. The brothers were seemingly more concerned with struggling against each other than with the future existence, welfare and strength of the people and the country as a whole.

It was Antipater II, one of the converted Edomites, whose advice Hyrcanus had followed when he made common cause with the Nabateans against Aristobulus.

Pompey had seemingly favoured Hyrcanus, and Aristobulus had apparently been taken to Rome. Julius Caesar defeated Pompey. It seems that Aristobulus was poisoned in Rome supposedly by supporters of Pompey. Caesar had been helped in Egypt by Hyrcanus and Antipater and subsequently confirmed Hyrcanus as high priest and ethnarch. But Antipater and his two sons (Phasael and Herod) gained much power and influence.

The title 'ethnarch' means 'head of the people' and presumably indicates that the holder of that position represents his people in relation to the foreign ruling power, possibly taking his orders from the local Roman governor in Syria.

Caesar was assassinated. Cassius who was apparently one of the conspirators gained control of Syria and Judea and tried to get as much money as he could out of the people of Judea. Antipater and his sons sided with him.

It seems to me that Antipater and his sons Phasael and Herod advised and acted throughout with complete disregard of the Jewish people, apparently concerned solely with gaining control over them, with their own personal power and influence.

(c) Civil War by Aristobulus' Son Antigonus Against Hyrcanus. End of Dynasty: Herod

It was Aristobulus II who started the civil war which in the end resulted in the country being overrun, the country and its people losing their independence to the Romans. His youngest son was called Antigonus.

When the Parthians invaded Rome's eastern provinces, Antigonus allied himself with them so as to replace his uncle Hyrcanus, so as to rule himself.

When Hyrcanus and Phasael were negotiating with the Parthians they were taken prisoner. Apparently Hyrcanus was mutilated by having his ears cut off so as to disqualify him from the priesthood. Aided by the Parthians, Antigonus was thus able to make himself king of Judea.

But Herod was able to escape and made his way to Rome so as to obtain political backing and military assistance. He was given the title 'king' by the Romans. This was in 40 BCE. Herod returned to Israel with some Roman legions and started to take the country from Antigonus. After the Romans defeated the Parthian armies they were able to considerably reinforce the Roman legions which were fighting Antigonus. Jerusalem was taken by Herod and the Romans after a siege lasting five months and Antigonus was defeated. During the course of his campaign against Antigonus, Herod had also married Mariamne (6th generation), a granddaughter of Hyrcanus II. Antigonus was put to death by Herod and so Herod ruled Judea for Rome, an Edomite king over the Jewish people.

Once again the Jewish people had been divided against each other by behaviour contrary to basic Jewish law and in this case the result was the ending of the rule of the Maccabean dynasty, of the revolt for the application of Jewish law in everyday life. The people were ruled by an Edomite king who may have been regarded as Jewish by some but whose whole actions showed that Judaism and behaviour according to Jewish law were very far from his thoughts.

The Struggle of the Maccabees

Mattathias, his sons and his grandson John Hyrcanus battled together and supported each other and John Hyrcanus was able to build the country and complete the work the others had started.

The country was built and enlarged until it became strong and independent through one central unifying purpose: to build a country in which Jewish people could live as Jews and practise their faith. Single minded, the members of the royal family were loyal to the ruler and as soon as one died the next one was ready to take over and was in turn supported by the rest of the family.

With Aristobulus I it seems that power had corrupted but he did not rule for long and Alexander Yannai was able to do very well indeed.

Following the popular rebellion for Judaism, for Jewish law and thus for freedom, the rulers formed a dynasty and a supporting establishment, had tasted power and meant to have it. Hence they battled for power with each other, allied themselves with foreign powers against each other. In so doing they divided the people and weakened all.

To begin with all were united and struggled against the brutal oppression. They struggled for Torah, freedom and the people. Against them were foreign invaders who believed in slavery and who were trying to impose their way of life through imposing their beliefs.

After three generations the situation had changed and we now see very clearly increasing internal confrontation, a struggle between people and Torah on the one hand against oppressive rulers and their oppressing establishment on the other.

The oppression of Jew by Jew, of the Jewish people by their own rulers and establishment, and the resulting struggle between them defeated both. It ended Maccabean rule, lost the land which had been gained, resulted in enormous hardship to the people. It resulted in the handing over of the country and its people to Herod and the subsequent introduction by Herod of 'hellenisation'. This meant the introduction and popularisation of a foreign ideology, supporting and based on slavery. It was indeed this which the Maccabees had struggled against.

The Jewish leadership, the Jewish establishment, supported centralised power, the oppressive ruling authority and its influence, since the ideas which were being imported helped them to oppress their own people. In so doing they disregarded the welfare of the people, disregarded Jewish law, disregarded the intent and purpose of Jewish law.

Outstanding is that the people were unable to restrain their leaders. The result was total destruction of people and country, and the dispersion of the Jewish people.

Rome and Herod

This is what Cecil Roth {47} says about Herod and his times:

> Herod was cold, calculating and cruel. He arrested and executed almost immediately 45 members of the leading aristocratic families of the realm. He appointed his wife's handsome young brother, another Aristobulus, to the high priesthood but he became popular and so Herod had him drowned. Herod also executed his own uncle, had the aged Hyrcanus (his wife's grandfather, formerly king and high priest) murdered and put to death his own wife, Mariamne, and followed this by eliminating her mother Alexandra. When Herod's own children by Mariamne, Alexander and Aristobulus, grew to manhood the two princes were charged with treachery and strangled in prison (7 BCE). The ultimate Roman overlordship was at all times plain. The tribute paid to them was heavy. Roman legionaries were never absent from Jerusalem, and Roman institutions prevailed in the country more and more. The old constitution of the country was overruled. The Sanhedrin was deprived of all executive or deliberative power, so that it became to an increasing degree an academic and religious council. The office of the high priesthood became less and less important.

It seems that Herod, an Edomite (Idumaean), one of the ancient enemies of Judaism and the Jewish people, had taken the country over and eliminated the opposition, the Jewish establishment, and the Maccabean line and then set about to try and destroy the religion, the hold which the religion had on the people, the people's beliefs, so as to do what the Greeks had tried to do, so as to render Jewish religion and Jewish beliefs ineffective.

> Herod was devoted to fashionable hellenic culture, to the complete neglect of everything Jewish. He did reconstruct the Temple in Jerusalem but in Sebaste he actually established a temple for the cult of the Emperor.

> The hellenisation against which the Maccabeans had fought became deeply implanted. When the king died in 4 BC, vast strides had already been made under his inspiration in the process which was to end with the final extrusion of Judaism from the country.

Herod re-established the state of Israel, but what he re-established was a secular state which gave equal if not more importance to other religions, which was a 'state like any other'.

He attempted to replace Jewish beliefs which demand freedom, secure independence and social security with those of a culture based on slavery, on the often inhuman exploitation of man by man. He brutally oppressed and exploited the people.

He moved far in the direction of negating Judaism and its protection and safeguards for the people and thus merely brought about the inevitable destruction of his regime and establishment.

'Inevitable' not just because it actually happened, but because what happened was predictable, happened in accordance with the social cause-and-effect relationship we discussed in the chapter 2.1.

Notes and Bibliography

Notes

<1> There is a later account which pointedly ignores Solomon's Hebrew servants {10}.
See also <6>.

<2> 1,000 men/ruler of 1,000.

<3> 1 score = 20.

<4> 1 talent = 3,000 shekels
200 targets @ 600 shekels = 120,000 shekels = 40 talents
1 lb (maneh) = 50 shekels
300 shields @ 3 lbs (maneh) = 300 x 3 x 50 = 45,000 shekels = 15 talents

<5> 666 talents = 666 x 3,000 shekels = 1,998,000 shekels
Say = 2 million shekels

<6> Once again the later Chronicles {21} tells a pointedly different story. See also <1>.

<7> Tabernacles

<8> Used throughout: Scriptures {63}; Talmud {64}

Bibliography

{1} 1 Samuel **22**, 2

{2} 1 Chronicles **28**, 1

{3} 2 Samuel **5**, 13

{4} 2 Samuel **20**, 24

{5} 2 Samuel **24**, 1; 1 Chronicles **21**, 1

{6} 1 Kings **4**, 6

{7} 1 Kings **11**, 28

{8} 1 Kings **5**, 27-30

{9} 1 Kings **9**, 15, 20-23

{10} 2 Chronicles **8**, 9

{11} 1 Kings **4**, 7

{12} 1 Kings **5**, 6-8

{13} 1 Kings **10**, 26

{14} 1 Kings **4**, 7-19

{15} 1 Kings **4**, 20

{16} 1 Kings **4**, 20; 5, 5

{17} 1 Kings **10**, 14-17

{18} Ency. Judaica **12**, 869

{19} 1 Kings **10**, 21

{20} 1 Kings **10**, 24-25

{21} 2 Chronicles **7**, 8-10

{22} 1 Kings **10**, 26-27

{23} 1 Kings **11**, 1-2

{24} 1 Kings **11**, 4, 8

{25} 1 Kings **11**, 3

{26} 1 Kings **3**, 1

{27} 1 Kings **7**, 8

{28} 1 Kings **6**, 2-3, 38

{29} 1 Kings **7**, 1-2, 6

{30} 1 Kings **8**, 65-66

{31} Midrash Rabba, Num **17**, 2

{32} Midrash Rabba, Lev **12**, 5

{33} 1 Kings **9**, 1-

{34} 1 Kings **11**, 9-

{35} 1 Kings **11**, 14-40

{36} Midrash Rabba, Ecclesiastes II, 3

{37} Ecclesiastes **1**, 12

{38} Ecclesiastes **2**, 10

{39} Moed Katan 9a; Sabbat 30a; Sanhedrin 107b

{40} 2 Chronicles **6**, 42

{41} Talmud Yerushalmi (Legends of the Jews, **4**, 165)

{42} 1 Kings **3**, 27

{43} 1 Kings **11**, 43

{44} Deut **17**, 14-20

{45} 1 Kings **12**

{46} 1 Kings **12**, 21-

{47} A Short History of the Jewish People, Cecil Roth, East & West Library, 1969

{48} 2 Kings **4**, 1

{49} 2 Kings **4**, 7-

{50} Amos **2**, 6-

{51} Amos **6**, 4-

{52} Amos **8**, 4-6

{53} Amos **2**, 4

{54} Amos **2**, 6-

{55} Amos **5**, 18-

{56} Hosea **4**, 1, 2

{57} Isaiah **5**, 8

{58} Isaiah **50**, 1

{59} Micah **2**, 2-

{60} Micah **3**, 5-

{61} Nehemiah **5**, 6-13

{62} Hebrew Law in Biblical Times, Ze'ev W. Falk, Wahrmann, 1964

{63} The Holy Scriptures, The Jewish Publication Society of America

{64} The Babylonian Talmud, Soncino Press, London

Chapter 2.3

At the Time of Jesus,
This is What Actually Happened in Israel:
The Truth about Hillel and his Times

Summary

Here Manfred Davidmann records a breathtaking journey of discovery through events which shaped today's world and today's problems. This is factual and conclusive, a documented statement of what Jewish writers then recorded about what had happened at about the time of Jesus to Jewish belief and practice, an exercise in biblical archaeology.

Fascinating is Manfred Davidmann's fully documented record of previously undiscovered material in the Talmud about Hillel and his time. It is eye-opening to discover the truth about Hillel, about his origin and background, about his political beliefs, about the decisive struggle going on within Judaism at that time.

Torah law provides and ensures equality, independence, freedom from oppression and exploitation, and a good life of high quality. The Jewish establishment argued against such laws so as to expose the people to exploitation through need. The resulting struggle changed Judaism, determined the fate of the Jewish people and gave rise to Christianity.

Manfred Davidmann includes a clear, concise and factual summary statement outlining what the Talmud is and how it came to be written, describing its relative authority and that of its components.

Included also is a similar statement about the Halachah (code of Jewish rabbinical law). Manfred Davidmann shows how Torah, Talmud and Halachah are related to each other and states their relative scope and authority.

Also recorded at the time were extremely relevant statements about what a future generation would have to do to reverse the pattern of events and to establish a good life of high quality for all.

Arguments against Observing the Release (Shemittah) and Freedom (Yovel) Laws

We have seen the Jewish people struggle successfully for a Jewish way of life, both under David and under the early Maccabees. But we also saw that in each case they were weakened internally until they were defeated and destroyed by their enemies. In each case it was the Jewish rulers and their establishment which bypassed basic Jewish laws so as to oppress their people. <1>

These laws are not being observed today and here we begin by taking a close look at the reasoning of those who 2000 years ago, at about the time of Herod, argued against observing the Year of Release (shemittah) and the Year of Freedom (yovel) laws.

Arguments against Observance

All the Jewish people have to be living in Erez Israel

One argument <11> runs that Freedom (yovel) years were abolished because the Freedom laws ceased to apply when some of the land's inhabitants were exiled. The conclusion drawn from this was that the Freedom laws apply only when all the Jewish people are living in Erez Israel.

The scholars discuss this in the Talmud {1} as follows:
> 'For it was taught: When the tribe of Reuben, the tribe of Gad and the half-tribe of Manasseh went into exile, the Freedom years (yovel years) were abolished as it is said: 'And ye shall proclaim liberty throughout the land unto all the inhabitants thereof', That is at the time when all the inhabitants thereof dwell upon it, but not at the time when some of them are exiled.'

The point is then made that in addition the tribes have to be living in their allotted areas, without intermingling, for the Freedom laws to be applied:
> '.... therefore it is said: 'Unto all the inhabitants thereof', which means, only at the time when its inhabitants are there as they ought to be, but not when they are intermingled!'

While exploring possible interpretations the scholars are saying that the Freedom laws apply only when all the Jewish people are living in Erez Israel and when the tribes are separated and living in their originally allocated areas. This would amount to abolishing the application in practice of these important laws.

But it does not seem valid to deduce a negative statement from a positive statement in the way put forward by them and this is discussed in more detail in the section 'If One Lapses So Does the Other'.

The relevant laws are as follows {2}:

10) And you shall set apart the fiftieth year, and proclaim freedom throughout the land to all its inhabitants thereof; it shall be a Freedom year to you; and every man shall return to his family.

13) In this year of Freedom every man shall return to his inheritance.

It is seen that freedom from servitude and freedom from want (returning to his inherited land) have to be proclaimed every fifty years to all Hebrews living in Erez Israel. The plain meaning of 'all' is 'without exception', so that freedom has to be proclaimed without exception to every Hebrew living in Erez Israel.

Lapsed sanctity of land

A detailed, scholarly and comprehensive discussion {3} of the laws relating to the land can be found in the second volume of Dayan Grunfeld's 'The Jewish Dietary Laws'. By laws relating to the land I mean laws such as those about tithes, Shemittah and Yovel. It seems that there is some doubt about the extent to which the laws apply today in Erez Israel.

Whether or not the laws apply, and the extent to which they are applied, is said to depend largely on whether the sanctity of the land still continues in our day.

The people of Israel could not observe the laws of the land until the land had been conquered and distributed among them. The argument then runs that Jewish people need to observe the laws relating to the land only because of the conquest of the land.

We occupied the land, led by Joshua and Joshua 'sanctified' it. This 'sanctity' lapsed when Nebuchadnezzar took the land away from us by conquest.

We returned after the Babylonian exile, the return having been permitted by King Cyrus. Ezra then took possession and sanctified (made holy) the land, not by conquest but by occupying it.

The assumption that sanctification arises from the way in which the territory is taken over leads also to discussion about there being different degrees of sanctity in different territories dependent on the way in which they were occupied. Distinctions are then drawn between territories occupied by a king of Israel or by a prophet and whether they were occupied with the consent of a majority of Israel. From this are then defined different degrees of sanctity of lands occupied at different times.

There are some who hold that the sanctification of the Holy land by Ezra was not meant to last for ever and that it ceased with the destruction of the temple and the dispersion of the Jewish people Hence some say that the holiness of the land has lapsed so that the Shemittah (year of release) is nowadays a rabbinical ordinance.

On the other hand there are those who consider that Ezra sanctified the land for ever and that this sanctification was not interfered with when the Romans conquered the country. They say that the land was taken away from us but this time retained its holiness so that the laws of tithes and Shemittah (year of release) apply today.

I would like to resolve these conflicting viewpoints by looking at the problem from a different point of view, from a point of view which also incorporates the other two.

Sanctity is 'holiness' and this means 'degree of observance'. Hence sanctification (making holy) and sanctity (holiness) depend on observing the laws and on degree of observance.

If there are different degrees of sanctity in different territories, this means that there is a difference in the laws which are being observed and in the degree of observance.

The land is God's, the people are the servants of God and sanctity shows itself when and as long as people behave in a way which sanctifies. The land is only sanctified by those who observe God's laws and by the extent to which they observe them.

The laws relating to the land could only be applied after the land had been conquered and distributed, could only be observed after the people had received land and were working it. The land was thus sanctified by Joshua who established Jewish law as the law of the land, up to the exile.

It was later sanctified by Ezra who again established Jewish law as the law of the land, until the law ceased to be applied and observed as the law of the land. If since then the law was always followed by part of the population then the land kept its sanctity correspondingly.

We see that the land's sanctity becomes apparent and becomes effective dependent on the behaviour of its inhabitants, dependent on the extent to which the law is applied and observed.

Its sanctity thus depends on the application of Jewish law in the daily lives of the country's inhabitants. It thus depends on Jewish law being the law of the land and on its effective application.

Laws such as those relating to the Release Year (shemittah), the Freedom Year (yovel) and tithing are clearly stated in the Torah and we are obliged to follow them whenever we have the opportunity to do so, whenever the land is ours.

Prosbul

Take the key area of making money available to those in need, of making it available in a way which protects the borrower from being exploited by the lender.

The law is very definite. Debts have to be cancelled every seventh year and immediately following the laws about the release from debt (in the Release year) we find the following:

> If there be among you a needy man, ... you shall ... surely lend him sufficient for his need ... . Beware that there be not a base thought in your heart, saying: 'the seventh year, the year of

110

release, is at hand'; ... and you give him not ... . You shall surely give him, ... I command you ... 'you shall open your hand to your poor and needy brother ...'

The Torah thus clearly lays down {4} that debts must be cancelled every seventh year and warns against refusing aid, against refusing to lend because the year of release approaches and we are commanded to satisfy the needs of the poor.

But about 2000 years ago Hillel at about the time of Herod (the Helleniser) instituted a proceeding called the 'Prosbul' for avoiding the release of debts in the Release year. Information about the Prosbul is recorded in the Mishnah which was collected and edited by Rabbi about two hundred years later:

(A loan secured by) a Prosbul is not cancelled {5}. This was one of the things instituted by Hillel; for when he observed people refraining from lending to one another, and thus transgressing what is written in the law, 'beware lest there be a base thought in thy heart', ... he instituted the Prosbul.

This is the formula {6} of the Prosbul: 'I declare before you, so-and-so, judges of that place, that touching any debt that I may have outstanding, I shall collect it whenever I desire.

Samuel, almost a contemporary of Rabbi's, made some outstanding decisions which show deep concern for the people and their welfare . The principles he announced included that a person is assumed innocent until proved guilty and he rigorously opposed exploitation of the people through higher prices due to seasonal demand or scarcity, due to prices being raised by traders for items required seasonally in connection with religious practices. He said
'This Prosbul is an assumption on the part of the judges {7}; if I am ever in a position, I will abolish it'
as the judges are seizing money wrongfully.

Hillel's Prosbul enabled those who had money to lend it without fear of losing their money during the Release year. However, the cancelling of unpaid debts during the Release year protects those who are in need against economic and later more direct oppression and enslavement by those who have money. Hence in instituting the Prosbul, Hillel withdrew an essential protection from the people, bypassing the application of a basic Torah law.

Lending money is very much a voluntary matter and is difficult to enforce. It is very much a matter between the individual and God, between the individual and his conscience, particularly so when the money is being lent without charging interest. One would like to know much more about how and under what terms those who needed money were able to obtain it in the days of Hillel. However, later Jewish communities up to and including the present time found other ways of helping those in need. Much voluntary time and effort is spent in collecting money for the needy, in helping those in need via the community.

If One Lapses So Does the Other

It has been argued by Rabbi {8} that we can deduce from the Torah that when the Yovel (freedom year) is not being observed then the Shemittah (release year) is not to be observed.

The argument is based on one of the Shemittah laws {9} which details how debts should be released:

> At the end of every seven years you shall make a release.
> And this is the manner of the release:
> every creditor shall release that which he has lent his neighbours;
> he shall not exact it of his neighbour and his brother;
> because the Lord's release has been proclaimed.

The argument runs as follows:

1. Of the two expressions 'release', one refers to the Shemittah and the other to the Yovel, the land having to lie fallow in both.
2. It follows that at a time when Yovel is observed the Shemittah also has to be observed.
3. It then follows that when the Yovel is not being observed the Shemittah is not to be observed.

Rabbi's argument is also quoted {10} as showing that one need not observe the Shemittah laws which cancel debts. The argument is based on the same text and is identical to the one already given:

1. The text indicates here two kinds of release, one the release of land and the other the release of debts.
2. When the release of land is being observed the release of money is to be observed.
3. It follows that when the release of land is not being observed that the release of debts is not to be observed.

The reasoning is identical and I will now discuss the three steps one by one.

1. The text refers only to the release from debt. It {11} defines the way in which the release is to be carried out, namely that all creditors should under all circumstances release all that has been lent to fellow-Hebrews.

The other different meanings {12,13} assigned to the word 'release' are largely arbitrary and unrelated to the meaning of the text. It is not surprising that 'release' is said to mean Yovel on the one hand and Shemittah on the other, the return of every man to his land on the one hand and the release from debt on the other, rest for the land on the one hand and release of money on the other.

2. This step says that it follows that if the first is being observed then the other has to be observed.

    One fails to see how the second step follows from the first and there is no such relationship between the laws mentioned.

    Take the Yovel and Shemittah laws.

    The Torah clearly states that the Yovel laws have to be observed and that the Shemittah laws have to be observed, separately and individually, because the Torah states them. There are certain relationships between them: each Yovel follows seven Shemittah years and the land rests both in the Shemittah and in the Yovel years. But they need to be observed individually and separately as part of Torah legislation and nowhere does it say that observing one set of laws depends on observing the others.

3. This step concludes the argument by saying that it follows that if the first is not being observed then the second must not be observed.

    The kind of conclusions reached here are that if the Yovel is not being observed then the Shemittah must not be observed, that when the resting of the land (say Yovel) is not being observed then the release of money (Shemittah) must not be observed.

    The previous statement (step 2) did not make sense and even if it did this one would not follow from it. It is not possible to argue from a positive statement, such as the previous one, to one containing two negatives like this one. The second statement of negatives does not follow and is purely arbitrary.

    The following examples illustrate the point:

    (a) 'I am eating while I am walking' is a statement about an actual situation. It simply does not follow that 'when I am not eating then I must not walk'.

    (b) I take my laundry to the launderette and while it is in a washing machine I go and do my shopping. It does not follow that I do not go shopping unless my washing is in a washing machine or that if I do not wash my clothes then I do not go shopping.

113

(c) The same kind of reasoning {14} as is put forward by Rabbi led a court to conclude that there was no need to keep the Sabbath during the Shemittah year.

Rabbi Zera asked:
Wherein did they err when they decided that no Sabbath is to be kept in the seventh (Shemittah) year?

In the following text {15}: 'In ploughing time and in harvest thou shalt rest'.

By arguing that:
'When ploughing is carried on, Sabbath is to be observed but when no ploughing is carried on Sabbath is not to be observed.'

This court, like Rabbi, arrived at a conclusion which contradicts the law and is in conflict with it. The actual law states that the Sabbath has to be observed: 'Six days thou shalt work, but on the seventh day thou shalt rest; in ploughing time and in harvest thou shalt rest.'

It is of interest that Rabbi's argument was also not accepted {16} by the scholars, who are of the opinion that the law of Shemittah is valid as Torah law, independently of the law of Yovel.

We may conclude that the Torah clearly states that each of these laws is to be observed. It does not say that one set should not be observed or that the other should not be observed or that if one is not being observed then the other must not be observed.

Torah and Rabbinical Law

Torah Law

We have seen that what little we understand in depth of Torah law is enormously important. That which appears less relevant seems to be so because we do not as yet understand its impact and intent. Attempts to modify and change the application of laws when one's understanding of the resulting consequences is limited can lead to making misleading and destructive changes. The Torah is very clear on this point:
'You shall not add {17} to the word which I command you, neither shall you diminish from it, that you may keep the commandments of the Lord your God which I command you'.

Whenever I mention the Torah I am referring to the Pentateuch, that is to the five books of Moses. The Torah is the basic constitution which safeguards the rights of the people and points the way ahead while on

114

this as a foundation has been built the vast body of common and case law which has grown up and which applies the law under present conditions.

The authority for such changes comes from the Torah {18}. In matters of dispute or doubt which cannot be resolved with reference to existing law, then the priests the Levites and the judge of the day will decide the matter. The law they will teach and the judgement which is made are binding and have to be followed.

It seems to me that they are thus authorised to modify the application of a Torah law so as to keep it effective in achieving its intent in the light of changing conditions. They may not change the basic constitution, they may not change Torah law.

They may modify the application of a law and do so by rabbinical ordinances. The resulting body of common and case law is called 'Halachah'.

Rabbinical Decisions (Ordinances)

Some ancient decisions protect and strengthen the laws of the Torah. There are those which prohibit the doing of something and these are called Gezerot. Then there are decisions called Minhagim which generally approve but without adding to or subtracting from Torah law. Further there are Takonnot which are amendments to the halachic systems and which generally call for the doing of something.

Halachic legislation (rabbinical decisions) thus aims to resolve new problems (social, economic and moral) which find no answer in the Torah or in existing Halachah by amending the existing Halachah or by new halachic legislation in the spirit and intent of the Torah.

Emergency Legislation

The saving of life being all-important, our scholars have in the past decided in times of danger and need that certain regulations and laws need not be kept, or found ways of bypassing the effect of a law without abrogating it, adapting the use of a law to conditions existing in their days. The land was worked during a Shemittah year, for example, to protect the people from persecution at a time of occupation when the Romans insisted on collecting taxes. Another example is that people may defend themselves on the Sabbath.

One may have to fight so as to preserve one's way of life and in an emergency legislation may be enacted to be in force for a limited period, abrogating a positive precept or transgressing a negative precept, according to the need of the hour. Emergency legislation leaves the law in existence so that it can be applied again at some future date when the emergency is over.

I have seen it stated that there are times when it is better to break one law so that many should be kept, that one may break one Sabbath so that many should be kept. However, as the breaking of one Sabbath could cause the breaking of many others, who decides when, where, how and by whom the line should be drawn?

Rabbinical modification to the application of a Torah law would seem to be permitted in an emergency as long as it is clearly stated that the Torah says one thing while the deciding halachic authority decides otherwise, it being made clear that the ordinance is subordinate legislation.

The legislation aimed at overcoming an emergency may either strengthen or weaken the observance of the law. We need to overcome emergencies by finding ways which strengthen the application of the law.

While emergency legislation leaves the basic law in existence to be applied again at some future date when the emergency is over, there needs to be a clear statement of the limited period of time during which it is to remain in existence and of what any law is attempting to achieve so that its application can be judged by those who need to apply it, by those who need to consider it in relation to Torah law.

This would enable one to judge such subordinate legislation by comparing what it achieves with what it is intended to achieve and to judge the time when it is to be annulled, amended or superseded when the emergency, the need to save life, is over.

Relative Strength

We have seen that the Torah is the basic constitution which safeguards the people and points the way ahead. It may not be changed in any way either by adding or by taking away.

We have also seen that the Torah authorises rabbinical legislation modifying the application of a law so as to keep it effective in achieving its intent in the light of changing conditions.

Rabbinical ordinances are subordinate legislation. They may be abrogated or amended by other rabbinical ordinances.

Case against Observance

We are here dealing with Torah laws which establish and safeguard personal freedom of the people, namely freedom from need and oppression, servitude and want, laws which provide freedom and maintain independence, which lay the basis for a good life. These laws are:

RELEASE (Shemittah, every seventh year)

(a) Cancellation of all debts.

(b) Rest from work for a year.

FREEDOM (Yovel, every fiftieth year)

(a) Freeing all from having to serve others, from serving others.

(b) Restoring to each his source of independent income, his share of the national wealth, his land.

These laws are essential provisions which protect the people and are not on the whole being observed today. Those who wish to expose the people to need and servitude argue against the observance of these laws.

Take the Yovel laws. Two arguments are used against the observance of these laws:

1. Observance of the laws relating to the land, that is of the Yovel and Shemittah laws, depends on 'sanctity' of land, that is depends on whether the land was conquered or occupied, depends on who authorised the action and on who led it and the laws need not be observed because the land lost its sanctity.

   We have seen that this argument does not stand up to examination. Yovel (freedom) and Shemittah (release) laws are clearly stated in the Torah and we are obliged to observe them.

2. Yovel laws have to be observed only when all the Jewish people are in Erez Israel with the different tribes in their originally allocated areas. Only part of the Jewish people live in Israel so that the laws need not be observed.

   We have seen that this argument does not stand up to examination. Freedom has to be proclaimed each Yovel year without exception to every Hebrew living in Erez Israel.

We also saw that Torah laws may not be bypassed except in an emergency and then only while the emergency lasts. It is rabbinical ordinances which may be annulled or amended as the need arises.

Rabbi considers that Shemittah laws are rabbinical ordinances so that they can be modified regarding the release from work and cancelled in the case of the release from debt.

His argument showing that Shemittah laws are rabbinical ordinances is as follows:

> (a) Yovel laws are not being observed.
> (b) From the Torah we can deduce that if the Yovel is not being observed, then the
> Shemittah is not to be observed.
> (c) But Shemittah laws are (or were) being observed
> (d) presumably because the rabbis said the Shemittah should be observed.
> (e) Hence as long as the Yovel laws are not being observed the Shemittah laws are
> only rabbinical ordinances.

The whole argument rests on the second step which states that one can deduce from the Torah that if the Yovel is not being observed, then the Shemittah is not to be observed. We have seen that this simply is not so, that each of these laws is to be observed. <2>

Consider the Release year (shemittah) laws. Hillel instituted the Prosbul and we saw that this bypasses the Torah Shemittah law that all debts have to be cancelled every seventh year.

We are told {19} that Hillel instituted the Prosbul 'for the better ordering of society'. The questions which immediately come to mind are

> 'Better' from whose point of view?
> 'Better ordering' by whom of whom?
> 'Better ordering' by whom of what?
> Who benefits, who loses?

What stands out is that in instituting the Prosbul, Hillel bypassed a law which provides essential protection for the people. He favoured the rich at the expense of the poor. He exposed the people to exploitation through need.

The questions which now arise are what reason he may have had for doing this and whether he had the authority to institute the Prosbul in the first place.

If the Prosbul had been intended to overcome an emergency then it would have only temporary validity and should have been annulled when the emergency was over.

If Hillel had intended to change the application of the law so as to keep it effective in achieving its intent in the light of changing conditions, strengthening the law instead of weakening it, he would have instituted ways of making the money available to those who needed it.

One may also consider that the authority to modify the application of a law in the light of changing conditions is limited to modifications aimed at achieving the intent of the law, so that Hillel erred when he instituted the Prosbul, having no authority to do so.

We see that no valid case has been made out and no valid argument has been advanced against observing the Yovel and Shemittah laws. The Shemittah (release) and Yovel (freedom) laws are Torah laws and need to be observed.

Prosbul

One's understanding of basic intent of any part of the Torah can only be an interpretation in the light of one's own knowledge and understanding at the time and this has been so since the Torah was written. Hence if a basic Torah law safeguarding the people has been bypassed then its application should be restored when the reasons for the modification to its application have disappeared or when one's understanding of the law and its intent has deepened and become more complete.

It follows that whichever way we look at it, Hillel's ordinance 'Prosbul' should be regarded as being null and void.

So before looking at how the laws can be applied successfully and effectively under present conditions we need to see and understand what happened in the past and why they are not on the whole being applied today.

Hillel and his Times

In the previous chapter we came to the conclusion that Hillel in instituting the Prosbul withdrew an essential protection from the people, exposing them to exploitation through need. He did so by abrogating a basic Torah law and we saw that he had no authority to do so, that he had no authority to institute the Prosbul.

We further saw that in attempting to show that Hillel was entitled to institute the Prosbul, Rabbi used a process of reasoning which is illogical and that his argument does not make sense.

We concluded that no matter which way we look at the situation, whether from point of view of applying Torah law or of protecting the people or of reversing the present trend so as to regain our strength, that the Prosbul should be regarded as being null and void, that we need to apply Torah law so as to safeguard the interests and welfare of the people under present-day conditions.

Hillel's and Rabbi's views did not go unchallenged but apparently the law followed Hillel and the release from debt is not observed today. Hence if we are to apply Torah law successfully then one would like to understand how Hillel's ordinance 'Prosbul' could have found acceptance, how Rabbi was able to put forward his line of reasoning and to get it accepted.

The people had suffered much under Seleucid rule and had been subjected to cruel persecution directed against their beliefs. We saw that the struggle against hellenisation under the leadership of the Maccabean dynasty had at first been successful. However, later generations of the Maccabean leadership and the establishment of the day were putting their own power and privileges above Jewish law. The Jewish leadership was divided amongst itself, the leaders were struggling against each other for power, and had greatly assisted the Roman occupation of the country.

We also saw that the Maccabean leadership had been replaced by the descendants of traditional enemies of the Jewish people, namely by converted Edomites, by Herod and his family.

The Romans occupied the country and oppressed the people, the Edomite establishment did what it could to turn people away from the Jewish religion and towards beliefs which sanctioned and approved the brutal exploitation of one man by another, the people were divided against each other.

This process of hellenisation was attacking the people's beliefs and strength from within, being fostered from above and from outside.

These times were very difficult and crucial for the Jewish people. This was the time preceding the destruction of Jerusalem, the destruction of the Second Temple, preceding untold brutal suffering of the Jewish population.

The Talmud

Hillel apparently lived in Jerusalem just before or during the time of Jesus.

It is during the following 200 years that the Mishnah was compiled, written down and edited. The Mishnah is a collection of legal decisions. It was finally edited by Judah haNasi who selected some decisions but rejected others and is known to have excluded many legal decisions <3>.

The compiling of the Mishnah was followed by the compiling of the Gemara which is a record of later discussions, arguments and stories relating to the Mishnah, written down many years afterwards.

Mishnah and Gemara recorded together are called the Talmud. The Gemara, and thus the Talmud, was compiled both in Jerusalem and in Babylon.

To compile the Gemara and add it to the Mishnah so as to compile the Talmud took another 200 years in Jerusalem and about 300 years in Babylon.

To compile the whole Talmud thus took about 400 years in Jerusalem and about 500 years in Babylon.

There are some basic rules of controversy in the Talmud:

1. The earlier scholars (tanna, tannaim) whose views and decisions are recorded in the Mishnah may not express a view which runs counter to a passage in the Torah <4>.
2. Later scholars (amora, amoraim) whose views are recorded in the Gemara cannot contradict a mishnah, tanna, tannaim, or an accepted baraita unless he cites another tannaic source in support of his contention.

In other words, the Talmud is subordinate legislation when compared with the Torah.

The Mishnah is closer to the Torah, is closer to being a body of legal decisions and a legal framework than the Gemara. The Mishnah carries greater authority than the mass of the Gemara.

On the other hand the Gemara is far-ranging, containing allegorical stories of often uncertain significance, containing much discussion and quoting scholars who lived hundreds of years earlier whose sayings and decisions had up till then been handed down only by the spoken word, had not previously been written down.

However, Hillel's descendants 'ruled' during the whole of the completion of the Talmud in Erez Israel. This Talmud, called Jerusalem Talmud or Talmud Yerushalmi, is considerably shorter than the Babylonian Talmud and is also considered to have a considerably lower level of learning and authority. The Babylonian Talmud is generally regarded as far more authoritative than the one produced under the spiritual leadership of the descendants of Hillel.

The Mishnah records legal decisions and traditions handed down previously by word of mouth. They were committed to writing when disputes arose between scholars about judgements which had been made in the past, about their meaning and their application. These disputes began at about the time of Hillel, increased and became more intense as time passed and this is reflected in the Talmud.

The Five Pairs (Zugot)

The law was guarded and preserved, that is passed on, by the prophets who battled on the side of Torah and people against the oppressing and thus irreligious establishment of their day. They battled against the irreligious and thus antisocial practices being condoned and spread by the establishment among the people so as to oppress the people. The keepers of the law who passed on the law were those who led the people in battle for God, for justice and the people.

The Mishnah in a few terse sentences {20} lists those who passed on the law from the time of Moses to the time of Hillel and Shammai and beyond, giving also some idea of the people concerned by quoting their sayings, perhaps the one considered most important or most characteristic.

Listed are five pairs (zugot) of people who in successive generations apparently transmitted the law from Simeon the Just. These are the only pairs of this kind mentioned in the whole of the Talmud. The last pair consists of Hillel and Shammai.

What we see here is a connected sequence which is intended to put across a meaningful story and lesson. It always has been difficult to criticise or accuse either one's employer or the ruling power and in addition this was written at a time of defeat and persecution. The message is there but it is hidden. It has to be decoded and explained.

The decoding of such an ancient message is fascinating in itself. Significant is that the last of these pairs was Hillel and Shammai, but the importance of this particular message lies in its relevance to what is taking place today.

By the time we will have reached the end of this section we will have a much better understanding of Hillel, of what he represents and stood for, of the confrontation between the opposing views of Beth Hillel and Beth Shammai, of what happened to Judaism and the Jewish people before the destruction of the Second Temple, of events which took place in Israel about 2000 years ago at the time of Jesus, during the five hundred years the Talmud was written and of what has been taking place in Israel in recent years.

Simeon the Just and Antigonus

The way in which the law was handed down from pair to pair, from man to man, is illustrated by figure 1 which shows the people and the relationship between them. It also illustrates the meaning of the whole sequence.

Now let us take the matter further by looking at what we are told about the people concerned. Let us look at what their names and sayings tell us about them and of the sides they represent. The Mishnah does not waste words and much is put across in a few terse sentences.

Simeon the Just said that the world was based on the Torah, divine service and the practice of kindness. He believed that the freedom and protection the law provides is essential, that the world is based on it. The world depends on the law, on it being observed and thus applied, and on the practice of kindness. This is a statement of the Jewish position.

Alexander the Great (of Macedon) conquered Israel. When he died his empire fell to pieces. Macedon was then taken over by one of his generals, called Antigonus. His dynasty included three kings called Antigonus and ruled Macedon until it became a Roman province in 168 BCE. This coincided with the Maccabean uprising.

It was from Macedon that Alexander had spread their hellenistic ideas of a way of life based on slavery, based on the exploitation of one man by another. Antigonus' dynasty and kings called Antigonus ruled Macedon until the Maccabean uprising.

The mishnah refers to Antigonus 'of Socoh'. This place is also mentioned in a passage in I Samuel.

It was after David had been anointed by Samuel {21} that
> 'the Philistines gathered their armies to battle, and they were gathered together at Socoh, which belonged to Judah'.

The Jews were struggling against the influx of Greek ideas and against the descendants of Greeks. The Philistines of that time were the Greeks.

It was after a Jewish way of life had been established in Israel that the Greeks gathered their armies for battle. They gathered them in Macedon, sweeping outwards from there against the Persian empire and against Israel, attempting to impose their beliefs and way of life on the Jewish people.

'Antigonus of Socoh' stands for the core of that which opposes and struggles against Jewish beliefs of freedom, justice and good life for all, stands for an ideology based on oppression and slavery.

So as to leave us in no doubt about this, the mishnah clearly announces what he stands for by his saying: Do not serve for pay, serve without expecting pay. Expect only to receive an unconditional gift to which you have no claim and fear 'heaven'.

'Be afraid and serve for the crumbs you may be thrown' is clearly the opposite of Jewish law.

Figure 1

PAIRS (Zugot)

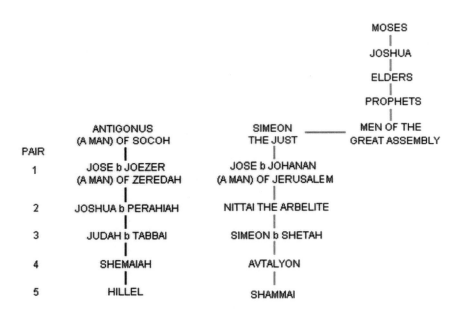

Antigonus learns from Simeon the Just. He may have taken over some of Simeon's ideas but if so then only so as to in due course weaken or replace the essence of Simeon the Just's teachings. He is setting himself up in opposition to justice and freedom.

Antigonus 'received from' Simeon the Just and the first pair received from them. Each of the next four pairs received from the previous one.

That Antigonus 'received from', that is 'learnt from' Simeon the Just does not mean that he 'followed the teachings of'. From this time onwards the unity of the transmission is broken and the law is handed down in parallel streams.

Justice and freedom are from then on under attack by an internal opposition which wishes to weaken or reverse the intent of the law, the application of the law of Moses, of the word of God, so as to be able to oppress so as to exploit. From then on we have successive pairs representing the struggle between the opposition on the one hand and the laws of freedom on the other.

Antigonus of Socoh would seem to stand for hellenisation, increasing weakening of religion, increasing oppression and exploitation of the people, would seem to stand for central authoritarian rule and establishment.

The two opposing ideologies have been defined. A foreign ideology which stands for oppression and exploitation of people but which apparently hides behind a mask of religious orthodoxy is marshalling its forces. It is camped on Jewish soil, it attempts to spread within the Jewish people. In reality it opposes those Jewish laws which safeguard independence, freedom and justice.

The First Pair

This brings us to the first of the zugot, to the first pair, namely to Jose of Zeredah and Jose of Jerusalem.

When the mishnah says that Jose of Zeredah and Jose of Jerusalem 'received from them' it does not mean that they each followed the teachings of the other two, but it means that Jose of Zeredah followed Antigonus while Jose of Jerusalem followed the teachings and tradition of the law of Moses by following the teachings of Simeon the Just.

The arrangement and content of the mishnahs also make the point. There are two mishnahs for each pair. The first lists both men and this is followed by the saying of the first of them. The second mishnah gives the saying of the second of the pair. In the case of Hillel there are an extra two sayings but this does not alter the argument. The arrangement implies that the first of the pair has something in common with both streams while the second of the pair takes his ideas of law and justice straight in line from Simeon the Just. Figure 2 illustrates this point.

The message is once again driven home by the place names. The place names in the first pair tell their own story. Jerusalem on the one hand is opposed by Zeredah on the other.

Jerusalem is the 'basis', the 'foundation'. Zeredah is a place of 'anxiety', that is a place where people are oppressed.

Here a native of Zeredah starts a sequence which aimed to overturn Jewish law, which was followed by the destruction of Jerusalem and of the second Temple and the dispersion and persecution of the people.

Only one other native of Zeredah is mentioned in the whole of the scriptures. It was Jeroboam of Zeredah who took ten of the twelve tribes away from king Solomon's son after the death of king Solomon. This division of Solomon's kingdom turned Jews against Jews. Immediately Jeroboam had established his authority over the ten tribes he modified Jewish worship. He also made {22} two calves of gold for the tribes to worship saying to them 'Behold the gods which brought you out of Egypt'.

He divided the people against each other and turned them against God the moment he succeeded in gaining control. The mishnah is saying repeatedly that this is what the followers of Antigonus are aiming to do.

Meaning of the Sequence

The names tell us what happened, tell the whole sequence of events and this is illustrated by figure 2.

Jose is the aramaic form of Joseph meaning 'may God add'. The two sides confront each other, each praying to their 'god' for greater numbers and strength.

The Jewish side is centred on Jerusalem. Judaism is a way of life, strengthens people, is the source of freedom and good life. It had been established, 'God has favoured' it.

The subverting antisocial ideology which wishes to put the clock back to exploitation of man by man is driven by its own 'god', its own source of strength. It is helped, it gains strength and praises its god, it gets the upper hand (god has granted).

Then it takes over, it is 'made bright'. It overturns the law from within, Jewish law and freedom are 'laid waste'.

What we have seen is the ruling establishment taking over and altering religious precepts so that the religion becomes the servant of the establishment (government or state) instead of serving God and people, resulting in oppression, exploitation and desolation and destruction.

What we have been told is how the religion was weakened from within, what was behind it and who did it. The whole sequence defines Hillel's position: He represents that which at that time weakened and overturned the intent and meaning of Jewish law.

The same sequence is used again elsewhere in the mishnah {23}. Its intended meaning is now much clearer.

Figure 2

NAMES OF THE PAIRS

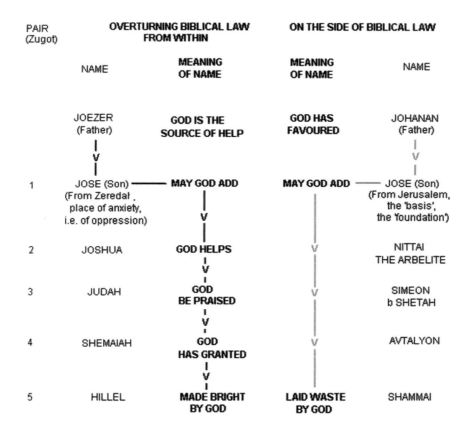

PAIR (Zugot)	OVERTURNING BIBLICAL LAW FROM WITHIN		ON THE SIDE OF BIBLICAL LAW	
	NAME	MEANING OF NAME	MEANING OF NAME	NAME
	JOEZER (Father)	GOD IS THE SOURCE OF HELP	GOD HAS FAVOURED	JOHANAN (Father)
1	JOSE (Son) (From Zeredat, place of anxiety, i.e. of oppression)	MAY GOD ADD	MAY GOD ADD	JOSE (Son) (From Jerusalem, the 'basis', the 'foundation')
2	JOSHUA	GOD HELPS		NITTAI THE ARBELITE
3	JUDAH	GOD BE PRAISED		SIMEON b SHETAH
4	SHEMAIAH	GOD HAS GRANTED		AVTALYON
5	HILLEL	MADE BRIGHT BY GOD	LAID WASTE BY GOD	SHAMMAI

Only the five pairs are listed. This list is identical to the one we have discussed apart from the addition of one person. But here we are told that the former (of each pair) were princes (Nasi) and the latter were heads of the court (Av Beth Din).

We are also told that there was a difference of opinion between the members of each pair concerning whether 'the laying on of hands' may or may not be performed. In the first three pairs it is the Av Beth Din who says that the laying on of hands may be performed but in the next two pairs it is the Nasi who says so.

Introduced opposite Hillel is Menahem who agrees with Hillel's point of view. Menahem is followed by Shammai.

It has never been satisfactorily explained why the laying on of hands should be such an important matter or why successive pairs should disagree about this matter over five generations. According to Maimonides the laying on of hands refers to 'the ordination of elders' but it is perhaps more likely to refer to the ordination of the religious hierarchy.

If the laying on of hands means the ordination of elders or say rabbis then those who say that it may be performed are those who have the authority (power) to do so. It is they who are ordaining elders or rabbis and who are thus gaining influence. Those who say it may not be performed do not have the authority (power) to ordain elders or rabbis, are not doing so and are losing what influence they have.

On that basis the authority rested with the Beth Din and thus with the Av Beth Din for three pairs. In the last two pairs it is the Nasi who has the authority, who has the power, who decides.

The sequence is illustrated by figure 3. It is in complete agreement with the story told by the names of the pairs.

There are considerable differences of opinion about what the terms Nasi and Av Beth Din mean. I have seen Nasi referred to as President of Palestinian Community and also as elected Head of Sanhedrin. I have seen the Av Beth Din referred to as Head of Sanhedrin and also as second to the Nasi.

However, we now have a much clearer picture. What we see is that the word Nasi (prince) stands for the ruler and his establishment. It is they who wish to oppress so as to exploit. They are prevented from doing so by Jewish law and negated it and/or bypassed the protection it offered the people.

In addition we are here told that Menahem agreed with Hillel and that when Menahem 'went forth' Shammai 'entered'. The name Menahem means 'consoler' or 'comforter'.

Authority had passed from the head of the court to the prince. The head of the court was completely subservient to the prince, that is served the prince. He comforted or consoled, that is tranquillised, the people.

Menahem was followed by Shammai. The law had been turned upside down, had been 'laid waste'.

Figure 3

LAYING-ON OF HANDS

PAIR	NASI SECULAR PRINCE	IN POWER, HAS AUTHORITY (See note 1)		AV BETH DIN HEAD OF RELIGIOUS COURT
1	JOSE b JOEZER OF ZEREDAH	NO	YES	JOSE b JOHANAN OF JERUSALEM
2	JOSHUA b PERAHIAH	NO	YES	NITTAI THE ARBELITE
3	JUDAH b TABBAI	NO	YES	SIMEON b SHETAH
4	SHEMAIAH	YES	NO	AVTALYON
			Agreed with Hillel	MENAHEM
5	HILLEL	YES	NO	SHAMMAI

Note 1 Should laying-on of hands be performed,
that is who has authority to ordain.

Looked at together with the other names, it confirms the story, it tells us another aspect of what happened. The religious dignitaries served the secular rulers first and foremost. The essence of the law was overturned and the religion (Jewish law) is used to tranquillise the people instead of protecting them from oppression and exploitation.

The mishnah clearly shows that Jewish law and the people are opposed by the rulers and their establishment. Wishing to exploit the people they wish to eliminate those provisions of the law which protect the people, that is wish to alter the basic constitution, the Torah. We have seen the mishnah tell us that they succeeded in introducing their antisocial ideas into Judaism and that it was done at the time of Hillel. It is Hillel who represents that which weakened and overturned the intent and meaning of Jewish law.

We saw earlier that when Hillel instituted the Prosbul he bypassed an essential protection of the people. Now we know much more about Hillel and his time. We can see why he did it, who benefited and whom he really served.

And now we can go on to explore what else he instituted and what the mishnah tells us to do in the circumstances.

Hillel's Ordinances

We have already come a long way together and now have a much better understanding of what happened to the Jewish religion at about the time of Hillel and also a better understanding of what Hillel represents. The different pieces of the puzzle fit together. Once Hillel's position has been understood it is seen that the mishnah makes the point again and again.

An ideology opposed to Jewish law, hiding behind a mask of religious orthodoxy, succeeded in weakening the application of the law. The message of the mishnah is that it was Hillel who represents this opposing ideology, that he represents the rich, the establishment and those who wish to exploit others, that it was Hillel who overturned much which is central and essential in Jewish law.

Take the case of Hillel's ordinances. There are apparently only two ordinances recorded in the mishnah as due to Hillel. The first is the Prosbul, the second concerns the redemption of town houses. These changes of the law are far-reaching and of great importance, and this applies particularly to the Prosbul.

The owner of a town house could sell it but was entitled {24} to buy it back from the buyer at any time during the first year. If he did not buy it back then the sale was legally binding and permanent.

Apparently the buyer used to hide himself on the last day of the year. This prevented the owner from returning the money, that is from buying it back from the buyer, so that the house became the buyer's permanent property.

Here Hillel ruled {25} that it was sufficient for the owner to deposit the money in a chamber. He was then entitled to break down the door of the house and occupy it while the buyer could collect the money whenever he wanted.

Here Hillel ruled to strengthen the law of the Torah against those who had found a way of bypassing its application. The buyer wants to keep

130

the house but Hillel ruled in favour of strict application of the law, in favour of the original property owner.

In the case of the Prosbul we saw that Hillel ruled so as to weaken the law by instituting a way of bypassing its application.

It is those in need who had to borrow to survive and in the case of the Prosbul Hillel ruled in favour of the rich.

In the first case he ruled to strengthen the application of the law, in the second he ruled to weaken it. What both cases have in common is that Hillel ruled in favour of the established property owner, in favour of the rich.

There can be no doubt about what Hillel stood for, about which side he is intended to represent. In the confrontation between slave-owners and God, Hillel serves and legislates for the slave-owners, the rich, the establishment, those who wish to exploit others.

But there are no dissenting opinions recorded in the mishnah, there is no protest by Shammai.

Controversies between Hillel and Shammai

Now here is something quite remarkable. In the whole of the mishnah there are recorded only three controversies between Hillel and Shammai themselves. Almost forgotten, seldom quoted, they can be found right at the beginning of the volume called Eduyot {26}, in the first three mishnahs.

Eduyot is one of the earliest of the tractates of the Talmud. It was probably put together at least in some preliminary way shortly after the destruction of the second Temple. Indeed it may well be the earliest of the tractates of the Talmud. The tractate 'Abot' also seems to be one of the earlier tractates and it contains the information about the pairs {27}.

These two tractates, Eduyot and Abot, are located {28} side by side in the same volume of the Talmud and consist only of mishnahs without gemara {29}. It is the first few mishnahs in each of these tractates which tell us about Hillel and Shammai and about the confrontation between them.

Now looking in more detail at what Eduyot tells us about Hillel and Shammai, we find them described in a very remarkable and unique way. They are called 'Fathers of the world' {30}.

The patriarchs have been referred to {31} as 'fathers' but the term 'Fathers of the world' would seem to have a more general, more fundamental, more all-embracing significance. Particularly so as the term has not been applied to anyone else and has not been used elsewhere in the mishnah.

As it was God who created the world the term 'Fathers of the world' cannot relate to the creation of the world.

Hillel and Shammai are opposed to each other, are intended to represent opposites, put forward opposing points of view. It would seem that the two sides they represent are the basic fundamental powers struggling against each other. The state of the world depends on the balance between them and it is for this reason that Hillel and Shammai are called 'Fathers of the world'.

The Torah defines both sides in a number of different but completely consistent ways:

'gods' of Egypt, 'other gods'	God
Oppression and slavery	Freedom and independence
Amalek	Jewish people
Hillel	Shammai

While the Torah clearly defines the two sides and is on the side of freedom and the people, it is the Talmud which tells us about Hillel and Shammai and about which side they represent.

Once again the stage has been set, the two sides have been defined.

Now let us look at what the mishnah tells us about the controversies between Hillel and Shammai, looking in some {32} detail at the first three mishnahs.

Each of these mishnahs contains a different controversy between Hillel and Shammai. Bearing in mind that these are the only three controversies between them recorded in the Talmud, what is unexpected but immediately apparent is that they do not seem to be of breathtaking importance. They are not matters of life and death. The three disputes are unconnected with each other, are unconnected with the main theme and message of the Torah.

But let us look at this in a different way. What these three controversies have in common is that they are unconnected with each other and with the main theme and message of the Torah. This is so because they were chosen like this so that they would not be censored, so that they would remain unaltered, so that the message could be preserved and passed on unaltered to future generations. The subject matter of the disputes is immaterial to the message.

We can now look in more detail at the message in the first three mishnahs.

One point stands out straight away. These are the only three recorded controversies between Hillel and Shammai and in each case the 'Sages' say that neither of them is right, that the law is different. This is far removed from the often repeated statement that the law is according to Beth Hillel which, however, is based on later statements in the gemara which cannot overrule a mishnah. What these first three mishnahs have in common is that after Hillel and Shammai state the law as they see it we find '... but the Sages say: neither according to the opinion of the one nor according to the opinion of the other, but ...'. (See figure 4).

Hillel and Shammai state their 'opinion' but the 'Sages' differ.

It seems significant that in the first two mishnahs it is Shammai who states his opinion first while it is Hillel who differs, while in the third mishnah Hillel states his opinion first with Shammai then contradicting Hillel. I put it to you that this signifies a change in the relative positions of the two, that this signifies a change in authority. It is he who is in authority who speaks first to state his opinion. It is the opposition which contradicts.

The story would seem to be rather similar to that recorded in the sequences about the zugot. What we see is a transfer of authority from Shammai to Hillel together with some indication of what took place.

In the first mishnah, the 'Sages' state the law as being according to a position which has moved a little from Shammai's towards Hillel's position, that is Hillel's point of view has gained some following.

In the second mishnah the authority is still with Shammai but the Sages state the law as being half-way between the opinions of Hillel and Shammai. This would seem to indicate Hillel's following and authority at that point of time.

The same mishnah states that the ruling was revised after the measures had been increased. The Sages then stated that 'five are liable', but that R. Jose {33} said 'Five are exempt, five and more are liable'.

A footnote in the Soncino Talmud points out that the measures changed at Sepphoris. As far as I can make out, what happened was that Vespasian together with his son Titus set out to subdue Palestine. Sepphoris anticipated an attack by spontaneously surrendering and it was by way of Sepphoris that Vespasian penetrated the region. The Jewish members of the municipality were apparently replaced by gentiles. It was this war which resulted in the destruction of Jerusalem and of the second Temple (66-70 CE).

It seems that the Jewish religious establishment simply allowed Hillel's point of view to take over (spontaneous surrender to the Romans).

The Sages stated the law very clearly saying that a certain law applies to a quantity of five or more. But here now appears R. Jose who contradicts the Sages by saying that five are exempt, five and more are liable. What he is saying muddles the law up, gives rise to dispute and controversy since he is saying that five are both exempt and liable.

The result is illustrated by the third mishnah. Hillel is in authority and states his opinion first while Shammai contradicts. The Sages, however, again disagree with both Hillel and Shammai but in this case do not state any ruling whatsoever.

We are given an indication of their reasons in the odd measures Hillel and Shammai use. Hillel used the 'hin', a measure which was apparently derived from the Egyptian {34}, and the mishnah states that he used it because 'a man must speak in the language of his teacher'. Shammai talks in terms of a dry measure (kab) for measuring a liquid. On this basis it seems that Hillel when in authority acts for the oppressing and exploiting rulers while Shammai is making mistakes. Here the Sages do not agree with nor do they support either the one or the other.

However when 'two weavers' from the 'dung-gate' in Jerusalem state a different quantity using a different measure 'in the name of Shemaiah and Avtalyon' then the Sages confirm their statement.

However, the unit 'log' used by the two weavers appears to have been used only in the Torah for measuring or stating oil in connection with the temple offering for the cleansing {35} from leprosy.

Shemaiah and Avtalyon were the pair which preceded Hillel and Shammai. Hence this part of the mishnah seems to indicate that when the people reverse the trend and state the law in accordance with the Torah's intent that the Sages agree with them and the law regains its authority based on the power of the people.

Figure 4   CONTROVERSIES BETWEEN HILLEL AND SHAMMAI

MISHNAH	IN AUTHORITY	OPPOSING	THE LAW ACCORDING TO THE 'SAGES'	OTHER POINTS MADE BY THE MISHNAH
1	Shammai	Hillel	Has moved a little from Shammai's towards Hillel's position	
2	Shammai	Hillel	Half-way between the opinions of Shammai and Hillel	Unconditional surrender to 'Romans' (Balance then moves to favour Hillel who has gained a slight majority and authority passes to Hillel) — Appearance of scholar R. Jose who confuses the law
3	Hillel	Shammai	Do not make any ruling	Hillel supports the oppressing and exploiting rulers, Shammai makes mistakes, and the sages do not agree with either — When the people reverse the trend and state the law in accordance with its intent then the law regains its authority based on the power of the people

Serving the Establishment

We have seen that the mishnah tells us much about Hillel, tells us something quite fundamental. Two sides are facing each other. One of these is represented by Hillel and it is this which infiltrated Jewish thought and religious belief and succeeded in bypassing some of the law's essential provisions.

Up to now we have looked at what the mishnah says. However, the gemara is in some ways less formal, further away from the events, contains discussion between differing viewpoints and stories and in this way may be more descriptive and may indeed tell us more about what happened at the time.

We are told {36} that it was related about Hillel that:
> He hired for a certain poor man who was of good family a horse to ride upon and a servant to run before him. On one occasion he could not find a servant to run before him, so he himself ran before him for three miles.

This story is used in the gemara in connection with a quotation from the Torah {37} to make the point that the community should help those in need. This is interpreted to mean that while on the one hand one should not give to the extent that the poor become rich, the rich should be maintained at the level of luxurious living to which they are accustomed.

The gemara arrives at this conclusion by quoting the Torah {37} and interpreting it by saying that 'sufficient for his need' means that one needs to maintain him but does not make him rich while 'in that which he wants' can be interpreted to mean even a horse to ride on and a servant to run before him if that is what he has been used to, since that is what Hillel did.

The story of Hillel producing for an impoverished gentleman a horse and a servant and then himself taking the place of the servant and running before the gentleman is, in my opinion, too far-fetched to be taken at its face value.

It would seem highly unlikely that the community's money would have been used to provide luxury items like a horse and a servant for a poor member of the establishment as a matter of public charity <5>. But then the poor can be taxed and can be taxed heavily.

It is a discussion about an isolated sentence from the Torah without regard to the context or the intent of the text. To understand the meaning and intent of the text, one needs to look at the previous verse and indeed also at the following three. These few verses are an impassioned plea to provide for the poor and to look after their needs. It concludes with the commandment to 'open your hand unto your poor and needy brother'.

I would interpret the statement that one should 'lend him sufficient for his need in that which he wants' by saying that the word 'wants' may well mean 'lacks' and may well refer to a need of which the impoverished may not be aware of. When one is starving one looks for food but there may be much else which is badly needed.

The story relates how Hillel provides for the establishment, provides a servant for them and serves them himself. The community's money comes from all and what Hillel did was to take away from the community so as to give to the establishment. In other words, the community became the servant of the establishment and this is the point of the story.

The intent and clear meaning of the law is to protect the poor from need and thus to protect them from exploitation. What Hillel did was to turn the law upside down. The gemara argues that the community, the bulk of the people, can according to Hillel be exploited so as to maintain and keep the rich in the style to which they are accustomed.

The gemara says so very forcefully by referring to the particular verses I have already mentioned. It is in this impassioned plea and commandment to help the poor that we find the statement to give even when the Year of Release (shemittah) approaches. It is this which was bypassed by Hillel's Prosbul. It was this Prosbul which bypassed an essential protection for the people and in so doing laid them open to oppression and exploitation. It was in this way that Hillel made the people serve the establishment and so provided the establishment with their horses and servants.

Teaching the Torah

The gemara also tells {38} that when a certain person asked Shammai to make him a proselyte 'on condition that you teach me the whole Torah while I stand on one foot', Shammai refused to do so. But when this person asked Hillel, he was told by Hillel

> What is hateful to you, do not to your neighbour; that is the whole Torah, while the rest is the commentary thereon; go and learn it.

Hillel is using two negatives (do not to your neighbour what you do not like) and this is not a valid way of making meaningful or positive statements.

There are both positive and negative commandments, there are positive and negative parts of the law. The positive statements tell one what has to be done to achieve a good life and secure future. The negative laws protect society, protect individuals from being harmed by others.

Hillel has not only left out the positive commandments but also has put the personal feelings of an individual above the essential provisions which protect society, has placed the individual's opinion above the word of God.

Hillel's statement puts the individual's likes and dislikes above the law and we know that people can be brainwashed into liking and pursuing behaviour which produces pleasure and profit to themselves at someone else's expense, at the cost of injuring those to whom it is being done. His statement would allow a sexual pervert to spread his perversion, would allow someone who is doing harm to himself by the way in which he is behaving (without perhaps being aware of it) to behave in a similarly harmful way towards other people.

What one does and does not do is not determined only by personal feeling and choice but is laid down and limited by the law of God, of the Torah. Shammai refused to teach the Torah under the stipulated conditions because the law in itself is a matter more important than the length of time a person who is not a Jew can stand on one foot.

The statement attributed to Hillel bears a certain resemblance to the following quotation from the Torah {39}

> You shall not take vengeance, nor bear any grudge against the children of your people, but you shall love your neighbour as yourself: I am the Lord. You shall keep My statutes.

It is not just the middle part of this statement which Hillel reversed. Our attention is being directed towards the context in which that which he reversed appears in the Torah. He also legislated against the people in favour of the rulers and served the rulers instead of God, failing to keep God's statutes.

What we have seen is that Hillel served the rulers and those who supported the rulers. We saw that it was done by subtly misrepresenting the Torah so that it was applied in a way which weakened its application, so that it was applied in a way which served the establishment instead of protecting and serving the people, instead of serving God.

So now we know about Hillel and what he stood for, we have had an indication of what was done and of the methods used to do it. But the gemara tells us much more so that there can be no doubt left about what went on, about how in those days the application of the law was turned upside down.

Hence now we take a closer look at what else the gemara tells us about how Hillel came to be 'appointed'. We want to find out what happened so as to ensure that it does not happen again.

Hillel's 'Appointment'

The mishnah described how the 'deeply orthodox' Hillel gained a following. It points its accusing finger at Hillel, at our own establishment. How come we ever allowed ourselves to be so blinded by our establishment?

The gemara tells us much the same.

There is a long and involved mishnah which states and discusses the rules for what may and may not be done on the Sabbath when preparing the Passover offering. The gemara states that on {40} one occasion the 'Bene Bathyra' had forgotten these rules and did not know whether the preparatory work could be carried out on the Sabbath. Inquiring whether anyone knew, they were told that a man who had just come up from Babylonia and who was called 'Hillel the Babylonian' had served 'the two greatest men of the generation' and that he would know. So they summoned him and asked him. He answered them by means of two abstract logical arguments. 'They immediately set him at their head and appointed him Nasi (prince) over them'.

He then lectured them the whole day on the laws of Passover, on the laws of the festival which celebrates the freeing of the Jews from slavery in Egypt. He told them that it was because they {40} 'did not serve the two greatest men of the time, Shemaiah and Avtalyon', that he came up from Babylonia to be prince over them.

The story relates how Hillel gained control and became prince:
1. He was taught by Shemaiah and Avtalyon,
2. he took over from the Bene Bathyra, having
3. persuaded them to hand over by means of hermeneutic rules for interpreting the law.

So what we shall do now is to look at each of these three aspects in turn. Let us begin with Shemaiah and Avtalyon. What does the gemara tell us about them?

(1) Shemaiah and Avtalyon

The first thing which strikes one is that the gemara does not see Shemaiah and Avtalyon as representing opposite sides. This fully agrees with the meaning of the mishnah about the zugot (see figures 2 and 3).

It is appreciated that Shemaiah and Avtalyon do not really differ, that they represent the same side, that authority has passed to the rulers and their establishment, that what is being attempted is a process of brainwashing the population into blindly following the establishment's upside down version of Jewish law. The gemara understandably is very bitter about it.

(1a) The Two Sides

This story is straightforward and tells much.

All the people followed the high priest who stood {41} for God and Torah.

Shemaiah and Avtalyon were descended from heathens. When the people saw them they forsook the high priest and followed them.

In due course Shemaiah and Avtalyon visited him to make the point that many people support them, that they will now 'take leave of the high priest', that is go their own way and take over.

He to them: May the descendants of the heathen come in peace!

They to him: May the descendants of the heathen, who do the work of Aaron, arrive in peace, but the descendant of Aaron, who does not do the work of Aaron, he shall not come in peace!

Shemaiah and Avtalyon are doing the work of Aaron. The high priest who is descended from Aaron does not do the work of Aaron.

Scripture tells us {42} that 'Moses saw that the people were broken loose - for Aaron had let them loose for a derision among their enemies'. In other words, Moses knew that it was Aaron, the religious establishment, who had permitted the people to break loose from Jewish law, who had allowed them to follow the golden calf of the establishment.

Shemaiah and Avtalyon say that they are doing the work of Aaron, meaning by this that they are leading the people away from Jewish beliefs and towards following the establishment's views.

The high priest is on the side of Torah, does not do what Aaron did, does not betray people and God.

The two sides are once again defined. Shemaiah and Avtalyon are clearly represented as the enemy within the Jewish people, as the secular establishment and as that part of the religious establishment which serves the secular establishment.

It is they who are attempting to overturn the Torah's social laws, doing so from within the Jewish people.

(1b) Identities and Purpose

The gemara links Shemaiah and Avtalyon with some other people and tells us that both were descended from Sennacherib {43} as follows:

- Naaman was a resident alien.
- Nebuzaradan was a righteous proselyte,
- the descendants of Sisera studied Torah in Jerusalem;
- the descendants of Sennacherib taught Torah to the multitude; who were these? - Shemaiah and Avtalyon.
- The descendants of Haman studied Torah at Bene Berak.

It is heart-warming to see such devotion to the law, to see such famous people spending their lives in the service of God. But take a second look. Remember it was written during times of greatest distress and persecution. The real message is very different.

'Naaman was a resident alien'. It all depends what you mean by 'resident alien'. But I suppose it doesn't matter how you translate the Hebrew word, it doesn't matter whether you call him resident alien or foreign settler or what have you. Naaman commanded the forces of the king of Aram. It was Naaman who {44} commanded the forces which defeated the king of Israel. To call the foreign conqueror a resident alien is quite an understatement but makes the point very effectively as long as you understand the language.

'Nebuzaradan was a righteous proselyte', and this means that he was 'one who accepts all the laws of Judaism with no ulterior motive'. Nebuzaradan was captain of the guard of Nebuchadnezzar, king of Babylon. He commanded the forces which burnt down Jerusalem and destroyed the first Temple. The people were killed or enslaved and carried off to Babylon, only the poorest were left behind to serve as unskilled labourers. The Temple treasures were also taken to Babylon. That was the end of the kingdom of Judah and of the first Temple {45}. Nebuzaradan is here called a righteous proselyte: In fact it was he who destroyed the Temple.

Sisera commanded the forces of Jabin, king of Canaan {46}. We read that 'the descendants of Sisera studied Torah in Jerusalem': For twenty years he harshly oppressed the children of Israel although he was defeated in the end.

The descendants of Sennacherib, namely Shemaiah and Avtalyon, taught Torah to the mass of the people.

All of those mentioned so far commanded those who attacked the Jewish people so as to destroy them. Haman also wanted to destroy the Jewish people and in this way destroy the religion, the practice and application of Jewish law in everyday life. We are being very pointedly told that Shemaiah and Avtalyon are like the others, that they are attacking Judaism and the Jewish people. They spread their poison from within, taught their kind of law 'to the multitude', spread dissension within the Jewish people from the inside.

Sennacherib was king of Assyria (including Babylonia) from 705 to 681 BCE. He attempted to take Jerusalem with his Assyrian army but failed. The biblical story is that he defeated Judah and exacted a heavy tribute from Hezekiah, but that he was defeated by an act of God and returned to Nineveh. Scripture tells us that {47}

> So Sennacherib, King of Assyria, departed, and went and returned, and dwelt at Nineveh. And it came to pass, as he was worshipping in the house of Nisroch his god, that Adrammelech and Sarezer his sons smote him with the sword; and they escaped into the land of Ararat. And Esarhaddon his son reigned in his stead.

The siege took place in 701 BCE, Jerusalem was not captured and Hezekiah sent his submission tribute to the king of Assyria in Nineveh. It seems that Sennacherib's son Esarhaddon succeeded to the throne about eight years after Sennacherib's death. The land where the Jews landed after the deluge, when they founded a new community after the destruction of Judah, was Babylon. It seems that Adrammelech and Sarezer escaped to Babylon.

What I have said so far is taken largely from scripture. Sennacherib's unsuccessful siege of Jerusalem is apparently known also from the Assyrian accounts. Assyrian sources, as far as I know, tell of a revolt against Sennacherib and of his murder but it is not known whether there was only one murderer or more murderers or whether they were sons of Sennacherib. Esarhaddon seems to have had a struggle with his elder brothers but the assassination of Sennacherib is not mentioned in his annals. Assyrian records do not mention a son of Sennacherib called Adrammelech and the name is unknown as an Assyrian personal name.

However, the stories in the gemara need to be looked at in the light of knowledge known or supposed at the time. They are likely to be based on contemporary writings and their meaning and message fairly clear at the time.

This is what we are told {48}:

> On his return to Assyria, Sennacherib found a plank, which he worshipped as an idol, because it was part of the ark which had saved Noah from the deluge. He vowed that he would sacrifice his sons to this idol if he prospered in his next ventures. But his sons heard his vows and they killed their father, and fled to Kardu, where they released the Jewish captives confined there in great numbers. With these they marched to Jerusalem, and became

142

proselytes there. The famous scholars Shemaiah and Avtalyon were the descendants of these two sons of Sennacherib.

Of course this sounds quite improbable. You might call it an old wives' tale. But old wives' tales are records of tradition with a kernel of truth which remains misunderstood until modern science catches up. This story needs to be regarded from the point of view of those living at the time.

Remember also that here they were undoubtedly trying to say something of considerable importance in a way which could be understood by themselves but not by the ruling power and which could not be held against them by their own establishment.

There is indeed quite a parallel between what happened to the descendants of Sennacherib and to Assyria when compared with what the story tells. We have a good amount of information about what happened {49}.

We are told that the Assyrian king found a plank, which he worshipped as an idol, because it was part of the ark which had saved Noah from the deluge.

> This describes in religious language what Esarhaddon did in fact. He had succeeded to the throne and was determined to prevent his sons from struggling with each other for power, he was determined to prevent civil war. He arranged matters accordingly and the empire's subject rulers had to agree to abide by this Pax Assyriaca. When he died his two sons ruled side by side for 17 years. Ashurbanipal from Nineveh and Shamash-Shum-Ukim from Babylon.

> In Noah's ark the animals came in two by two, there was peace between the different animals. The 'plank' found to save them from destruction was the peace treaty which prevented the struggle for power between the two brothers. It was worshipped by the king 'as an idol' which tells that he forced his subject rulers to obey and follow it, to adhere to its provisions.

He vowed that he would sacrifice his sons to this idol if he prospered in his next ventures.

> This tells that if successful and thus having an empire to leave them then his two sons would be sacrificed to this idol, to the idea of peace in the realm. Neither would have complete power but there would be peace.

His sons heard his vows and they killed their father, and fled to Kardu.

> In the year 652 BCE war broke out between the two brothers. After some years of bloody warfare the one in Nineveh emerged

143

victorious. But the throne of Babylonia was seized by Nabopolassar who established the Chaldean dynasty in Babylon, successfully defended Babylonia's newly-won independence and finally eliminated and took over Assyria itself. Power and control had moved to Babylon.

It so happens that Babylonia had been called {50} Kar-duniash sometime before. 'Kardu' clearly refers to Babylon.

The sons didn't abide by their father's peace treaty, and killed the father, which means that in breaking the peace, in warring with each other, they destroyed Assyria and destroyed their father's dynasty. They fled to Kardu which denotes the passing of power from Nineveh (Assyria) to Babylon and this is in full agreement with the biblical version I mentioned earlier.

In Kardu (Babylon) they released the Jewish captives confined there in great numbers. With these they marched to Jerusalem, and became proselytes there.

The mentioning of 'Jewish captives' confirms that Kardu stands for Babylon. But it so happens that Nabopolassar's son was Nebuchadnezzar who succeeded to the throne of Babylon and conquered Jerusalem and Judah, who destroyed the first Temple with brutal destruction of the people and exile to Babylon. The Babylonians must certainly have marched to Jerusalem in considerable numbers. This is what the story tells us. 'Becoming proselytes' refers to the destruction of the Temple in Jerusalem and the vicious brutal slaughter and enslavement of the population.

The statement that Shemaiah and Avtalyon descended from those who led their people in battle against the Jewish people and who destroyed the Temple, Jerusalem and Judah, bearing in mind that what is indicated is that they 'descended from them' meaning 'followed their ideas, had the same intentions', is a very grim accusation indeed.

When the gemara {51} talks about a certain man 'who has come up from Babylonia, Hillel the Babylonian by name, who served the two greatest men of the time, ...' then the references to Hillel as having come from Babylonia and being called 'the Babylonian', as having served Shemaiah and Avtalyon take on a far more sinister meaning than has been supposed so far.

The descendants of Haman studied Torah in Bene Berak. Haman 'the Agagite' is presumably called this to indicate descent from Agag the king of the Amalekites {52}. Scripture tells how he set about to exterminate all the Jews in Persia. It also tells how his plans backfired. Haman was he who led this attack on the Jews. It seems that his descendants studied Torah in Bene Berak but this I will discuss in more detail later.

The term 'descendants' appears to be used so as to indicate those who followed the ideas, who had the same purpose as those whom they followed and Naaman, Nebuzaradan, Sisera, Sennacherib and Haman were all powerful enemies of the Jews, had all tried to destroy the people, had succeeded or failed in varying degrees. The sum total of the harm actually done or intended by those here mentioned is almost unimaginable. To see Shemaiah and Avtalyon mentioned in such company confirms all that we have said about them and tells much more.

What is absolutely staggering is that such heartfelt protest against the actions of the secular and religious leadership should have been kept hidden for so long.

We have seen who Shemaiah and Avtalyon were, whom they represent, and what is said about them. None of it is pleasant, it is all pretty horrifying.

(2) Bene Bathyra

We are told by the gemara that the Bene Bathyra listened to Hillel's abstract arguments and immediately set him at their head and appointed him 'Prince' over them.

He immediately told them that he ruled over them because he had served Shemaiah and Avtalyon, while they had dared not to serve them. This would seem to make the point that the Bene Bathyra were on the side of Torah and people.

The gemara does not tell us who the Bene Bathyra were. This may have been common knowledge when the gemara was written but it has been lost.

However, just who the Bene Bathyra were, is in fact obvious. The hebrew 'bene bathyra' states that they are the children or sons of the Covenant, of those who carry out the brit. The Bene Bathyra are those who follow the word of God, who adhere to the laws of the Torah including its social laws and its social system.

(3) Bible Interpretation

The Bene Bathyra allowed abstract rules <6> of bible interpretation to confuse the law and handed over their authority.

We have already seen that a religious establishment which served the secular establishment gained control. They took over from a religious establishment which served God and people.

We have also seen that this secular-establishment serving religious establishment abrogated the social laws and social system of the Torah, doing so by abstract, illogical and invalid arguments.

So here we are told that Jewish belief and practice now serves its establishment instead of serving God and people and that it was abstract, illogical and invalid rules of bible interpretation which had brought this about.

Hermeneutic Rules

'Hermeneutics' is said to be <7> a way of bringing out and explaining the meaning of the Torah by means of a number of rules of logic and association.

Hillel argued with the Bene Bathyra by means of hermeneutic rules. He was apparently the first, or one of the first, to apply such rules not just for explaining the Torah but for deriving new meaning and new laws.

It seems that Hillel introduced the application of hermeneutic rules (rules of logic and association) for determining new laws. It is from about this time that argument began amongst the scholars about the meaning of the law. It is a tannaitic tradition that the great Sanhedrin decided any matters that had to be resolved but that as the pupils of Hillel and Shammai increased so controversy increased in Israel. Suddenly there were many differences which had to be resolved <8>.

In other words, before these rules of logic and association were introduced, the law seems to have been decided according to the Torah and in line with its intent.

But the use of abstract rules of logic and association resulted in laws which were unrelated, or perhaps even outside or opposed to the meaning of the original text of the Torah, and in this way controversy increased in Israel.

Indeed, it seems {53} that there developed two schools of interpretation:

> R. Ishmael and his academy endeavoured to uphold modes of interpretation that would maintain the legal and logical meaning of the scriptural passages concerned. R. Akiba and his academy adopted modes of interpretation that widened the meaning of the scripture far beyond the terms of the written text, even when the conclusion was not altogether in keeping with the general meaning of the verse, expounding every seemingly superfluous

word or phrase and the occurrence of every synonym or repetition of a word or even letter.

There are thirteen rules and these are external teachings, that is external to the Talmud. It seems that at least some of the rules have Greek parallels {54}. However, the gemara {55} quotes one, namely 'the meaning of a passage is to be deduced from its context'.

Another rule draws conclusions from comparing similar phrases appearing in different parts of the Torah. This rule is called Gezera Shava. From the similarity of words or phrases occurring in two often unrelated passages it is inferred that what applies in the one applies also to the other. Where this rule is used to draw conclusions regardless of the context then the results are sometimes truly astonishing.

Examples of such reasoning are Hillel's arguments before the Bene Bathyra, Rabbi's arguments <9> supporting Hillel's Prosbul, R. Simeon's ruling about using flesh cooked in milk {56} and one which states {57} that the words 'release: release' refer to oaths.

What is even more astonishing is that some people can accept the end result without even observing how far removed the conclusion is from the spirit and intent of the law. How come we ever allowed ourselves to be confused in this way?

Notes and Bibliography

Notes

<1>   See chapter 2.2:
        'History Speaks: Monarchy, Exile and Maccabees'

<2>   See 'If One Lapses, So Does The Other', p.104

<3>   Tosefta and Beraitot (Baraita)

<4>   Pentateuch

<5>   And yet this is being done on a vast scale in Israel. See 'The Way Ahead for Israel; Vol. 1: Causes of Present Problems' by David Baram

<6>   The same point is also made by the mishnah, e.g. 'Controversies between Hillel and Shammai', mishnah 2. See what happened at Sepphoris.

< 7> Sometimes the word 'exegesis' is used when referring to a commentary on scripture. The word 'interpreting' means 'bringing out and explaining the meaning of'.

< 8> The mishnah makes the same point. See 'Controversies between Hillel and Shammai', mishnah 2. See my discussion of R. Jose's version of the law.

< 9> See 'If One Lapses So Does the Other', p.104

<10> Talmud: The Babylonian Talmud, Soncino Press, London.

<11> Laws of the Year of Freedom (yovel year)

Bibliography

{ 1}   TB, Arakin 32b

{ 2}   Lev 25, 10, 13

{ 3}   Soncino, London, 1972

{ 4}   Deut 15, 7-11

{ 5}   TB, Shevi'it 10, 3

{ 6}   TB, Shevi'it 10, 4

{ 7}   TB, Gittin 36b

{ 8}   Jerusalem Talmud: Shevi'it 10, 2

{ 9}   Deut 15, 1-2

{10}   Babylonian Talmud: Gittin 36a, Moed Katan 2b, Kiddushin 38b

{11}   Kiddushin 38b

{12}   Jerusalem Talmud: Shevi'it 10, 2

{13}   Babylonian Talmud: Gittin 36a, Moed Katan 2b, Kiddushin 38b

{14}   TB, Horayoth 4b

{15}   Exod 34, 21

{16}   Dayan Grunfeld, Dietary Laws, Vol. 2, p.106 (TB: Moed Katan 2b; Gittin 36a).

{17}   Deut 4, 2

{18}   Deut 17, 8-11

{19}   TB, Gittin 34b

{20}   Aboth **1**, 1-15

{21}   1 Samuel **17**, 1

{22}   1 Kings **11**, 26; 12, 20, 28

{23}   Hag 16a

{24}   Lev **25**, 29-30

{25}   Arakin 31b (Kodashim 3)

{26}   Tractate

{27}   Zugot

{28}   Order 'Nezekin'

{29}   Babylonian Talmud

{30}   Eduyot **1**, 4

{31}   Legends of the Jews **5**, p.378

{32}   Eduyot **1**, 1-3

{33}   Name means 'He shall add'

{34}   Haim Herman Cohn, Associate Professor of Law, Hebrew
        University, Ency. Judaica **16**, 388

{35}   Lev **14**, 10, 12, 15, 21, 24

{36}   Kethubot 67b (Nashim **2**, p.410)

{37}   Deut **15**, 8 (7-11)

{38}   Shab 31a

{39}   Lev **19**, 18-19

{40}   Pes 65b (Moed **2**, Pesahim p.333)

{41}   Yoma 71b (Moed **3**, Yoma p.339)

{42}   Exod **32**, 25

{43}   San 96b (Nezekin **3**, p.652)

{44}   2 Kings **5**, 1

{45}   2 Kings **25**, 8-22

{46}   Judges **4**, 2-3

{47}   2 Kings **19**, 35-37; Isaiah **37**, 36-38; 2 Chronicles **32**, 20-21

{48}   Legends of the Jews, L. Ginzberg, **4**, 269

{49}   Ency Judaica, **16**, 1503-,

{50}   Ency Judaica **16**, 1499

{51}   Pes 66a (Moed **2**, Pesahim p.334)

{52}   1 Samuel **15**, 8

{53}   Ency Judaica **8**, 1417

{54}   Sanhedrin 88b (Nezekin **3**, p.586)

{55}   Hul 63a

{56}   Hul 116a (p.639)

{57}   Shebuoth 49a (p.303)

One Law for All:
Freedom Now, Freedom for Ever

Summary

Manfred Davidmann here uncovers the innermost secrets of the Talmud, secrets which were buried and hidden there and whose existence had been forgotten for close to 2,000 years until Manfred Davidmann published his work.

This is again a fully documented record of previously undiscovered material in the Talmud, about the decisive struggle then going on within Judaism.

The central theme which emerges is again that Torah law provides and ensures equality, independence, freedom from oppression and exploitation, and a good life of high quality. The Jewish establishment argued against such laws so as to expose the people to exploitation through need.

The resulting struggle changed Judaism, determined the fate of the Jewish people and gave rise to Christianity and it is this struggle which is exposed here to the light of day.

Manfred Davidmann's work is factual and conclusive, a documented statement of what Jewish writers then recorded about what had happened at about the time of Jesus to Jewish belief and practice, an exercise in biblical archaeology.

The Talmud contains key social and historical information carefully written by those who decided to record what was happening to Jewish belief and practice in the time just preceding and during the origin and formation of Christianity. It is these records which later evolved into the Talmud.

Here Manfred Davidmann brings us into contact with the work and mind processes of those who 2,000 years ago exerted their combined mental powers to record how and why their country and freedom had been lost and how and why religious belief and practice changed fundamentally.

These are important records and they took steps to ensure that what they recorded would not be changed or obliterated, distorted or misrepresented. They did so to enable a future generation to reverse the trend of events and move towards a good life of high quality for all.

You can see here how the Talmud refers in one detailed example to early Christians and their beliefs. You can see codes used by the early writers of the Talmud to ensure that later generations could not distort or misrepresent the message which was really there. And you can see how they linked relevant stories and arguments in the same way as was used contemporaneously by Christian gospel writers.

We see a religious establishment which to an increasing extent supported the secular establishment line and weakened the application of basic Jewish law.

There are two sides, two policies. 'Power and wealth for a few at the expense of the many' on the one side, 'Freedom, independence and a good life for all' on the other.

So controversies arose about the meaning of Jewish law, about how and whether certain Torah laws should be observed.

They argued in religious terms about social and political policies. You can see here, for example, how the Talmud records

> That wealth and fund-raising were more important to Beth Hillel than learning and wisdom

> The bitter feelings of ordinary people about what establishment scholars were doing to Torah and people

> That Beth Hillel lost the argument that the law followed them. The argument clearly and without any doubt concludes that the law follows Beth Shammai.

In the Talmud are also recorded earlier decisions which applied Torah law to everyday matters which had not been written down before to this extent. The Talmud is thus also a record of what previously was oral law.

But some scholars attempted to provide their own statements with an authority they did not otherwise have. They did so by claiming that they were stating laws given verbally to Moses about 1,500 years earlier which had been handed down verbally over this period without having been written down.

You can see here how this practice was scathingly condemned in the Talmud.

Also recorded at the time were statements about what a future generation would have to do to reverse the pattern of events so as to establish a good life of high quality for all.

One of these, that about R Johanan b. Zakkai and his disciples, is here shown to state that the Torah is to be taught to all who are unaware of its social laws and social system. The observance of these is to be re-established.

There is a striking similarity between events then and today.

Success and strength of a community depend on observing the social laws and social system. So Manfred Davidmann states that observance of the social laws and social system of the Torah needs to be re-established under present conditions (see Policies for a Better Future *)

* In 'Judaism: Basis - Past - Present - Future, Part 2'
Manfred Davidmann
ISBN 978-0-85192-061-0
see chapter 7: 'The Way Ahead: Policies for a Better Future'

Controversies

We have already come a long way together.

We saw <2> that a process of hellenisation was attacking the people's beliefs and strength from within, being fostered from above and outside.

The Jewish leadership was affected and corrupted. They knew that Jewish law protected the people and gave strength to resist oppression. So the leadership attempted to weaken and bypass the basic social laws of the Torah.

We saw <3> that much information was left for us in the Talmud and we now have a better understanding of its meaning. We now have a much better understanding of what happened to Judaism and the Jewish people before the destruction of the second Temple about 2000 years ago at about the time of Jesus.

The Jews believed in and practised freedom and independence for all. The Greeks organised their society on slavery. The mishnah told us about the impact of this foreign ideology and way of life on Judaism and how after some considerable time some fundamental social laws were turned upside down. It was done from within and the greater understanding which we obtained made us look more closely at what we know about Hillel. We now know much more about Hillel and about whom he and his side serve.

Behind a mask of religious orthodoxy they serve that part of the Jewish establishment which wishes to oppress the people, they serve that foreign ideology which stands for oppression and exploitation. They are against Jewish laws which safeguard independence, freedom and justice.

The gemara tells us that Hillel and his side did not serve God, Torah and the people but that from under a mask of religious orthodoxy they served the establishment and legislated in its favour. The gemara ranks Hillel and his side among the most vicious enemies of Judaism and of the Jewish people. They obscured and at times bypassed some basic laws and the intent of the law by using illogical reasoning.

It is small wonder that controversies started and it was from this time onwards that disputes multiplied.

We are now expecting to see the two sides arguing with each other, and discrediting the other side, would expect to see this done in a way which is clear and to the point but without being obvious.

Remember that we are here discovering and seeing a bitter struggle for power, for control of people and resources, between the oppressors on the one hand and those who wish to free themselves and be free, and that this struggle takes place first at the level of men's minds for men's minds so as to gain influence, and that it then expresses itself in the reality of living, in the kind of life people lead and the kind of freedom which they have, in the quality of their lives.

Controversies Increased

So now we will look in somewhat greater detail at how the controversies increased and at the point of view of the followers of Hillel, that is of the establishment, which was against the law of Moses.

We will see how the conflicting points of view, both for and against the law of Moses, are reflected in the Talmud by looking at some of their arguments.

Credit for Work Done

The gemara {1} tells us that when the Nasi (prince) belittled two scholars who had responsible positions in the academy, they tried to get their own back. So he expelled them from the academy.

However, they showed how knowledgeable they were by writing down answers to problems he could not solve and threw the answers in.

So he readmitted them but imposed upon them the penalty that no traditional statement was to be reported in their name. One of them was to be designated as 'others', the other as 'some say'.

This is a nasty piece of work as the prince, the establishment, is robbing the knowledgeable opposition of credit for their knowledge, is in fact preventing their names from getting known and their knowledge and learning from being acknowledged.

This is a political weapon as the establishment is robbing the opposition of their reputation and influence.

But this is not all. The gemara also relates {2} the names of the 'anonymous' rulings in the Mishnah, Tosefta, Sifra and Sifre <1> and mentions that all of them are taught according to the views of R. Akiva.

This seems to complete the process we have just seen applied. The term 'anonymous' indicates that the author is not known but here the anonymous rulings are now credited to the establishment side.

It is not just that the establishment is attempting to prevent the opposition from making itself heard and gaining influence. It is the establishment which aims to profit from the good work done by the opposition.

Hillel's Disciples

We are told {3} that Hillel

> had eighty disciples. Thirty of them deserved that the Divine Presence should rest upon them as it did on Moses our teacher. Thirty of them deserved that the sun should stand still for them as it did for Joshua the son of Nun. Twenty were of an average character.
>
> The greatest of them was Jonathan b. Uzziel, the smallest of them was Johanan b. Zakkai.

Then follows a list of the subjects studied by Johanan b. Zakkai which includes many subjects such as the study of the Torah, astronomy and geometry as well as a number of highly esoteric subjects including the language of demons and the whisper of palms.

He studies in order to fulfil {4} the scriptural text 'that I may cause those that love me to inherit substance and that I may fill their treasuries'.

The point is then made that

> If the least among them was so great, how great must have been the greatest among them!

Such praise warms the cockles of one's heart. Such greatness, such learning, such wisdom. Dewy eyed we see and read about such vast learning, about such vast knowledge, skill and ability in the least of all his disciples. If the least of them was so great, then what a great man Hillel must have been and his other disciples. Dewy eyed we have read about one who is great among the great, a leader of his people, a shining example for the future.

The eye blinks and blinks and we take another look. Right at the back of our minds there is a persistent nagging sound, the soft ringing of an alarm bell. Things are not what they seem. Is this praise objective? Is this praise intended to be taken seriously? It is too lavish to be either sincere or intended.

Thirty of Hillel's disciples are said to have been as worthy as Moses. But the Torah {5} states clearly

> 'And there hath not arisen a prophet since in Israel like unto Moses, whom the Lord knew face to face; in all the signs and wonders, ... before the eyes of all Israel.'

156

If thirty of his disciples were like Moses and another thirty like Joshua, then how come their names are not household words? If they ever existed, what were their names? What did they do or write? How come we do not know them?

The whole of the Talmud from the first page to the last page contains none of the teachings of Jonathan b. Uzziel and yet he is said to be so much greater than Johanan b. Zakkai who is much better known.

This story from the gemara undoubtedly makes a point and it is very clearly stated, but it is far removed from praising the disciples of Hillel for their knowledge and practice of the Torah.

The key lies once again in the quotation from the scriptures. Johanan b. Zakkai was very learned and he studied much so as to enrich his followers. But the great Johanan b. Zakkai is here regarded as the least successful of the followers of Hillel.

And now we see why Jonathan b. Uzziel whose teachings have not found a place in the Talmud is here said to have been so very great. A few lines earlier on {6} we find Jonathan b. Uzziel in effect taking away two-thirds of the estate of someone on Shammai's side. It seems that of the total amount he kept one-third, gave one-third to the 'Temple' and returned one-third to the other side.

Both are said to be followers of Hillel and the whole story contrasts two different ways of enriching the followers of Hillel. The 'greatest' is he who enriches them. Study of the Torah and learning are not the way to gain riches for one's side and that is why they regard the learned R. Johanan b. Zakkai as the least successful among them.

Scholars' View of People

The gemara also tells us {7} about how the scholars felt about the people. It is the scholars who recorded that ancient tradition handed down as a matter of law that

> a man should 'always sell all he has and marry the daughter of a scholar', so that 'his children will be scholars'

> but he should not marry the daughter of an ordinary person (country folk) as his children would be ordinary people.

> To marry the daughter of an ordinary person is a repulsive and unacceptable thing.

> Let him not marry the daughter of an ordinary person because they are detestable and their wives are vermin and (so that he

will not be cursed for) of their daughters it is said {8}, 'cursed be he that lieth with any manner of beast'.

It is also taught that scholars do not reveal a secret to ordinary people, do not appoint them as guardians for orphans, do not appoint them as stewards over charity funds, and must not join their company on the road.

It is a baraita that Rabbi said that an ordinary person may not eat meat, for ... whoever engages in (the study of) the Torah may eat meat but he who does not engage in (the study of) the Torah may not eat meat.

The gemara continues by quoting R. Eleazar who said that 'an ordinary person, it is permitted to stab him on the Day of Atonement which falls on the Sabbath'.

In case we think he did not mean it the gemara records that his disciples asked him whether the ordinary person should be slaughtered to which he replies that slaughter requires a benediction while (stabbing an ordinary person) does not require a benediction.

The scholars also recorded that 'greater is the hatred with which ordinary persons hate the scholar than the hatred with which the heathens hate Israel'.

They are making the point that the religious learned hierarchy should intermarry among itself, keep itself to itself. In this way would be created an inter-bred and inter-married establishment (class) which will look after its own interests and support itself at the expense of the common people who would be uneducated and powerless to resist.

It is clear that the scholars themselves do not love the people and we are here told far more about the scholars' attitude towards the people than about the attitude of the people towards the priestly hierarchy.

All this is very far removed from the kind of social system described and laid down in the Torah. It is very clear that what we see here is not a united people guided and led by a learned leadership applying the law of the Torah but a priestly hierarchy serving the establishment and a hard-pushed and oppressed people reacting to this.

Divine Right (Heavenly Voice)

I find that whenever I understand a little more of the meaning of the Talmud, I admire what is there. Bearing in mind the times of persecution in which it was written I admire the courage of those who struggled to ensure that the law should never be forgotten regardless of what the reformists who controlled religious life were doing to it.

We find the arguments between the two sides recorded in the Talmud, we find one of the two sides using all means at their disposal for shaping and twisting the image of the law to favour the establishment point of view but we also find that their attempts at arguing their point of view are countered and turned against them.

Knowing the importance of this written work for the future of the Jewish people, they did what they could to make it proclaim their own particular side's message. However, we are dealing with much more than remote abstract arguments. At stake is the way of life of a whole people. On one side is God, Torah, people, freedom and independence, on the other side is rulers, establishment, oppression, exploitation, and slavery. The Talmud has remained unaltered since those days and the picture has been preserved for us.

Reputation is No Proof

Here is one example.

When some scholars who wished to have their own particular arguments adopted quoted them in the name of some learned and highly respected authority who had lived long before and whose views were likely to carry great weight, then this was countered by the simple statement {9} that the authority of the person quoted did not constitute proof.

This is clear and to the point. Any case has to be decided on its merits and we do not accept a decision merely because of the reputation of the person saying so.

Either One or the Other

The gemara elsewhere {10} quotes a baraita (external teaching) that
> 'as a general principle, the halachah follows Beth Hillel. If one prefers, however, to adopt the rule of Beth Shammai, he may do so, and if he desires to adopt the rule of Beth Hillel he may do so. ... either one must follow Beth Shammai both where they are more severe and more lenient or Beth Hillel both where they are more severe and more lenient'.

In other words, the law generally follows the establishment point of view but one can either follow Beth Hillel or one can follow Beth Shammai.

One belongs either to one side or the other, either favours the establishment or favours Jewish law and the people.

Voted into Power

And then the 'Heavenly Voice' makes its appearance {11}:
> Since the death of the last prophets, Haggai, Zechariah and Malachai, the Holy Spirit departed from Israel; yet they were still able to avail themselves of the Heavenly Voice. Once when the scholars were met in the upper chamber of Gurya's house at Jericho, a Heavenly Voice was heard from Heaven, saying: 'There is one amongst you who is worthy that the Divine Presence should rest on him as it did on Moses, but his generation does not merit it.' The scholars present set their eyes on Hillel the Elder. ...

Remember that the mishnah {12} clearly stated that the law of Moses had been handed down in unbroken tradition from Moses to the prophets. From them it was handed down {12} to the men of the Great Assembly and to Simeon the Just.

But in this gemara we are told about a Heavenly Voice which could be heard after the prophets had died.

On one occasion a Heavenly Voice was heard to say in one meeting place that one of the scholars there at the time was as worthy as Moses. The scholars who were there all looked at Hillel, that is voted for him.

The supporters of Hillel seem to be arguing that a supernatural voice proclaimed someone to be as worthy as Moses and that all those present voted for Hillel.

Can be Outvoted

Then we have this fascinating mishnah {13}:
> And these are the halachoth which they stated in the upper chamber of Hananiah b. Hezekiah b. Garon, when they went up to visit him. They took a count, and Beth Shammai outnumbered Beth Hillel; and on that day they enacted 18 measures.

To me the meaning of the mishnah is fairly plain. It makes a great deal of sense. The followers of Hillel, of the establishment, here outnumber the followers of Shammai who stand for Torah and the people. The followers of Shammai, having equal standing, get together and by visiting as a group are here able to outnumber and outvote the followers of Hillel and are able to pass measures which favour Shammai's point of view, which support God, Torah and the people.

It is the majority which counts and one way of outwitting and overcoming the establishment and its upside-down version of the Torah is to act together and to outvote them in this way.

It is accepted that Beth Shammai are greater {14} in 'wisdom' than Beth Hillel, that Beth Shammai are more worthy because they have greater understanding of the Torah and of its intent.

We have seen that argument and decision cannot now be based on the authority of some ancient scholar and this includes Hillel himself.

Each case has to be decided on its merits, people are free to choose which side they prefer and the law is decided by majority vote.

However, the followers of Hillel (Beth Hillel) represent the establishment's point of view. They are trying to prove that they have the right to have their opinions shape the law regardless of the opposition. But the law now clearly states that they can be outvoted and they do not like this one little bit.

By Divine Right

We saw that a vote decided that Hillel was as worthy as Moses, presumably from the point of view of determining the law. But this was a matter of voting and votes can go against one. So Beth Hillel prepared a new and more forceful argument {15} to prove that their point of view was always to be accepted.

The gemara tells that for three years there was a dispute between Beth Hillel and Beth Shammai with each of them claiming that the halachah was in agreement with their views. A Heavenly Voice then announced that the views of 'both are the words of the living God, but the halachah is in agreement with the rulings of Beth Hillel'.

The gemara then says that the Heavenly Voice decided that the law was to be fixed in agreement with Beth Hillel's rulings because they were kindly and modest, studied their own rulings and those of Beth Shammai, and even mentioned the words of Beth Shammai before theirs. We are then told that this teaches that one is rewarded for being humble, for not seeking greatness, for not attempting to influence the course of events, for accepting what happens to one.

The gemara concludes by telling that Beth Hillel and Beth Shammai argued {15} for two and a half years the question of which was better: For man to have been created or for man not to have been created. Beth Shammai are said to have argued the point of view that 'it were better for man not to have been created' while Beth Hillel maintained that 'it is better for man to have been created'. The gemara states that 'they finally took a vote and decided that it were better for man not to have been created'. In other words Beth Shammai won the vote.

161

The gemara concludes by saying that 'but now that he has been created, let him investigate his past deeds or, as others say, let him examine his future actions'.

We saw earlier on that it was a vote by those present which indicated that a Heavenly Voice had, in their opinion, referred to Hillel as being so very worthy. We also saw that Beth Hillel could legally be outvoted. So here Beth Hillel attempt to avoid this possibility and the Heavenly Voice is much more direct: Both sides are equally worthy but the law follows Beth Hillel because it is the Heavenly Voice which says so.

Some reasons are given but on the surface these do not seem very relevant when you consider the bitter struggle between the two sides and what is at stake. Significant is that there is nothing here about following the law or justice or observance, that the reasons do not say that they acted for God, Torah and people, or that they ruled justly or impartially. We saw that in reality money was more important to them than the study of the Torah.

The message here is in what these reasons are supposed to teach: Reward comes from serving and from submitting. Do not attempt to compete with us, to change matters or to improve your lot or that of others.

They are saying that as long as people believe this the people will behave in the way they want people to behave, that people will suffer and serve, and will love it.

Then follows the argument about whether man should have been created. Beth Shammai outvote Beth Hillel. Beth Shammai have won.

The gemara concludes by saying that this is irrelevant since real life is in accordance with Beth Hillel's point of view.

So the message this gemara attempts to have accepted as a matter of agreed law is an argument by Beth Hillel:

1. What Beth Hillel say is law because a Heavenly Voice said so.
2. Reward comes from serving and submitting. Do not attempt to improve your lot or to change the set-up.
3. If Beth Shammai outvote Beth Hillel then the law is still according to Beth Hillel because the Heavenly Voice said so.

This argument has now cut across the whole position of Beth Shammai. Beth Hillel and the establishment rule by 'divine right' and what can possibly be said against such logic?

The answer was clear, to the point and completely convincing:

The Torah Decides

The gemara quotes a baraita (external teaching) {16} which records that R. Eliezer put forward 'all the arguments in the world' and when the scholars did not accept them he called upon the 'supernatural' to back his point of view. Then a carob-tree was torn out of its place, a stream of water flowed backwards, the walls of the schoolhouse began to incline, all to support his point of view, but the walls were stopped from falling by R. Joshua. The scholars pointed out that 'supernatural' events could not decide a question about the law one way or the other.

Finally R. Eliezer called upon heaven to prove that the halachah (law) agreed with him and a Heavenly Voice cried out saying 'Why do you dispute with R. Eliezer, seeing that in all matters the halachah agrees with him!'. But then R. Joshua arose and called out: 'It {17} is not in heaven!'.

R. Jeremiah then explains that this means
> That the Torah (the basic constitution) had already been given at Mount Sinai; we pay no attention to a Heavenly Voice because You have long since written in the Torah at Mount Sinai, 'After the majority {18} must one incline'.

The text indicates that supernatural events are not relevant to a discussion of a matter of law as they do not prove the matter one way or the other.

Having failed to impose his opinion on his colleagues by the force of supernatural events, we then see R. Eliezer claiming that he is always right because a supernatural voice says so.

Figure 1

BETH HILLEL'S CLAIMS TO RULE BY DIVINE RIGHT

		Argument	Reference
1		Reputation of a scholar is not a proof	(Megillah 20a)
2		Law is generally according to Beth Hillel but support either one side or the other	(Rosh Hashanah 14b)
3	Claim	Heavenly Voice: "Someone is as worthy as Moses". By vote: Hillel!	(Sanhedrin 11a)
4	Reply	Beth Shammai can outvote Beth Hillel	(Shabath 13b)
5	Further claim	Heavenly Voice says that the law is according to Beth Hillel. The voting strength is not important. Love to obey.	(Erubin 13b)
6	Final reply	We do not listen to or follow heavenly voices. Voting is important. Must not support or follow those who are against Torah.	(Baba Mezia 59b)

But the supernatural may be on the side of good or on the side of bad. Just like supernatural events, supernatural voices do not prove a matter of law one way or the other. R. Joshua makes the point clearly and strongly. The Torah was given at Sinai in written form, it protects the people, it cannot be superseded or overruled by supernatural voices.

This means that a Heavenly Voice cannot give overriding authority to an individual scholar's opinion (or to the opinion of a group) when compared with the law of Moses. It also effectively disproves any claim by Hillel's followers to be right because of the authority given to them by a Heavenly Voice, that is to rule by 'divine right'.

And then R. Jeremiah explains that what R. Joshua's statement means is that we pay no attention to a Heavenly Voice because God wrote in the Torah that one must follow the majority.

Superficially it seems that R. Jeremiah's explanation raises other points. A majority may be corrupted, may be for or against Torah. The authority of a majority depends on whether it is representative, whom it represents and to what extent it is aware of the facts and background of the problem being voted on.

But the Torah text he quotes adds another dimension as it lays down that one must not follow a multitude to do evil or to pervert justice.

In other words the Torah clearly states that one must not follow those who wish to do evil or pervert justice, and this includes those who wish to pass laws which negate or counter the laws of the Torah.

The whole dispute has now been finally decided (see figure 1 which summarises the whole sequence of Beth Hillel's claims and the way they were proved to be invalid and rejected) and we are told that 'God laughed in that hour'. And sure enough there is no come-back, no further argument in support of Beth Hillel's claims.

For Torah and People

Opposition can be Proved Wrong

There is in the Talmud a very charming story which in a most beautiful and sensitive way utterly condemns those who argued for the establishment against the Torah.

Abaye {19} argued for Hillel's Prosbul, arguing for bypassing a basic Torah law so as to bypass an essential protection for the people. In the same discussion R. Nahman makes the point even more strongly. He would even go so far as to bypass the law automatically and permanently, in this way annulling it completely.

Now that you have the background, here is the story:

> Four scholars once sat together {20}. They were studying. Feeling the need to appoint a head they agreed among themselves that whoever would make a statement which could not be refuted shall become head. The statements of all of them were refuted, but that of Abaye was not.

> Abaye held up his head and we see Abaye as a great scholar, the only one whose argument could not be refuted, the future head of the academy.

At this point Rava, who is one of the others, calls out to him 'Nahmani, begin and say something'.

To call Abaye by the name Nahmani amounts to calling him 'You who wishes to annul the law'.

One could argue that the person who says nothing cannot be proved wrong. Abaye, however, said quite a lot at different times and is quoted a considerable number of times in the Talmud.

In other words, he is not refuted as long as he keeps silent.

His colleague Rava is clearly making the point that whenever Abaye, that whenever he who wishes to annul the law, says something that then he is wrong and can be refuted.

Establishment is to Blame

R. Jonah {21} is lecturing at the entrance to the Nasi's house and in this way very pointedly accuses the Nasi, and thus presumably the Nasi's house which is his establishment, of neglecting the poor.

He is lecturing about what is meant by the verse 'The just are concerned about the troubles of the poor' but the wicked are not {22}. He is saying that

God knows that dogs do not get much food.
It is usual to throw raw meat to a dog.
How much?
Give it a little and then immediately drive it off!
'None are poorer than a dog and none richer than a swine'.

The poor are likened to dogs and are badly fed and badly looked after. The rich are likened to swine, to the beast most disliked by observant Jews. The Prince, the establishment, stand accused of neglecting the poor.

The Torah itself accuses the religious establishment with considerable force:

When the people saw that Moses was so long in coming, they demanded a god from Aaron. Aaron asked the people for their gold, and they gave it to him. With this he made them a god of gold whom they worshipped instead of the one God, doing so at their request. They exclaimed that it was this god of gold who released them from slavery.

Aaron asks Moses not to blame Aaron but to direct his anger against the people for it is they who are set on evil. Moses knew differently {23}:

166

'Moses saw that the people were broken loose, for Aaron had let them loose for a derision among their enemies'.

Moses knew that it was Aaron who was responsible.

The Torah indicates clearly that the establishment attempts to deny responsibility but that when people are out of control it is because the establishment let them get out of control.

Listen to Jose of Maon preaching {24} in the synagogue of Maon:
> There will come a time when God will judge the priests, the people, the Nasi and his establishment. The priests did not toil in the Torah because they did not receive the priestly dues from the people. The people did not give the priestly dues because the establishment took away everything. God then judges the establishment and condemns them.

This is very clear and to the point. The Nasi and his establishment are here openly accused of taking everything the people had so that people cannot even pay the priestly dues. And 'when Rabbi heard of this, he became enraged'.

Then Rabbi attempts to defend himself by saying that the leader (Nasi) is like his generation. But Jose of Maon points out that 'according to the garden so is its gardener', that is that one judges the leadership by the condition of the people it leads.

Two Sides, Two Laws

Two Sides

On the one hand we have the Jewish people who are protected by Jewish law from need and from being exploited because of need. On the other we have the rulers and their establishment who wish to oppress their people so as to exploit them.

Two sides do not engage in such bitter controversy without very real cause. What is at stake is on the one hand power and wealth for a few at the expense of the many; and on the other hand freedom, independence and a good life as against oppression and exploitation.

In fact it was the enemy from outside who had infiltrated and corrupted the Jewish secular establishment which then attempted to eliminate the application of the basic laws on which the strength and freedom of the people rests.

The two religious factions we have been discussing are the two sides in this struggle for the application of basic Jewish law. We need to be very clear about what the sides stand for and what they are really aiming at, about the effect of their rulings. One judges people not by what they say but by what they do, one judges by the effect of their actions, by who benefits.

From about the time of Hillel onwards we see a religious establishment which to an increasing extent supported the secular establishment line and weakened the application of basic Jewish law. Hence disputes arose because opposing 'schools of thought' started to argue about the meaning of the law. In essential matters we saw that Beth Hillel ruled so as to favour the establishment point of view.

The Jewish establishment misguided and misinformed the people. What Hillel and Beth Hillel attempted to do was to convert Jewish law and religion into a spineless, toothless, tranquillising religion which served the establishment instead of serving God and the people.

It went hand in hand with a movement towards concentrating on matters of minute and detailed observance which replaced the application of basic teachings and in this way led people astray.

They attempted to invalidate the basic provisions of the five books of Moses, that is of the Torah, through abstract unreal logic and legal fictions aimed at superseding the Torah. In this way they created a labyrinth of enormous proportions in which disappeared the real identity of the two sides, in which were hidden the essential laws which were turned upside down, being laws which protect the people and which underlie the freedom of the people. The purity and vision, the essence and intent of the law were hidden under a smokescreen of abstract illogical reasoning unrelated to the Torah or to the needs of the people.

The Torah is entirely on the side of freedom and people, on the side of that which is good and humane. What we see is an enormous change from the beauty, clear meaning and intent of the Torah.

Having already discussed the greater authority and importance of the mishnah, we have also seen that the gemara is much more far-ranging and that it contains fact and fiction, discussion, argument and political propaganda.

In the gemara we can at times see scholars looking at a statement from a purely logical point of view, arriving at conclusions by logical deduction and reasoning regardless of whether they are either reasonable or even possible.

We see unconnected meanings assigned to biblical or scriptural passages which are quoted merely to back an argument, to 'prove' the scholar's point, to give an appearance of validity to the argument being put forward.

But they also back their arguments by what are often improbably detailed stories about meetings between people and about events which took place some 100 to 300 years before, and about what people said then, to illustrate their points and to lend authority to their opinions.

I am talking about that part of the gemara which attempts to diminish and overrule the beauty and wholesomeness of the Torah and what it stands for, that is that part of the gemara which attempts to serve the oppressor.

It was originally decided to write down the law so that it should not be forgotten because the law was becoming like two laws. The mishnah was completed first. The gemara hundreds of years later.

The Talmud was then 'frozen' ('canonised') and one has to appreciate that this not only helped the establishment to keep the law in an upside-down state but at the same time preserved the law and the recorded arguments for Torah, for the people, for God.

The Written Word and Oral Traditions from Moses

Rabbi Akiva b. Joseph is quoted a considerable number of times in the Talmud and was apparently tortured to death by the Romans. He seems to have been very much an exponent of interpreting the law by means of abstract rules of interpretation which disregard the meaning of the passage being interpreted. He seems to have derived much 'law' in this way which is quite unrelated to (and I would suggest often far removed from and contradicting) the original Torah.

The gemara {1} tells us that when Moses ascends (to receive the Torah) he finds God engaged in affixing coronets to the letters. Asking God, in effect, why he spends his time doing this he is told hat after many generations there will arise a man, Akiva b. Joseph by name, 'who will expound upon each tittle heaps and heaps of laws'.

Heaps and heaps of laws which are not in the Torah, a second set of laws which are unrelated to and thus at times contradicting the laws which God is just about to give Moses.

Moses says he would like to see Akiva b. Joseph and his wish is granted. So he sits down behind eight rows of disciples in Rabbi Akiva's academy. Moses, that mind which wrote the Torah some of whose social laws about behaviour and equality and freedom are only now beginning to be paralleled by social science, is ill at ease because he is unable to follow their arguments. In other words some of their arguments do not make sense.

However, when they came to a certain subject and the disciples asked the master 'Whence do you know it?' they were told by Akiva b. Joseph that 'It is a law given to Moses at Sinai (but not written down)'.

So Moses returns to God and says: You have such a man and you are going to give the law by me! To which God replies that without any possibility of argument his law will be the Torah of Moses.

This is very cutting comment on those who followed R. Akiva. It makes the point that when the arguments they put forward could not be proved, they attempted to cloak them with an authority they did not otherwise have, by saying that the laws were given verbally to Moses about 1,500 years before and had been handed down verbally over this period without having been written down.

Moses then has one further request. He now asks that having been shown Akiva's law, he would like to be shown Akiva's reward. This request is granted also and he sees 'them weighing out his (Akiva's) flesh at the market stalls'.

'Lord of the Universe', cried Moses, 'such law and such a reward!'. God tells him that beyond any argument such is his decision.

The story clearly makes the point that it is because Akiva distorted the Torah, because he replaced God's law with Akiva's, that he was punished by being tortured to death.

The whole story is a most scathing commentary on the kind of law the followers of Hillel, of the establishment, derived by abstract rules of interpretation. It removes all credibility from claims that their opinions should be regarded as laws because they were given by God to Moses some 1,500 years earlier, having been handed down by word of mouth without having been written down, over so many generations.

The Rambam, Maimonides, makes much the same point. He said that whenever there is an argument (in the Talmud) about a particular law said to be a 'halachah handed down to Moses at Sinai' then it clearly cannot have been given to Moses. In other words, only those laws handed down orally and about which there is no argument are laws given by God to Moses. This reduces the number to a very few indeed and is acceptable as a definition as it apparently rules out and eliminates most of the political propaganda, downrating it from the level of law to the level of political argument.

Earlier on we saw the gemara listing the enemies of Judaism. The statement that 'the descendants of Haman studied Torah at Bene Berak' undoubtedly refers to R. Akiva's academy. Those who studied there are included among the worst enemies <1> of the Jewish people.

However, now we have a much better understanding of the underlying reasons for listing R. Akiva with enemies of Judaism.

We know that verbal communication from person to person is very unreliable, that those who hear may use the same word but understand quite different concepts, see quite different meaning in the same word. Hence information passed on by word of mouth is distorted and gets more and more distorted as time goes on.

Verbal communication is notoriously inaccurate and nowadays we know not to follow information which is spread by word of mouth alone. We know that rumours exaggerate and distort and are likely to be highly misleading.

Verbal contracts are liable to be misunderstood and are open to misinterpretation. Written contracts are preferred.

We now know the value of the written word, the value of the written message. The written word is there, it cannot be distorted. If misunderstood or misreported then it can be referred to and explained. It is because of this, because of the greater reliability of the written word, that when the establishment's arguments appeared to spread so that the Torah looked like becoming two laws that the mishnah was compiled and written down, that the Talmud was completed and frozen. It was 'canonised', that is preserved without further change so that we can now understand what took place.

The gemara makes much the same point, convincingly. It relates {2} a number of different arguments between two of the scholars. The same two scholars hold conflicting points of view in each of the three cases which are quoted. In each case they jump up and take an oath, each swearing by the Temple that he heard his ruling from Rabbi.

It may be that a particular argument has been misunderstood by one of them but this does not really matter. No matter which way one looks at it, the gemara in this way clearly illustrates how quickly arguments can develop and wrong ideas be introduced and passed on when one relies on the verbal transmission of information.

The reputation of a scholar does not prove an argument reported in his name. We do not listen to a 'Heavenly Voice'. Similarly the claim that a particular law was transmitted verbally over about 1,500 years does not constitute a proof nor does it lend authority to that 'law'.

Then and Now

Important People on Each Side

Here is another example, this time taken from the Midrash Rabba. The midrash {3} lists six pairs, as follows:

Pair

1	Rebekah	Kohath
2	Levi	Amram
3	Joseph	Joshua
4	Samuel	Solomon
5	Moses	Hillel
6	R. Johanan b. Zakkai	R. Akiva

Each pair once again consists of opposites <2> and this is illustrated by figure 2. The midrash in this way makes the point that just as the first four pairs are opposites, so are the last two pairs. Moses gave the law while Hillel negated it. R. Johanan b. Zakkai taught to re-establish the law while R. Akiva taught and obscured it.

The midrash then comments on the lives of the last two pairs, that is of Moses and Hillel, R. Johanan b. Zakkai and R. Akiva.

Their lifespans are divided into three parts and the midrash lists the experience gained and work done during the three main parts of their lives. They all served Israel during the last part and prepared themselves for this task during the first two parts of their lives.

This is illustrated by figure 3. You can see how useful the midrash considers their service to have been by comparing the knowledge and experience each brought to the task of serving Israel. Hillel and R. Akiva are scathingly condemned, Moses and R. Johanan b. Zakkai are given credit for their knowledge and practical experience of life and for their deep concern for people.

Figure 2

SIX PAIRS OF OPPOSITES

Rebekah	Grandson Levi fought for family purity and justice	Grandson Korah rebelled against Moses and the law of Moses	Kohath
Levi	Struggled for family purity. Took chief part (with his brother Simeon) in avenging the attack on Dinah	Married his aunt which is contrary to the law of Moses	Amram
Joseph	Established the people in Egypt	Established the people in Erez Israel	Joshua
Samuel	Anointed David who unified the country	Oppressed the people so sorely that they rebelled and the country was split up	Solomon
Moses	Instrument for giving the law	Instrument for negating the law	Hillel
R. Johanan b. Zakkai	Taught to re-establish the law	Taught and obscured the law	R. Akiva

Figure 3

MIDRASH'S COMPARISON BETWEEN MOSES AND HILLEL, R. JOHANAN b. ZAKKAI AND R. AKIVA

WORDS OF THE MIDRASH

Moses	Lived in Pharaoh's palace. Then lived in Median.	Lived in Babylon. Then served the scholars ('Sages').	Hillel
R. Johanan b. Zakkai	Was engaged in commerce. Then studied the Torah.	Was an ignoramus. Then studied.	R. Akiva

MEANING OF THE MIDRASH

Moses	Learned and experienced the ways of rulers and establishment. Then learned and experienced the life of the people.	Learned from Babylonians. Learned from serving scholars.	Hillel
R. Johanan b. Zakkai	Learned and experienced commercial life. Studied the law of Moses (which safeguards and protects people).	Learned nothing. Just studied (studies not related to law of Moses).	R. Akiva

174

Some Beliefs of the Essenes

This is how the Essenes, one of the Jewish sects of the time, saw what was taking place. Their Qumran (Dead Sea) scrolls were written before the Talmud, closer to the events, written before the destruction of the country by the Romans, describing the same kind of confrontation in religious language.

These Qumran scrolls talk about the 'teacher of righteousness' who led, guided or inspired 'the children of the light'. He seems to have been called the 'Prophet of Light'. Opposing him was a 'Prophet of Darkness'. The followers of each were apparently called 'Children of Light' and 'Children of Darkness', respectively.

It seems that on the one hand we have darkness, namely those who wish to oppress and exploit, opposing those who are represented by light who struggle for freedom. The 'teacher of righteousness' apparently brought out the essential meaning of the law but was unable to reach and convince the people.

It seems that the Essenes opposed slavery as a matter of principle. Here is what Philo says about the Essenes {4}:

> Not a single slave is to be found among them, but all are free, exchanging services with each other, and they denounce the owners of slaves, not merely for their injustice in violating the law of equality, but also for their impiety in annulling the statute of Nature, who motherlike has borne and reared all men alike and created them as genuine brothers, not in mere name but in reality, though this kinship has been confused by the triumph of malignant covetousness, which has wrought estrangement instead of affinity and enmity instead of friendship.

Philo says that they believed that all are equal and that as a result they freely co-operated with each other. All are equal as a matter of right but it is greed which causes some to oppress others and this causes conflict instead of co-operation.

They also recorded their ideas on how to struggle for light and against darkness.

The two sides are clearly defined. The struggle is the same. The prophet of light, like Shammai, was unable to reach and convince the people and darkness descended.

This outline summary of some of the information from the Qumran scrolls is in line with what the Talmud has told us about the two sides.

The same two sides are struggling with each other. On the one side are those who oppress so as to exploit while on the other are those who wish to be free and independent, who wish to have a high standard of living and satisfying lives.

And of course the same struggle is being fought today. The environment has changed, the sides are still the same. Freedom, good life and security depend on following the law of Moses.

Quoting out of Context and from Uncertain Sources

So now let us move into the twentieth century. The same struggle is there. Its effects can be seen all around us.

Much else has been written during the last two thousand years and arguments are often put together, argued or illustrated by odd quotations from different sources which sound good and seem to support the point of view being put forward. Closer examination reveals that quotations are being misapplied, being used in a way or for a purpose which is far removed from the meaning of the original text. Quoting out of context and quoting from uncertain sources can be highly misleading.

Here are some examples of omissions which I have come across and which illustrate how easy it is to unintentionally quote from incomplete or mistaken sources.

The mishnah tells us that {5} R. Johanan b. Zakkai received the tradition from both Hillel and Shammai, and this probably does not mean that he actually studied under them but means that he knew both their teachings. However, a chart which shows the various tannaim in relation to each other {6} lists R. Johanan b. Zakkai as one of Hillel's disciples and this is highly misleading.

I also came across another example, namely an extensive table {7} which illustrates the history of the Jewish people from the time of the patriarchs to modern times. The prophets are mentioned. Mentioned are Shemaiah and Avtalyon, Hillel and the death of Jesus. Mentioned are many cultural achievements ranging from the writing down of the Mishnah and the completion of the Talmud, up to modern times. Mentioned is the exodus from Egypt and its Pharaoh Rameses II. Completely ignored and left out are the Torah given by the hand of Moses at Sinai, and Moses.

Here are just two examples which I happen to have noticed, in the Jewish prayerbook.

Every morning during the preliminary morning service the Jew is asked to repeat thirteen abstract rules <4> for interpreting the law of Moses. It is rules such as these which were used to derive new meaning regardless of the actual intent and context of the law.

Why should these be included in the daily prayer? Presumably they were included in the first place so as to condition Jews into accepting without question the results of such abstract reasoning.

We saw that Solomon bitterly oppressed his people. He taxed them heavily and introduced compulsory labour service. He ignored basic Jewish law and weakened its application so as to oppress the people. We also saw that the result was that people and country split up into two kingdoms which were destroyed one after the other.

We now know {8} that those who wish to weaken the freedom and independence of the people condone and encourage permissive (promiscuous) behaviour.

Pointedly we are told that the 'Song of Songs' was written by Solomon. Is it not time it is seen for what it so obviously is and deleted from Jewish prayers?

Here is another example. Take that most important and momentous occasion of the blowing of the shofar at Rosh Hashana. It is preceded by a prayer {9} addressed 'To the chief musician: a psalm of the sons of Korah'.

But it was Korah who rebelled against Moses.

So here is a psalm of the sons of Korah, that is of the followers of a man who rebelled against Moses.

I put it to you that it is a psalm by the followers of Korah who rebelled against Moses and that it is not addressed to God. It is addressed to the chief musician. The chief musician? Just who is the chief musician of those who follow a man who rebelled against the law of Moses?

Do Jews really address anyone but God before blowing the shofar on Rosh Hashana (New Year) and Yom Kippur (Day of Atonement)?

Two Sides

Clearly and without doubt we see two sides struggling against each other. This is a world-wide struggle and powerful forces are battling on each side. The two sides faced each other at the time of Moses, the same two sides are locked in combat in our days.

On one side are those who see people as beasts of burden which merely exist so as to slave for and serve their masters, are those who wish to oppress so as to exploit. On the other side are those who see people as free and independent human beings who should have a good life here on earth.

I have shown that the history of the struggle for freedom, independence and good life is clearly described in Torah, Scriptures, Midrash, Talmud and external writings. The Mishnah names the two sides

Hillel

> 'Made bright by god', that is 'favoured by god', that is the rulers, the rich, the establishment.

Shammai

> 'Laid waste by god', that is the poor, the oppressed, the underdog, the enslaved.

The gemara at times considers that both are right, that is that both sides are different aspects of the same situation, and much argument is spent in reconciling the possible opposing arguments and situations.

But we are engaged in a struggle not just against the enemy outside but also against the enemy within who has injected some of his ideology into our belief and practices.

This means that one has to face up to the fact that there are two sides, that there are those among us who behave without consideration for their fellow beings, who wish to oppress so as to exploit, who wish to persuade and condition us into behaving contrary to Jewish law, who want us to forget its meaning and intent.

Look at it this way. That both sides are different aspects of the same situation can be illustrated by the example of two people sitting in a room facing each other. Each of them describes 'the room' by describing what he sees by looking forward without turning his head. They can argue long enough about who is right and who is wrong. In fact both are right and by putting their points of view together they can both see the whole room much more clearly and comprehensively.

This works well if both describe reality but what if one of them is colour blind or the other falsifies what he sees because he wants a bigger share of the room? To avoid misleading conclusions, wrong solutions and bad decisions one should first assess the bias and reliability of statements and of arguments being used, before attempting to reconcile conflicting arguments and interests.

Hence one has to have clear aims and standards, needs to be able to assess what is right and what is wrong.

Rights and Wrongs

God is the God of freedom and the Torah clearly states this a number of times. Here are some examples:

> I am the Lord your God, who brought you forth out of the land of Egypt, to give you the land of Canaan, to be your God. {10}

> I am the Lord your God, who brought you out of the land of Egypt, out of the house of bondage. You shall have no other gods before me. {11}

This quotation is the first of the Ten Commandments. When Moses brought the tables of the law he brought 'freedom upon the tables'.

In other words, following the provisions of the law results in freedom and ensures it, ensures strength and security.

The statement that there is one God and one God alone who delivered us from slavery in Egypt means that only these laws, only this code of behaviour, enables you to gain freedom and stay free.

If you follow advice given by those who want you to behave differently then you are in fact praying to another god, no matter whether this so-called 'god' attempts to influence you through the attitudes and opinions of your external enemies or through opinions and practices being spread internally.

The Torah makes the points very clearly.

> The Lord will have war with Amalek from generation to generation {12}.

> Remember what Amalek did to you by the way as you came forth out of Egypt; ... . Therefore it shall be, when the Lord your God has given you rest from all your enemies roundabout, in the land which the Lord your God is giving you for an inheritance to own it, that you shall blot out the remembrance of Amalek from under heaven; you shall not forget. {13}

'Amalek' may be a real people but the name Amalek means 'A people which licks up' or 'which exhausts' {14} but also means 'labour that is irksome' {15} and it can also mean 'A people who rule', 'A people who lick, who suck empty the people, who exhaust the people' {16}. One is drawn to the conclusion that 'Amalek' refers to those who rule, refers to the establishment, refers to those who serve the rulers, who wish to exhaust their people, who wish to oppress and exploit.

In addition there is the statement in the Torah that on your way to freedom it is they who attacked and wished to delay and destroy you, it is they who have to be fought throughout the ages until they are utterly and completely defeated.

Particularly relevant seems to be the statement that as soon as there is peace from war around one's border that then it is time to deal with the enemy within, to blot out the memory of 'Amalek' within one's own borders.

Not only are there two sides but it is clearly stated that they are bitter enemies and that the only way in which freedom can be reached and made secure is to follow the one and only God, to follow without wavering, bypassing or side-stepping the code of behaviour which leads to freedom, independence and good life, namely the law of Moses.

The Majority Decides

We have seen that there are two sides in bitter conflict with each other and that the resulting confrontation cannot be ignored. There are rights and wrongs and the law of Moses takes a clear stand. God and Torah are completely on the side of freedom, independence and good life for all.

However, the people are oppressed, the application of the law has been modified so that it serves the rulers and the establishment, the law is generally according to Beth Hillel.

The mishnah, however, clearly states that Beth Hillel can be outvoted <3> {17}. It is the majority which decides.

While we are told that Beth Shammai passed eighteen measures, the actual measures are not listed in this mishnah and thus are not relevant to its argument.

So this mishnah is important because it clearly lays down that Beth Hillel (the establishment side) can be outvoted and that laws which reflect Beth Shammai's viewpoint (that of God, Torah and people) can be enacted in this way.

Elsewhere <3> {18} in the mishnah there is a more detailed discussion of the whole matter of deciding the law in accordance with the opinion of the majority.

It lists the recorded disputes between Hillel and Shammai. In the whole of the Talmud there are only these three disputes between them and in each case the scholars ('sages') agree neither with the one nor with the other, listen to them but decide independently.

The mishnah then makes the point that the opinions of Hillel and Shammai were recorded so as to teach the following generations that 'a man should not persist in his opinion' for Hillel and Shammai did not persist in their opinion.

The mishnah then clearly defines that the law must be according to the opinion of the many, that it is the opinion of 'the many' which decides the law.

The point that 'a man should not persist in his opinion' could be interpreted as meaning that one should be flexible, that one man's point of view is not enough, is incomplete and unlikely to be balanced, that one should learn from others. It indicates that confrontation and conflict are to be replaced by accepting the point of view of the majority, are replaced by voluntary restraint and co-operation.

'The halachah must be according to the opinion of the many'. The majority is followed.

But the decision of a court can be set aside by a decision of another court as long as the second court is both greater in wisdom' and greater in numbers. The mishnah states that both these conditions must be fulfilled.

The mishnah also states that although the law is according to the opinion of the many, the opinion of a single person among the many is recorded. In other words, although the majority opinion decides the law, the dissenting opinion is also recorded.

The dissenting opinion is recorded so that if later a man claims that this is what he has learned, that it may be pointed out to him that what he learnt was the opinion of the particular individual which was recorded although it had been set aside.

In other words it is on record that this particular viewpoint was considered at the time and rejected for recorded reasons in the light of knowledge and circumstances existing at that time.

One can now consider what is new and what has changed since the prior decision, one can now reconsider the decision in the light of knowledge and circumstances existing at this time.

The mishnah also makes clear that if a court prefers the opinion of the single person then it may depend on him, that it may accept his dissenting viewpoint.

In other words, a later court can override the earlier decision, now ruling according to what previously had been a dissenting opinion, as long as it is greater in number as well as in wisdom when compared with the first court.

'Wisdom' could be a compound of education, knowledge, common sense, experience, knowledge and understanding of the Torah. It refers to the members of the court. So how does one assess 'wisdom'?

When Beth Shammai outvoted Beth Hillel {17} it was accepted that Beth Shammai were greater in wisdom, that they had greater understanding of the Torah, of its intent, of implementing it effectively.

This is a key requirement.

Teach the People

The overriding assembly has to be greater in number and in learning and this is stressed a number of times. This points to the need for the majority to be educated, this being an essential protection against a misguided assembly or majority abrogating or bypassing essential laws such as those which protect the people.

The Torah is aware of the danger and states that one must not follow a multitude to do evil or to pervert justice, that we must not do that which is wrong.

We saw that the cause-and-effect relationship tells us what inevitably happens if we do that which is right or do that which is wrong.

We also saw that history fully confirms the drastic and bitter consequences of allowing our establishment to bypass the social laws of the Torah.

Hence the great importance of educating all the people in the real meaning and intent of the law of Moses, of them being shown the consequences of ignoring the law and the rewards for following it.

One Law for All

R. Johanan b. Zakkai

It has been suggested that R. Johanan b. Zakkai set up a new court or academy elsewhere after the destruction of the Temple and of Jerusalem. But we have not been given any information about his place of origin, about his family or about any regulations he may have issued before the destruction. If he was sufficiently learned and wise as would enable him to set up a new court or academy after the destruction, then how come nothing is known about him up to the destruction?

We are indebted to Josephus for much of our knowledge about what happened at the time the second Temple was destroyed and Herford {1} points out that Josephus does not mention R. Johanan b. Zakkai.

He was not a disciple of either Shammai or Hillel in any real physical sense and if he did exist then he was highly respected.

We are also told {2} that he had five disciples, their names, what he said about them, how he rated them and some of the things they said (figure 4). But nowhere else in Aboth is there a similar statement relating one scholar to another.

So the sequence is important and we now look in some detail at the five disciples:

Eliezer b. Hyrcanus

Joshua b. Hananiah

Joseph haCohen

Simeon b. Nathanel

Eleazar b. Arach

Each has been given a name which includes at least one name from among those few who, about 500 years earlier, had a non-Jewish wife but promised to divorce her and to return {3} to following the law of Moses.

That each one should have at least one name taken from that short list is more than coincidence. We are being told something important about his disciples, namely that each one of them left his ways behind and began to follow the law of Moses. And indeed it is the second part of the name which provides the vital clue. The picture which emerges is vital, important, fascinating and quite unexpected.

Figure 4

R. JOHANAN b. ZAKKAI'S DISCIPLES

Name	Said By Him	Said About Him
Eliezer b. Hyrcanus	Let the honour of your friends be as dear to you as your own. Be not easily provoked to anger. Repent one day before your death. Warm yourself before the fire of the wise but beware of them.	A plastered cistern which loses not a drop.
Joshua b. Hananiah	An evil eye, the evil inclination and hatred for (one's fellow) creatures put a man out of this world.	Happy is she that bare him.
Joseph haCohen	Let the property of your fellow be to you as if it were your own. Fit yourself to study Torah for it is not to you like an inheritance. Let all your actions be for the sake of heaven.	A pious man.
Simon b. Nathanel	Be careful with the reading of the Shema and with prayer. Make your prayer a plea for mercy, an entreaty for God is patient, compassionate, repents of the evil. Be not wicked in your own esteem.	Fears sin.
Eleazar b. Arach	Study the Torah. Know what answers you should give to the 'epicurean'. Know before whom you are working, who employs you, and who will pay the reward of your labour.	Like a spring which gathers force.

Eliezer b. Hyrcanus

R. Johanan tells us that he takes but does not give (a plastered cistern which does not lose a drop), that he carries more weight than all the 'sages' of Israel, and that he is descended from Hyrcanus. When you recall that Hyrcanus was in effect the last of the Maccabean kings you realise that we are talking about those who followed him, about the Jewish secular establishment.

That this is the intended meaning is fully confirmed by what 'Eliezer b. Hyrcanus' says:

1. The establishment looks after its members (Let the honour of your friends be as dear to you as your own).
2. Let your actions be determined by cold intellect instead of by warm emotions (Be not easily provoked to anger).
3. Sin against the law virtually all your life (Repent one day before your death).
4. Listen to the wise but beware of what they teach.

'Eliezer' means 'God is help' so that 'Eliezer b. Hyrcanus' as a name could refer to those who have power to direct and help, to those who are of the Jewish establishment.

Joshua b. Hananiah

On the surface, the comment 'Happy is she that bare him' does not tell us much about his academic progress and abilities, about his success in studying Torah and halachah.

However, his father's name 'Hananiah' means 'Graciously given of the Lord', we were told about him that 'Happy is she that bare him', and the common Greek form of the Hebrew name Joshua is Jesus.

I understand that in early Christian writings people who have evil eyes, who have eyes which offend, are people who have the wrong belief from a Christian point of view, and so the saying of Joshua b. Hananiah can be expressed positively:

His saying	Expressed positively
An evil eye,	Adopting the right belief,
the evil inclination	a corresponding right way of life
and hatred for (one's fellow) creatures	and love of one's enemies (fellow creatures)
put a man out of this world.	fit a man for the kingdom of heaven.

The message on the right is a summary of early Christian belief.

In other words, this disciple represents Christians and thus gentiles in general.

Joseph haCohen (Joseph the priest)

The only one whose father's name is not given, he is pointedly called 'the priest' although the Temple had been destroyed.

However, we are told that he is 'pious' which seems to mean that he is religious rather than observant, learned or wise.

His sayings are correspondingly vague. They sound good but do not stand up to closer examination.

'Let the property of your fellow be to you as if it were your own' can be interpreted to mean 'use it if you need it' as well as 'take it if you want it' and he could have quoted 'You shall not steal'. His saying bears a close resemblance to Hillel's equally vague and misleading <1> 'what is hateful to you, do not to your neighbour'.

To say that 'one has to prepare oneself for the study of the Torah because the Torah is not an inheritance' is vague and ambiguous. It sounds impressive but is misleading since the essence of the covenant is that every generation accepts the Torah's provisions as a matter of irrevocable law.

His next saying tells us much more about what he really stands for. He tells us to 'Let all your actions be not for the sake of Torah or God, but for the sake of heaven'.

He is telling us not to let our actions be determined by the Torah or by God but to do what 'heaven' tells us. 'Heaven' is to replace God and Torah, is the 'supernatural' behind the establishment, is that which attempted to entrench Beth Hillel <2> by 'divine right'.

His sayings are vague, confusing and misleading, against God and Torah. 'Joseph the priest' stands for the Jewish religious establishment which intentionally and unintentionally backs the secular establishment and confuses the law and other matters, who muddle things up.

This is confirmed by his name. We now understand why he is referred to as 'Joseph the priest'. The aramaic form of Joseph is Jose. We saw that it was R. Jose who confused the clarity of the law <3> {5}.

Simeon b. Nathanel

Here both names occur in the list of men in Ezra {3} so that the clue is possibly in the meaning of both names:

'Simeon' means 'Hearing with acceptance', and
'Nathanel' means 'Given of God', so that
'Simeon b. Nathanel' could very easily be intended to mean that here are those who hear with acceptance that which God gave, who hear and follow the teachings of the Torah.

The text confirms this interpretation. We are told that 'Simeon b. Nathanel' fears sin, while he himself states that one should plead with God for mercy, that one should trust in God to regret that which is evil, and that one should think well of oneself.

This seems to describe good God-fearing people who do that which is right according to the law but who quietly accept all that comes, good and bad, as coming from God, who accept the hardships of life without complaining.

Eleazar b. Arach

R. Johanan tells us that 'Eleazar b. Arach' is 'like a spring which gathers force' and that he 'outweighs all the sages of Israel and R. Eliezer b. Hyrcanus' put together. In other words, he outweighs the Israeli religious and secular establishment put together.

'Eleazar' means 'whom God helps'. 'Arach' means 'wanderer'. Hence 'Eleazar b. Arach' means those who are helped locally and who get on, wherever they happen to be living, among or from those who wander.

Clearly we are here talking about those who get on well among diaspora Jewry, we are talking about diaspora Jewry.

They say that a good way to follow is to have 'a good heart' and that one should stay away from the evil of 'an evil heart'.

To get on well they are told to study the Torah and to know how to reply to those Jews and gentiles who do not accept the Torah as their authority and guide, to those who deny God and his commandments.

Re-establish the Torah

The first chapter of Aboth begins with 'Moses received the Torah at Sinai ...'. We saw that this chapter tells about the way in which the five books of Moses, that is the law of Moses, was transmitted. It told us that an external ideology corrupted the Jewish establishment which in turn corrupted the application of the law. 'Shammai' has the last word, the law is to be kept alive {6}:
> Make your Torah established.
> Speak little but do much.
> Receive all men with a pleasant countenance.

Live according to the law of Moses, apply it but do not draw attention to yourself and be pleasant to all.

The second chapter of Aboth begins with {7}:
> Which is the right way that a man should choose for himself?
> One which is an honour to the person adopting it and honour to him from men.

This advocates that one should by one's behaviour seek the approval of those who rule and of other men, that one should act according to their standards.

This is the voice of the foreign subverting ideology, of the rulers and the Talmud here {7} refers to them as 'my master' <4>.

So the first chapter of Aboth begins with Moses receiving the Torah and describes how the application of the law was corrupted. The second chapter begins with a statement of opposing principle but in this chapter we are told what can be done to re-establish the application of the law of Moses.

R. Johanan b. Zakkai {8} 'received from' Hillel and Shammai. This does not mean that he 'studied under' but that he learned from their teachings, that he sees things as they are.

The same mishnah continues by giving us the only saying of his which is quoted in Aboth, namely
> If you have learned much Torah, do not claim credit for yourself,
> because for this were you created.

In other words, it is the Torah, God's law, the law of Moses which one should study, that it is one's purpose in life to study it because the knowledge it contains determines the quality of life of the people, because Jews have to follow the provisions of the Torah as a matter of law.

The mishnah concludes by telling us about his 'disciples'. In other words, the knowledge needs to be passed on to others so that it can be taught and applied.

We saw that each of the disciples had at least one name which came from a short list of those who had married foreign wives and who, regretting this, agreed to separate from them and to return to following the law of Moses. In other words, what they have in common is that they had assimilated, had worked for and supported the oppressor against God and Torah, that they had followed other gods.

The list of the groups of people whom the disciples represent and which we drew up from the analysis of the names, and of what is said about them, fully confirms this conclusion, and this is illustrated by figure 5.

The mishnah is in fact telling us that these groups need re-educating:
1. Secular establishment.
2. Gentiles.
3. Religious establishment which serves the secular establishment.
4. Those who follow the upside-down version of the law in good faith.
5. Diaspora establishment and people.

This is in full agreement with our various previous findings in previous reports and chapters.

The Torah is to be taught to all who have forgotten it, who are not yet aware of the overriding importance of the application of its teachings.

Figure 5

THE DISCIPLES

NAME OF DISCIPLE	DESCRIPTION OF GROUP THE DISCIPLE REPRESENTS	CORRESPONDING GROUP
Eliezer b. Hyrcanus	Those who have the power to direct and help from among the Jewish secular establishment	Secular establishment
Joshua b. Hananiah	Christians and gentiles in general	Gentiles
Joseph haCohen	The Jewish religious establishment which intentionally and unintentionally backs the secular establishment and confuses the law and other matters, who muddle things up	Religious establishment which serves the secular establishment
Simeon b. Nathanel	Good God-fearing people who do that which is right according to the law but who quietly accept all that comes, good and bad, as coming from God, who accept the hardships of life without complaining	The people who follow the upside-down version of the law in good faith, accepting without complaining that which life offers
Eleazar b. Arach	Those who get on well among diaspora Jewry (a spring which is gathering force and outweighs the secular and religious Israeli establishment)	Diaspora establishment and people

Tell the People

Moses and Freedom; Prophets, Exile and Persecution

First there is the period of the struggle for freedom under the leadership of Moses, including in this the wandering and struggle for survival and strength in the desert which converted a mass of rowdy slaves into tough nomadic fighting units having common aims, purpose and interests, free men all.

It must have been very difficult for them to appreciate that Moses based his work on a comprehensive understanding of life and of the underlying reality of life. It must have been completely beyond their comprehension at the time. However, the work of Moses, the word of God, was based on a deep appreciation of a reality whose existence they could not even suspect but which was understood or at least known intuitively by the prophets of the later two kingdoms.

Moses died before the country was conquered and things were never quite the same after that.

The next short period would be that under Joshua in which the Hebrew tribes battled with the inhabitants of Canaan and conquered much of the country. However, the conquest of Canaan under Joshua was not as purposeful, clear and directed as operations had been under Moses' leadership, nor was it complete.

What was lacking was the leadership which only Moses could give. The conquest proceeded slowly and painfully under some kind of loose tribal organisation with somehow ineffective co-ordination of the work and efforts of the people.

Then followed a period of about 200 years in Canaan in which the tribes struggled against their neighbours, the period of the so-called Judges. A kind of commonwealth perhaps, with some kind of co-operation between tribes in times of need, but avoiding central leadership. These 'Judges' were people who led the tribes in times of difficulty and trouble, appointed on a somewhat intuitive basis.

We next have the period of the monarchy and of the two kingdoms. The monarchy (Saul, David, Solomon) lasted for about 100 years. At Solomon's death the kingdom split up into two kingdoms called Judah and Israel (Samaria). Israel was destroyed after about 200 years and Judah was destroyed about 100 years after that.

Conditions worsened for the people because the rulers turned away from the law of the Torah and oppressed and exploited the people, particularly towards the end of the two kingdoms. The prophets clearly predicted the resulting fall and destruction of the kingdoms, screaming out their warnings against an establishment that would not listen so that the kingdoms were destroyed.

The fall of Judah meant the destruction of Jerusalem, mass deportation to Babylon, and the destruction of the first Temple.

Judges

In the period of the Judges we see the Hebrew tribes struggling with foreign tribes, doing so under leaders which were selected on the basis of what appears to be an intuitive supernatural 'trial-by-strength'. A struggle perhaps of the mind of the oppressors against the group mind of the people, a struggle which sometimes went one way and sometimes the other. One might describe this as a struggle for the soul of Israel. It could be described as a struggle of rule of the people and of the authority of God against the rule of the oppressor and centralised authority.

The 'Judges' seem to have come to the fore in times of trouble. They 'judged', that is determined the course of events. They did so not so much by conscious decisions but by what they did, by what happened to them, by what happened to those round about them with events relating to the people being reflected in an allegorical way in the events associated with these individuals. A kind of primitive 'trial by ordeal' which we left behind hundreds of years ago. Nowadays we know that 'trial by strength' is unjust, based on primitive superstition, on 'sorcery'.

After the death of Moses and during the period of the Judges it seems that there was a considerable amount of 'prophecy'. These were intuitive statements, were predictions of the future, probably both 'for' and 'against', probably sometimes the word of God and at other times the fabrication of the enemy. The indications are that what happened in the period of the Judges was sometimes for the people while at other times it was against.

It may be that they were attempting to find a way of duplicating Moses' special ability and power, or it may have arisen from the system of reward and punishment inherent in 'the blessing and the curse'. It may have been their way of attempting to lead and guide their people but we now know that relying on any one person leads to distortion, irrationality and dictatorship.

It seems to me that in the period of the Judges they were attempting to live and gain strength while following Jewish law, struggling for territory and freedom, aiming to do so without centralised leadership, that is aiming to do so democratically. We face the same situation, are facing and struggling against the same risk of centralised leadership taking over our democratic institutions.

It seems to me that central military rule solved their military problems, an in-between stage between the road to freedom they had trodden with Moses and the successful unification of the tribes and the liberation of the country under David. The central rulers grasped power and were corrupted. The increasing oppression under the monarchy took them back to the point of destruction and risk of extinction.

Role of the Prophets

In an earlier chapter <5> we discussed the warnings of the prophets about the consequences of particular kinds of antisocial behaviour, and said:

> A few quotations from the sayings of the prophets show clearly that the prophets were very much aware of the consequences of what was taking place. They pointed out what was bound to happen if the rulers, their secular and religious establishment and perhaps also the people continued to behave as they were doing and events proved them right. We would now say that intuitively or consciously they were aware of the social relationships, that they were aware of the social consequences of different types of behaviour.

> The prophets, motivated by a deeply-seated sense of social responsibility and urgency, by love of God, Torah and people, continued with increasing frequency and increasing urgency to warn of the inevitable consequences unless rulers and establishment changed their ways, pointing out that all the people would suffer horribly unless behaviour changed. They were bitterly opposed by the rulers and establishment of the day and struggled for God and people while alone and unsupported. They were not listened to, the rulers and their establishments continued to corrupt and oppress the people until both kingdoms were destroyed and the people most viciously dispersed.

> So far I have covered in outline some of the knowledge which we have from the warnings of the prophets about the behaviour of the Hebrew rulers and their establishment, a story of increasing oppression and exploitation of the people, of increasing disregard of basic Torah law, with consequences which were very clear to the prophets who warned and who appear to have had a clear understanding of the inevitability with which the law acts, of the inevitability with which the behaviour of the establishment caused

the effects which destroyed their people and thus the rulers and their establishment themselves.

Outstanding is not only that the warnings were ignored by the rulers and their establishment but that they actively opposed, harassed and persecuted the prophets as can be seen from the following examples.

Amos {9} states that the prophets were commanded to stop prophesying. He accuses the rulers of hating the person who reproves them in the gate (in public, to the people), of abhorring the person who speaks uprightly.

Micah {10} accuses prophets who mislead the people by crying 'peace' and emphasises that he is more qualified to prophecy than they. He points out that among the corrupt practices is that these prophets prophecy for reward, that they are against those who do not feed them and that priests teach for hire.

There are prophets and prophets and some make religious-sounding pronouncements which are really pro-establishment, antisocial and therefore anti-Jewish political propaganda spoutings under the guise of religious fervour.

Jeremiah {11} describes how the priestly establishment attempted to defeat him in argument. He curses them and asks God not to forgive them but to deal with them in the time of his anger. He is persecuted further {12} and again curses his persecutor, correctly foretelling the coming and imminent destruction of Judah and the exile in Babylon.

Here he clearly indicates his understanding of the intent of the law, that it is the basis of and underlies all freedom. His anger arises from his love and concern for the people because the establishment will not change their ways, because he has been unable to change the course of events.

In the next few verses he curses himself and his life because of the isolation and struggle and suffering he has to endure as a result of battling on the side of the people against an oppressive establishment, as a result of trying to save the whole people from being destroyed by the rulers and their secular and religious establishment.

The prophet accuses the rulers and the ruling level for what they do and holds them responsible for what their establishment does and thus for the practices of the people.

But the prophets did not accuse the people of failing to act.

This may well have been because it is the rulers and their establishment who attempt to manipulate the people into behaving in ways which weaken their resistance to oppression.

The People Have to Know

Moses had a central position, led his people selflessly, advised action. When he acted with the elders and his advice was followed the people went from strength to strength.

At the time of the judges an individual or a prophet was able to make himself known to the people in times of severe need and was backed by them. They were then able to defeat their enemies.

Under the monarchy we see authority taken away from the religious priesthood and administration by a central secular establishment which was battling not for the people but for itself. While being militarily effective it in the end took over the people, ruling over the people instead of leading for them. It established central rule which oppressed the people so as to exploit them for the benefit of the rulers and their establishment.

The prophets 'who speak the voice of God', who speak for freedom and for the people, were then considered unimportant and ignored, listened to only when it suited the ruler to do so.

The wheel has come full circle. The Hebrews having disregarded the law are once again oppressed and exploited but this time by their own ruling establishment. This now has a vested interest in rendering the Jewish religion ineffective as following Jewish law would protect the people from being exploited.

When the establishment of the day found ways of bypassing the law and thus of betraying the people, found ways of persuading the people to disregard the law, and when the prophets who warned against such practices were neither respected nor followed, then disaster, destruction and exile followed.

On the one hand we have Moses with full responsibility, acknowledged and followed by the people and thus able to lead his people to freedom. On the other hand we have Jeremiah, unable to affect events, crying out against having to lead a life of unrewarding labour for the people, crying out against having to live his life in shame as a result, wishing he had never been born.

The secular and religious establishments persecuted him because of his warnings.

His aim was to prevent disaster striking the whole people by changing their way of life, by changing the method of government by the rulers and their establishment. In foretelling disaster he aimed at preventing it.

The government would not listen, the establishment would not listen, the people would not support him, he was isolated and alone and had no responsibility, could not help the people. As a consequence the Temple, Jerusalem, the country and the people were destroyed.

It was those 'Jews' who did not observe the basic law, who stood to gain from exploiting people and who wished to exploit people, who grasped leadership and power in the past sometimes under the mask of religious observance. They then legislated against observance and superimposed obedience to themselves (leadership and its establishment under disguise of leader or state) as more important than Jewish law. They then proceeded to reduce freedom, oppressing the people so as to exploit them, and in this way defeated Judaism and the hope for achieving freedom and a good life for themselves, for the Jewish people and for the rest of humanity.

The prophets behaved very responsibly but had no authority, were isolated voices speaking for God and for the people, heartily disliked and at times persecuted by the rulers and their secular and religious establishment. The message did not reach the people. The people did not act. Our cause-and-effect relationship tells us that disaster and destruction were inevitably caused by the behaviour of the establishment and by the resulting behaviour of the people.

But on the other hand Moses was the acknowledged leader and his word was law. He was not part of the establishment and did not 'dictate'. His authority was derived from God, from the support of the people.

It was the people who supported Moses, who followed the law he stated, who backed him and supported him in times of need. It was those who were in distress who joined David. It was those who were oppressed who turned against central authority following the death of Solomon.

This, the support of the people, would seem to make the essential difference between defeat and destruction of Temple, Jerusalem and Israel on the one hand and victory against oppressing and exploiting dictatorships on the other.

What we have seen merely underlines the staggering catalytic potential of a mind like Moses, the extreme uniqueness of his presence, the overwhelming importance of what took place.

Clearly no artificial system could hope to even remotely approach the capabilities of the mind of Moses.

Consider what might have happened to the Jewish people and to freedom if Moses had been rejected by his people. We know what did happen when the prophets were persecuted, isolated and ignored, tottering to their graves as lonely, frustrated and bitter men because they had failed to wake and save the people.

The prophet must be known by the people so that they can learn to trust his knowledge, judgement and sincerity, so that they can back him. Those 'prophets', those teachers, who act from a deeply seated sense of selfless social responsibility, within the laws of the Torah and according to its intent and light, carry great responsibility for the present and future well-being of the Jewish people, indeed of all people.

They need the opportunity to have impact and to affect events, in other words their teachings and warnings must reach the people. They have to be respected by the people so that they will be listened to and followed, backed and supported, so that they can work effectively for the people.

Tell the People

It was the enemy from outside roughly 2,000 years ago which corrupted the Jewish establishment which in turn corrupted the Jewish religion and in so doing destroyed the Jewish people and itself.

Times were very different from a material point of view, from the point of view of style and standard of living. In any case they had to disguise much of what they said and we are now so far removed from their day and age that stories and events may well have had a meaning and implications which may at times have been lost, which we find difficult to understand, which may indeed be open to differing interpretations. But the mind has not changed, the basic conflict has remained the same, and from this point of view we are today engaged in the same struggle. Once this is understood the gemara as such becomes much more meaningful when it is seen to reflect the confrontation between opposing ideologies.

With regard to the Jewish people, Jew was turned against Jew, the establishment of the day in that way dividing the people and weakening them instead of uniting them and instead of leading them in the fight against the common enemy.

The establishment which is persuaded to bypass the provisions of the Torah and which is persuaded to oppress its people for the sake of its own power and material wealth, is serving the enemy of the people and of the country and thus of themselves. The result of such behaviour is, unquestionably as a matter of cold scientific social fact, the weakening and destruction of the people and of the country. A divided house falls and people who are battling against each other weaken themselves and are defeated and taken over by their enemies. The establishment itself is destroyed and replaced by another so that they do not gain from what they have done.

There is a striking similarity between events then and today. We see an establishment which has been warned and is being warned, a people who allow themselves to be led astray and do not act, a Jewish country threatened by powerful forces all around it, with world opinion being manipulated against it. The process must be halted and reversed before it is too late.

The success and strength of the community depend on the law being followed. Hence one has to make sure that no powerful elite may overrule the basic provisions of Jewish law once again, that the uneducated multitude may not be led astray once again. In other words, brainwashing is not education and one must convince the people. The knowledge which we now have has to be made common property and has to be spread.

A united people ably led are strong and remain so as long as the people are free, as long as the people follow the essential and basic laws of the Torah.

The Torah, namely the five books of Moses, is accepted by the Jewish people without question or doubt as the basic constitution, as the written word of God. There can never be defeat of the laws of the Torah, there can never be defeat of the kind of behaviour which is stated in the Torah. Defeat is unthinkable. In fact the corruption which would result from defeat would be so utterly inhumane and monstrous that it would be better to destroy the planet and Genesis states so very clearly.

The people need a clear statement of the basic intent of the law so as to judge events, alternative courses of action and subsequent legislation in the light of the intent of the Torah.

They need to be shown the Torah's view of a world in which people can live good and happy lives serving their community which exists to serve them.

Notes and References

CONTROVERSIES

Notes

    <1>   External to the Talmud

    <2>   See chapter 2.2:
            'History Speaks: Monarchy, Exile and Maccabees'
            Manfred Davidmann

    <3>   See chapter 2.3 :
            'At the Time of Jesus, This is What Actually Happened
            in Israel: The Truth About Hillel and his Times'
            Manfred Davidmann

References

{ 1} Horayoth 13b

{ 2} Sanhedrin 86a

{ 3} Baba Batra 134a; Sukkah 28a

{ 4} Prov **8**, 21

{ 5} Deut **34**, 10

{ 6} Baba Batra 133b

{ 7} Pesahim 49a

{ 8} Deut **27**, 21

{ 9} Megillah 20a

{10} Rosh Hashanah 14b

{11} Sanhedrin 11a

{12} Aboth **1**, 1-2

{13} Shabbat 13b

{14} Eduyot **1**, 4-6

{15} Erubin 13b

{16} Baba Mezia 59b

{17} Deut **30**, 12

{18} Exod **23**, 2

{19} Gittin 36a

{20} Horayot 14a

{21} Shabbat 155b

{22} Prov **29**, 7

{23} Exod **32**, 25

{24} Genesis Rabba LXXX (1)

TWO SIDES, TWO LAWS

Notes

<1>   See chapter 2.3:
      'At the Time of Jesus, This is What Actually Happened
      in Israel: The Truth About Hillel and his Times'
      Manfred Davidmann
      see chapter 'Hillel and his Times'. There see 'Identities
      and Purpose' in section on 'Hillel's Appointment'.

<2>   Like the zugot (five pairs) in the chapter referred to in
      note <1> above.

<3>   See also 'Can be Outvoted' in section on 'Divine Right' in
      chapter 'Controversies'

<4>   R. Ishmail's baraita (external teaching): "Rabbi Ishmail
      says that there are thirteen exegetical principles by
      which the law is expounded ....."

References

{ 1} Menahoth 29b

{ 2} Yebamoth 32b

{ 3} Genesis Rabba, Vayechi 10

{ 4} Quod Omnis Probus Liber Sit
      Philo
      (Ency. Judaica, 1973 Yearbook, p.152, Note 40)

{ 5} Aboth **2**, 8

{ 6} Ency. Judaica **15**, 801

{ 7} Ency. Judaica **8**, 767

{ 8} 'If You Want a Future, Read On ...'
(The Social Effects of Promiscuity)
David Baram
Social Organisation Ltd

{ 9} Psalms 47

{10} Lev **25**, 38

{11} Exod **20**, 2-3

{12} Exod **17**, 16

{13} Deut **25**, 17-19

{14} The Proper Names of the Old Testament Scriptures
Alfred Jones

{15} Bible Names
E. N. Hamilton

{16} Die Namen der Bibel
H. Schumacher

{17} Shabbat 13b

{18} Eduyot 1, 1-6

'ONE LAW FOR ALL' and 'TELL THE PEOPLE'

Notes

<1>   In chapter 2.3: 'At the Time of Jesus, This is What
Actually Happened in Israel: The Truth About Hillel
and his Times'
Manfred Davidmann
see ''Teaching the Torah' in chapter 'Hillel and his
Times'.

<2>   See 'Divine Right (Heavenly Voice)' in chapter
'Controversies'.

<3>   In the chapter referred to in note <1> above, see
'Controversies between Hillel and Shammai' in chapter
'Hillel and his Times'.

<4> The word 'rabbi' is frequently used in this way in the Talmud. To say that Judah haNasi and Rabbi are the same person is equivalent to saying that the Jewish establishment speaks with the voice of the rulers.

<5> In chapter 2.2: 'History Speaks: Monarchy, Exile and Maccabees'
Manfred Davidmann

see 'Warnings of the Prophets' in chapter 'Monarchy Followed by Two Kingdoms'.

References

{ 1} Pirke Aboth: Sayings of the Fathers
R. Traverse Herford
Schocken, 1945

{ 2} Aboth **2**, 8-14

{ 3} Ezra **10**, 22-31, 42

{ 4} Aboth **2**, 8-14

{ 5} Eduyot **1**, 2

{ 6} Aboth **1**, 15

{ 7} Aboth **2**, 1

{ 8} Aboth **2**, 8

{ 9} Amos **2**, 6-

{10} Micah **3**, 5-8, 11-12

{11} Jeremiah **18**, 18-23

{12} Jeremiah **20**

THROUGHOUT

{ 1} Scriptures: The Holy Scriptures, The Jewish Publication Society of America.

{ 2} Talmud: The Babylonian Talmud, Soncino Press, London.

Chapter 3

Jewish Belief and Practice

Summary

Here Manfred Davidmann provides the required background knowledge of the essential core of Jewish belief and practice and for drawing the only possible conclusion: The procedure called 'Prosbul' is invalid. So he annuls it in part 7. This decision will have far-reaching effects on what Jewish people believe and practice.

In part 1, Rab Judah's story is used to illustrate Maimonides' ruling that most of what is taught at present as valid 'oral law' is in fact invalid. The term 'oral law' here refers to Talmudic laws supposedly given at Sinai to Moses but not written down.

Part 2 describes the conflict at the time of Solomon between the Jewish establishment and the social laws of the Torah.

In part 3, Manfred Davidmann explains the social Cause-and-Effect relationship. The Torah states the social Cause-and-Effect relationship, clearly defining this as a fundamental scientific law which applies to all people everywhere at all times. The consequences of not following the social laws and the social system of the Torah are disastrous and unavoidable until behaviour changes.

Parts 4 and 5 clearly state the relative importance and authority of the Torah, the Talmud ('oral' law) and the Halachah (rabbinical decisions). You will find here short concise statements in plain and meaningful language, describing what Talmud and Halachah are, and what you would want to know about them and about their relative authority and significance.

In part 6 the Torah's essential social laws and its social system are outlined. These protect people against oppression and exploitation and they are stated in the Torah as human rights. They are outlined with respect to (a) wealth and (b) social security.

In Part 7, Manfred Davidmann proves that the Prosbul is contrary to the laws and the intent of the Torah, and that Hillel had no authority for making such a ruling. Manfred Davidmann then annuls the Prosbul.

At the core of the Torah are its social laws and its social system. The Cause-and-Effect relationship clearly shows that they have to be followed to ensure a good life of high quality for individuals and to ensure the survival of humankind on this planet under present conditions.

The events of history confirm the operation of the Cause-and-Effect relationship and people need to be made aware of the Torah's social laws and social system and of the need to follow them.

For more information see:

1. See chapter 2.1:
   'Struggle for Freedom: The Social Cause-and-Effect Relationship'
   Manfred Davidmann

2. See chapter 2.2:
   'History Speaks: Monarchy, Exile and Maccabees'
   Manfred Davidmann

3. In 'Management and Leadership: Local, National,
   Multinational (Global), Principles and Practice'
   Manfred Davidmann
   ISBN 978-0-85192-057-3
   see chapter 2: 'Style of Management and Leadership'

4. In 'Messianic Struggle: The Worldwide Struggle for a
   Good and Secure Life for All, Here and Now'
   Manfred Davidmann
   ISBN 978-0-85192-059-7
   see chapter 2: 'Social Responsibility, Profits and
   Social Accountability'

1. Rab Judah's Story

Rabbi Akiva is considered to have been tortured to death by the Romans, is generally represented as a Jewish sage and martyr. The Talmud, however, tells a different story.

The gemara (Menahoth 29b) tells us that when Moses ascends (to receive the Torah) he finds God engaged in affixing coronets to the letters. Asking God, in effect, why he spends his time doing this he is told that after many generations there will arise a man, Akiva b. Joseph by name, 'who will expound upon each tittle heaps and heaps of laws'.

Moses says he would like to see Akiva b. Joseph and his wish is granted. So he sits down behind eight rows of disciples in Rabbi Akiva's academy. Moses, that mind which wrote the Torah some of whose social laws about behaviour and equality and freedom are only now beginning to be paralleled by social science, is ill at ease because he is unable to follow their arguments. In other words some of their arguments do not make sense.

However, when they came to a certain subject and the disciples asked the master 'Whence do you know it?' they were told by Akiva b. Joseph that 'It is a law given to Moses at Sinai (but not written down)'.

So Moses returns to God and says: You have such a man and you are going to give the law by me! To which God replies that without any possibility of argument his law will be the Torah of Moses.

This is very cutting comment on R. Akiva's 'heaps and heaps of laws' and on those who followed R. Akiva.

Moses then has one further request. He now asks that having been shown Akiva's law, he would like to be shown Akiva's reward. This request is granted also and he sees 'them weighing out his (Akiva's) flesh at the market stalls'.

'Lord of the Universe', cried Moses, 'such law and such a reward!'. God tells him that beyond any argument such is his decision.

The story clearly makes the point that it is because Akiva distorted the Torah, because he replaced God's law with Akiva's, that he was punished by being tortured to death.

Added, after comments:

Rab Judah's story does not record actual events taking place at that time in the life of R. Akiva.

Rab Judah's story (Menahoth 29b) is a forceful argument against those scholars in the Talmud who tried to give their own personal opinions a semblance of validity and authority by claiming that what they were putting forward was a law given to Moses at Sinai but not written down.

Regarding this matter, Maimonides (Moshe ben Maimon, Rambam) recorded that whenever there is an argument about a particular law said to be a 'halachah handed down to Moses at Sinai' then it clearly cannot have been given to Moses. In other words, only those laws handed down orally and about which there is no argument are laws given by God to Moses.

To illustrate with greater clarity the point being made by Rab Judah, I am repeating below what I said before. This time, however, I have deleted references to 'R. Akiva' and substituted 'Jones', thus attempting to focus attention on Rab Judah's central point.

> The gemara (Menahoth 29b) tells us that when Moses ascends (to receive the Torah) he finds God engaged in affixing coronets to the letters. Asking God, in effect, why he spends his time doing this he is told that after many generations there will arise a man, Jones by name, 'who will expound upon each tittle heaps and heaps of laws'.

> Moses says he would like to see Jones and his wish is granted. So he sits down behind eight rows of disciples in Jones's academy. Moses, that mind which wrote the Torah some of whose social laws about behaviour and equality and freedom are only now beginning to be paralleled by social science, is ill at ease because he is unable to follow their arguments. In other words some of their arguments do not make sense.

> However, when they came to a certain subject and the disciples asked the master 'Whence do you know it?' they were told by Jones that 'It is a law given to Moses at Sinai (but not written down)'.

> So Moses returns to God and says: You have such a man and you are going to give the law by me! To which God replies that without any possibility of argument his law will be the Torah of Moses.

> This is very cutting comment on Jones' 'heaps and heaps of laws'.

> Moses then has one further request. He now asks that having been shown Jones' law, he would like to be shown Jones' reward. This request is granted also and he sees 'them weighing out his (Jones') flesh at the market stalls'.

'Lord of the Universe', cried Moses, 'such law and such a reward!'. God tells him that beyond any argument such is his decision.

For more information on 'halachah handed down to Moses at Sinai' see chapter 2.4:
'One Law for All: Freedom Now, Freedom for Ever'
Manfred Davidmann

2. King Solomon

King Solomon, greatly praised, of such wonderful wisdom, of great power, wealth and horses, having many wives. But his reign was immediately followed by the kingdom splitting into two kingdoms which fought each other, which largely disregarded Jewish law until both kingdoms were destroyed and the people exiled to Babylon.

On the surface it seems unlikely that the reign of one so great should have contained within itself the causes of subsequent weakness and destruction. But it did and we need to understand what happened to avoid history repeating itself, to avoid making the same mistakes again, to avoid weakness and destruction.

What then was it that caused the decline and destruction?

He had 40,000 'stalls of horses' and 12,000 horsemen and he also had 1,400 chariots, located in 'chariot cities' as well as with the king in Jerusalem.

'Raising a levy' seems to mean getting together people to labour for the king, this being compulsory (forced) labour. So Solomon conscripted 30,000 men which worked for him in Lebanon. They spent one month out of every three in Lebanon, 10,000 each month, in turn. In addition Solomon had 70,000 who 'bore burdens' and had 80,000 who were 'hewers in the mountains' besides 3,300 chief officers who ruled over the people that did the work.

Solomon had '700 wives, princesses and 300 concubines'. This is unlikely. I have seen it stated that his marriages were politically motivated but then how many countries and tribes surrounded Israel or were known? Only a few.

The king had a very great annual income in addition to that from merchants, traders, the kings of the mingled people, the governors of the country. Some of this additional income, if not all of it, must have come from the people of the country either directly or indirectly.

We are told that every man brought his present, 'a rate year by year' and the given figures confirm the thought. We are being told that he obtained his wealth by taxing the people, that this was paid as an annual tax and that this was a heavy burden on the people. And so the king 'made silver to be in Jerusalem as stones'.

His wealth is described as having been very great indeed. 'All king Solomon's drinking vessels were of gold, and all the vessels of Solomon's palace were of pure gold.'

The Torah (Deut 17:14-20) leaves little doubt about what a ruler in Israel must not do:

> He must not 'multiply horses to himself'.
>
> He must not 'cause the people to return to Egypt, to the end that he should multiply horses'. This means that he must not exploit, or oppress so as to exploit, the people for personal gain or for increasing his power over them.
>
> He must not 'multiply wives to himself' so that his heart is not turned away.
>
> He must not 'greatly multiply to himself silver and gold'.
>
> He must read this law 'all the days of his life' ... 'to keep all the words of this law and these statutes, to do them; that his heart be not lifted up above his brethren, ...'

The laws quoted here protect people and safeguard their strength and freedom.

What rulers and their establishment may do is clearly limited by these laws. They may not grasp power, may not oppress or exploit the people, may not behave promiscuously, may not enrich themselves.

Compare the kingship (i.e. government) laws with what we are told about Solomon. What we are being told is not that he had 1,000 wives, etc., but that he broke the laws of government which protect the people, that he oppressed and exploited the people.

The whole record of Solomon's reign shows a ruler who is more concerned with personal wealth and power than with leading the people towards a better life.

Solomon died but before his son Rehoboam could be installed, the people spoke to Rehoboam saying 'Your father made our yoke grievous; now therefore make you the grievous service of your father, and his heavy yoke which he put upon us, lighter and we will serve you'.

Rehoboam's answer was 'My father made your yoke heavy, I will add to your yoke; my father punished you with whips, but I will punish you with scorpions'.

Israel then rebelled against the descendants of David. and Solomon's kingdom split up into two separate kingdoms.

Scripture tells us that Solomon had a choice, namely to follow the law or not. He was warned about the inevitable consequences.

Just as Solomon was given a choice and judged according to the way in which he behaved, so here Solomon's son is given a choice by the people of Israel.

The information about Solomon comes from 'First Kings'. There is much else which confirms what has been said here. Just how 'wise' is a ruler who betrays his people and thus the foundation on which his home is built?

For more information
see chapter 2.2:
'History Speaks: Monarchy, Exile and Maccabees'
Manfred Davidmann

3. The Social Cause-and-Effect Relationship in the Torah

We saw (in Part 1) a statement from the Talmud which argued forcefully against an aspect of oral law, when compared with the laws of the Torah.

The scholars are arguing about whether some laws take precedence or which laws should be kept in preference. It is the social laws and social system of the Torah which are at the centre of confrontation and strife.

We then saw (Part 2) that Scripture tells us that king Solomon and later his son, were each given a choice, to follow the laws of the Torah or not. They decided not to follow them and Israel was in the end lost as a result.

So what does the Torah say about the consequences of keeping or rejecting the social laws and social system of the Torah?

If we want freedom, independence, good life of high quality, then we have to follow these laws. If we do not, then we lose freedom, independence, good life and the country in which we live. This Cause-and-Effect Relationship is stated as a scientific law. The consequences of our behaviour cannot be avoided but we can change the course of events by behaving differently.

Here are some relevant passages from the Torah in plain English as well as in the Torah's religious language. It will be seen that they clearly describe the relationship and the range over which it applies.

CAUSE-AND-EFFECT RELATIONSHIP IN THE TORAH

Extent to Which It Applies

The relationship applies:

Plain English	Religious Language
(1) to all without exception	... your heads, your tribes, your elders, and your officers, even all the men of Israel, your little ones, your wives, and your stranger that is in the midst of your camp, from the hewer of your wood to the drawer of your water; (Deut 29: 9-10)
(2) at all times, to the present as well as to the future	... with him that stands here with us this day ... and also with him that is not here with us this day (Deut 29: 14)
(3) here and now, wherever you may happen to be	... it is not too hard for you, neither is it far off. ... It is not in heaven ... neither is it beyond the sea ... (Deut 30: 11-14)
(4) to your mind (thoughts) and to your emotions (feelings)	(It) is very close to you, in your mouth and in your heart, that you may do it. (Deut 30: 11-14)

Introduction to Relationship

Plain English	Religious Language
You are unable (at your present stage of knowledge and	The secret things belong to the Lord our God; but the things that

development) to understand the Cause-and-Effect Relationship. However, the information given here enables you to see what will happen as a result of your behaviour.

Even if you do not see how that which happens results from your behaviour, the consequences of your behaviour are certain to occur and will be as stated.

are revealed belong to us and to our children for ever, that we may do all the words of this law. (Deut 29: 28)

I call heaven and earth to witness against you this day ... (Deut 30: 19)

Outline of Relationship

Plain English	Religious Language
The quality of your life can range from freedom and a good secure life at one end of the scale to oppression and enslavement at the other end.	See, I have set before you this day life and good, and death and evil, ... (Deut 30: 15) ... I have set before you life and death, the blessing and the curse; ... (Deut 30: 19)
Where you will be on this scale depends on the way you behave towards each other, that is on the extent to which you follow the law.	
Allow yourself to be persuaded into contrary behaviour and you will be oppressed and enslaved. Follow the law and you will be free and have a good life.	But if your heart turn away, and you will not hear, ... you shall surely perish; ... choose life, that you may live, ... (Deut 30: 17-19)

The Relationship

The actual results of behaviour both ways are listed and described, clearly and powerfully illustrating intermediate stages between the two ends of the scale. The results of observing the Law are described (Deut 28: 3-13), and so are those of disregarding the Law (Deut 28: 16-44).

The process is reversible. Increasingly disregarding the Law results in greater suffering and oppression (Deut 28: 49-66), increasingly behaving according to the Law results in greater freedom and a better life (Deut 30: 1-10).

The relationship is stated in a way which enables people to benefit from the effects of their behaviour, even if they do not understand the underlying interrelation.

History clearly and convincingly illustrates the working of the relationship through successive periods of exile and return to Erez Israel. The events speak for themselves. There is no need to keep repeating the same mistakes. We must do better this time.

We have seen here that it is up to us whether or not we follow the Law, and we know what the inevitable consequences will be, either way.

But which laws under what circumstances?

The Talmudic scholars argued about whether some laws took precedence, about which laws should be kept in preference, about Oral laws and Torah laws. Some scholars were motivated by love of God and people, others were politically motivated. However, some were so horrified by the destruction of the Second Temple and by the suffering of the people that they recorded what went wrong and how to correct matters.

For more information
see chapter 2.1:
'Struggle for Freedom: The Social Cause-and-Effect Relationship'
Manfred Davidmann

4. Talmud

The Talmud consists of 'Mishnah' and 'Gemara', recorded together.

The Mishnah records legal decisions and traditions handed down previously by word of mouth. They were committed to writing when disputes arose between scholars about judgements which had been made in the past, about their meaning and their application. These disputes increased and became more intense as time passed and this is reflected in the Talmud.

It took about two hundred years (roughly 1 - 200 CE) for the Mishnah to be compiled, written down and edited. It was finally edited by Judah haNasi who selected some decisions but rejected others and is known to have excluded many legal decisions (Tosefta; Beraitot).

The compiling of the Mishnah was followed by the compiling of the Gemara which is a record of later discussions, arguments and stories relating to the Mishnah, written down many years afterwards.

The Gemara was compiled and added to the Mishnah to form the Talmud, both in Jerusalem and in Babylon. This took about two hundred years in Jerusalem and about three hundred years in Babylon. So to compile the whole Talmud took about four hundred years in Jerusalem and about five hundred years in Babylon.

There are some basic rules of controversy in the Talmud:

1. The earlier scholars (tanna, tannaim) whose views and decisions are recorded in the Mishnah may not express a view which runs counter to a passage in the Torah.

2. Later scholars (amora, amoraim) cannot contradict a mishnah, tanna, tannaim, or an accepted baraita unless he cites another tannaic source in support of his contention.

In other words, the Talmud is subordinate legislation when compared with the Torah.

The Mishnah is closer to the Torah, is closer to being a body of legal decisions and a legal framework than the Gemara. The Mishnah carries greater authority than the mass of the Gemara.

On the other hand the Gemara is far-ranging, containing allegorical stories of often uncertain significance and containing much discussion. Scholars are quoted who lived hundreds of years earlier whose sayings and decisions had up till then been handed down only by the spoken word, had not previously been written down.

The Babylonian Talmud (Talmud Bavli) is considerably longer than the Jerusalem Talmud (Talmud Yerushalmi). The Babylonian Talmud is also considered to have a higher level of learning and greater authority when compared with the Jerusalem Talmud.

For more information
see chapter 2.3:
'At the Time of Jesus, This is What Actually Happened in Israel:
The Truth about Hillel and his Times'
Manfred Davidmann

5. Halachah (Jewish Law)

Torah Law

What we understand in depth of Torah law is important and relevant. That which appears less relevant is often so because we do not as yet understand its impact and intent. Changing the application of laws under such circumstances can lead to the making of misleading and destructive changes. The Torah is very clear on this point:

> 'You shall not add to the word which I command you, neither shall you diminish from it, that you may keep the commandments of the Lord your God which I command you'. (Deut 4: 2)

When I mention the Torah and Torah law, then I am referring to the Pentateuch, that is to the five books of Moses.

The Torah is the basic constitution which safeguards the rights of the people and points the way ahead. On this as a foundation has been built the vast body of Jewish common and case law which has grown up and applies the law under present conditions.

The authority for such changes comes from the Torah (Deut 17: 8- 11). In matters of dispute or doubt which cannot be resolved with reference to existing law, then the priests the Levites and the judge of the day are to decide the matter. The law they will teach and the judgement which is made are binding and have to be followed.

They are thus authorised to modify the application of a Torah law so as to keep it effective in achieving its intent in the light of changing conditions. They may not change the basic constitution, they may not change Torah law.

They may modify the application of a law and do so by issuing directives. The resulting body of common and case law is called 'Halachah'.

Halachah (Jewish Law)

Some ancient directives protect and strengthen the laws of the Torah. There are those which prohibit the doing of something and these are called Gezerot. Then there are directives called Minhagim which generally approve but without adding to, or subtracting from, Torah law. Further there are Takonnot which are amendments to the halachic systems and which generally call for the doing of something.

Halachic directives thus aim to resolve new problems (social, economic and moral) which find no answer in the Torah or in existing Halachah.

They do so by amending the existing Halachah or by new halachic legislation in the spirit and intent of the Torah.

Emergency Legislation

The saving of life being all-important, our scholars have in the past decided in times of danger and need that certain regulations and laws need not be kept. Or they found ways of bypassing the effect of a law without abrogating it, adapting the use of a law to conditions existing in their days. The land was worked during a Shemittah year, for example, to protect the people from persecution at a time of occupation when the Romans insisted on collecting taxes. Another example is that people may defend themselves on the Sabbath.

In an emergency, directives may be issued to be in force for a limited period. Emergency directives leave the law in existence so that it can be applied again at some future date when the emergency is over.

Halachic modification to the application of a Torah law would seem to be permitted in an emergency as long as it is clearly stated that the Torah says one thing while the deciding halachic authority decides otherwise, it being made clear that the directive is subordinate legislation.

Legislation aimed at overcoming an emergency may either strengthen or weaken the observance of the law. We need to overcome emergencies by finding ways which strengthen the application of Torah law.

Emergency legislation leaves the basic law in existence to be applied again at some future date when the emergency is over. Hence emergency legislation has to be accompanied by a clear statement of what it is attempting to achieve, and of the limited period of time during which the emergency legislation is to remain in existence.

This would enable one to judge such subordinate legislation in relation to Torah law, by comparing what it achieves with what it is intended to achieve, and to judge the time when it is to be annulled, amended or superseded when the emergency, the need to save life, is over.

Relative Strength

We have seen that the Torah is the basic constitution which safeguards the people and points the way ahead. It may not be changed in any way either by adding or by taking away.

We have also seen that the Torah authorises halachic legislation modifying the application of a Torah law so as to keep the law effective in achieving its intent in the light of changing conditions.

Halachic legislation is subordinate legislation and as such may be abrogated or amended by other halachic legislation.

For more information
see chapter 2.3:
'At the Time of Jesus, This is What Actually Happened in Israel:
The Truth about Hillel and his Times'
Manfred Davidmann

6. The Social Laws and the Social System of the Torah

6.1 Wealth

God promised the Hebrews the land of Canaan (Erez Israel), the Torah clearly laying down its borders. All the land was to be allocated to Hebrews and the land was divided among them, each family receiving land in proportion to its size.

Except for Levites, every family had its own plot of land, the land having been shared out fairly. Each family had its own independent source of income. Each family independently controlled its own share.

Each family has the right to work the land and to its produce. This right is hereditary and passes to one's heirs, but laws prevent the division of land from becoming unfair, prevent the accumulation of land in the hands of a few, prevent land passing from tribe to tribe.

The laws about ownership of land deal with the means for generating income and wealth. They are important because it is through accumulated wealth that power accumulates to exploit others, to oppress, and to oppress so as to exploit.

As time passes some people gain wealth and power, others fall into poverty and need, and the equal, fair and appropriate distribution of land has to be restored. This is done in several different ways.

In every fiftieth year (Year of Freedom; Yovel; Jubilee) those in service are released from their labours. They then return to their hereditary plot of land as free men, returning to their land and means of livelihood as free people free of all debt.

Ownership of land reverts to its original owners and in this way land is not allowed to accumulate in the hands of a few who could use it to exploit and oppress others.

The owner cannot sell the land to another Hebrew or to a non-Hebrew. He can only transfer the use of the land for a limited period, which cannot be longer than to the next Year of Freedom (Yovel year), since the original owner or his heirs return to their allocated plot of land in that year (Lev 25: 13-16).

Selling the use of the land in this way amounts to leasing it to a tenant, the lease terminating at the Year of Freedom. The land itself cannot be transferred permanently, cannot be sold.

That only the use of the land is transferred and not ownership is underlined by the owner's right of 'redemption'. He and his relatives for him have the duty and right at any time to terminate the lease by paying back to the tenant an amount corresponding to the unexpired part of the lease (Lev 25: 23-28).

This section of the Torah then clearly states that land cannot be sold and defines leasehold giving the maximum length of the lease. It also defines the owner's right of terminating the lease to regain possession while protecting the tenant from financial loss.

The Torah states that the land belongs to God, that the Hebrew who uses land is God's tenant (Lev 25: 23). Hence he may continue to use the land as long as he keeps the conditions of the agreement. So the Torah clearly states that the Hebrews who dwell in the country may use the land only as long as the law is followed, as long as they observe God's laws. This corresponds precisely to how ownership is defined in other countries: A tenant may continue to work the land but only as long as he keeps the terms of the lease.

Land provides independent income and security. Jewish law lays down that the land is to be shared out fairly among the population. It states how ownership is to be controlled so that land cannot accumulate in the hands of a few at the expense of the many.

Jewish laws of leasehold maintain a fair distribution of wealth so that wealth cannot be used to exploit or to oppress. The grim consequences of not keeping such Torah laws cannot be avoided (See 3. Social Cause-and-Effect Relationship in the Torah).

For more information
see chapter 2.1:
'Struggle for Freedom: The Social Cause-and-Effect Relationship'
Manfred Davidmann

6.2 Social Security

We saw that the whole of the land of Israel was divided, fairly and equally, among the Hebrews living in Israel (Part 6.1: Wealth), and that this fair and equal division of the land was to be re-established at regular intervals at the Year of Freedom (Yovel Year).

Now we are looking at the Torah's system of social security. This supports and backs Hebrews who are falling on bad times. The laws of the Torah help Hebrews to maintain their freedom and independence as owners farming their own land, supporting their families in this way. The laws provide an essential safeguard against domination and exploitation by others. A person's need must not be used to exploit him.

Protection against Eviction

If a Hebrew sinks into poverty and his means fail, then he has to be supported. He is to be helped to keep and regain his independence.

A tenant (ger toshav: 'stranger who is a settler') cannot own land. He is a tenant whose lease expires at the next Year of Freedom.

And the Hebrew whose means have failed is to be treated like a tenant whose lease expires at the next Year of Freedom and who is working independently on his own account. He may be sharecropping or paying an annual rent for the use of the land, to his creditors.

As long as he works the land and farms it as a tenant he may in this way regain his financial strength and redeem his own property in due course.

Providing and 'Lending' Money

In addition to being protected against eviction, a Hebrew in need of finance, in need of money, has to be helped. To assist him is not optional but obligatory. One is merely doing one's duty in providing funds, in giving loans.

But he must not be charged interest nor may one profit from supplying him.

When lending money to those who need it one may not press for repayment, particularly so when one knows that the borrower is unable to pay.

So interest-free loans are to be provided to those who need them. Hebrews must not charge each other interest nor pay interest to each other.

However, one may charge interest when lending to a foreigner and foreigners have to repay their debts. Presumably because they are not Hebrews and thus do not adhere to benevolent Jewish law.

Release from Debt every Seventh Year

Unpaid debts are cancelled at the end of the Year of Release (Shemittah Year). This does not apply to unpaid wages or credit for day by day purchases but means that a lender is legally prevented from collecting all debts which have not been repaid by the end of the Year of Release.

In any case one may not press for payment and no creditor would seem to have the right to press for payment of a debt during the seventh year.

Only money lent to Hebrews is released (cancelled) during the Year of Release. Rashi considers that it is a positive command to ensure repayment of debts by non-Hebrews, presumably because they themselves do not release debts and do not adhere to other benevolent Jewish laws such as those which forbid charging interest on loans.

One needs to release all debts without quibble or precondition, without trying to avoid or modify the release of those whom one has in one's power because of their indebtedness.

Conditions of Employment

If a Hebrew continues to sink into poverty in spite of assistance and aid, becoming unable to support himself and his family, then he is forced by need to serve others.

His need must not be used to exploit him. He is to be employed as a hired servant and must not be treated harshly.

Re-establishing the Fair and Equal Division of the Land

Hebrews are to be freed from working for others, and from having to work for others, in each Year of Freedom.

In that year all those who had fallen on bad times and had had to lease their hereditary land to others, were freed from any service commitments and returned to their own land.

In this way they regained possession of their own land, regained freedom and independence.

What we have in the Torah is a comprehensive and fair social system. So why are the social laws and the social system of the Torah not being applied under present-day conditions?

For more information
see chapter 2.1:
'Struggle for Freedom: The Social Cause-and-Effect Relationship'
Manfred Davidmann

7. Hillel's Prosbul

Whichever way we look at it, Hillel's 'Prosbul' is now null and void

We saw earlier {1} that

> Jewish laws of leasehold maintain a fair distribution of wealth so that wealth cannot be used to oppress or to exploit.

> The Torah's system of social security supports and backs Jews who are falling on bad times. Interest-free loans are to be provided to those who need them. Jews must not charge each other interest nor pay interest to each other. Unpaid debts are cancelled after a period of time which cannot exceed seven years.

> In the Torah is a comprehensive and fair social system. The laws safeguard against domination and exploitation by others.

> The grim consequences of not keeping such Torah laws cannot be avoided.

However, the social laws and the social system of the Torah are not being applied under present-day conditions. The reason is that about two thousand years ago an individual called Hillel decided that wealthy Jews did not have to keep the laws of the Torah, that they could ignore the social laws which protected the working population from oppression and exploitation.

The Torah states that loans which have not been repaid have to be cancelled. Hillel decided that loans do not have to be cancelled, that wealthy Jews could legally enforce the repayment of loans at any time. In this way Hillel annulled a central and essential law which safeguarded and protected the working population.

The wealthy and the establishment of the day liked this idea and Hillel's viewpoint was taught, managed to establish itself, and has been taught since then.

Hillel's procedure 'Prosbul' for avoiding the release of debts in the Release year is recorded in the Mishnah. This also records his reasons, thus:

> (A loan secured by) a Prosbul is not cancelled. This was ... instituted by Hillel ...; for when he observed people refraining from lending to one another, and thus transgressing ... the law, ... he instituted the Prosbul.

There were wealthy Jews who refused to lend funds because the Release year, in which debts would be cancelled, was approaching. So Hillel decides that they can collect their debts any time they like as long as they state this in writing.

He sees wealthy people breaking the law. So he decides that they do not have to keep the law, that they can bypass the application of the law, is in effect annulling the law.

Suppose that stealing is a problem. If one were to follow Hillel's example, then one could rule that people can legally help themselves to other peoples' possessions as long as they deposit a written statement of their intentions in a local Registry.

Hillel sees there is a problem. The rich are breaking the law. Hillel abolishes the law!

Tannaim may not express a view which runs counter to a passage in the Torah. Hillel ruled against Torah and people and in favour of the rich.

We are also told that Hillel instituted the Prosbul 'for the better ordering of society'. The questions which immediately come to mind are
'Better' from whose point of view?
'Better ordering' by whom of whom?
'Better ordering' by whom of what?
Who benefits, who loses?

What stands out is that in instituting the Prosbul, Hillel bypassed a Torah law which provides essential protection for the people. He favoured the rich at the expense of the poor. He exposed the people to exploitation through need.

The questions which now arise are what reason Hillel may have had for doing this and whether he had the authority to institute the Prosbul in the first place.

If the Prosbul had been intended to overcome an emergency then it would have only temporary validity and should have been annulled when the emergency was over.

If Hillel had intended to change the application of the law so as to keep it effective in achieving its intent in the light of changing conditions, strengthening the law instead of weakening it, he would have instituted ways of making the money available to those who needed it.

One may also consider that the authority to modify the application of a law in the light of changing conditions is limited to modifications aimed at achieving the intent of the law.

So Hillel erred when he instituted the Prosbul, having no authority to do so.

Take the key area of making money available to those in need, of making it available in a way which protects the borrower from being exploited by the lender.

The law is very definite. Debts have to be cancelled after a period of time which cannot exceed seven years. And immediately following the laws about the release from debt (in the Release year) we find the following:

> If there be among you a needy man, ... you shall ... surely lend him sufficient for his need ... . Beware that there be not a base thought in your heart, saying: 'the seventh year, the year of release, is at hand'; ... and you give him not ... . You shall surely give him, ... I command you ... 'you shall open your hand to your poor and needy brother ...'

The Torah thus clearly lays down that debts must be cancelled and warns against refusing aid, against refusing to lend because the Release year approaches and we are commanded to satisfy the needs of the poor.

* **It follows that whichever way we look at it, Hillel's procedure**
* **'Prosbul' is now null and void, that it has been annulled by**
* **this decision.**

References FOR PART 7

{1} See

Part 3 (above): Social Cause-and-Effect Relationship in the Torah.

Also

Part 6 (above): Social Laws and Social System of the Torah (Wealth; Social Security)

Chapter 4

Causes of Antisemitism

Summary

Here Manfred Davidmann shows that there are two separate root causes
of antisemitism, and these he describes clearly.

These two distinct causes one would normally not consider in relation to
antisemitism. But one can quickly see that what is usually talked about
or considered in relation to antisemitism are only side-effects and
symptoms.

The conclusion is that while one of the causes is of international concern
and can be remedied by increasing peoples' awareness, the other is
under the control of the Jewish people and can be remedied from
within.

The Law Defines Human Rights

The Torah's social laws and social system <1> include a statement of
fundamental and scientific social laws of behaviour, of human rights, of
social and community organisation.

It is the social laws of the Torah which in effect state that all are equal, that no person may exploit another or oppress so as to exploit. All have the right to be free and independent masters of their own fate and there has to be a system of social security which guarantees not just freedom from need but also protection against loss of material and spiritual independence. In effect, oppression can be and has to be resisted, struggled against and opposed.

The essential social provisions of Torah law are clear and to the point. This is what the Torah lays down as a matter of law {1}:

1. The community has to provide ('lend') money to those who need it, free of interest.
2. All such loans, if outstanding, are to be cancelled every seventh year.
3. The country's wealth, and this applies particularly to productive capital such as land, belongs equally to all and needs to be shared out.
4. Inhabitants are also entitled to have a sabbatical year every seventh year. During this sabbatical year they are entitled to be freed from work at the expense of the community.

Every person is entitled as a matter of right to social security. This means that people are entitled to be supported by the community not only when they fall on hard times but also to maintain their independence as independent breadwinners for their families. For example, the community has to provide backup funds to those who need them and they have to be provided as and when required.

To prevent people being exploited through their need these funds have to be provided without charging interest and such 'loans' are cancelled every seventh year if the borrower has been unable to repay them.

It is the inhabitants who keep the social laws, who keep Torah law, who are entitled to these rights.

Dictatorship

Obviously it is not surprising that those who follow and keep the social laws of the Torah have in the past been persecuted by dictatorships of both right and left, by those who wish to establish and support such dictatorships, by those who wish to oppress so as to exploit people. Openly under dictatorship and in more hidden ways under other forms of government.

The Jewish religion keeps alive the knowledge of these human rights and social laws, as Jews read the whole of the Torah each year from beginning to end at weekly services. Jews also celebrate every year the exodus from Egypt, that successful rebellion of slaves against their overlords when God freed the slaves.

Hence dictatorships both of the left and of the right, or those who approve or condone such systems, persecute Jews so as to discredit and wipe out from human memory that which the Jewish religion teaches, namely the social laws and social system of the Torah.

Consequences of One's Behaviour
(Social Cause-and-Effect Relationship)

So far we have had a look at the social laws and system of the Torah. But the Torah also clearly states the consequences of keeping or rejecting the social laws and social system of the Torah. {1}

In the language of religion the Torah states a fundamental scientific law, the Social Cause-and-Effect Relationship {1}, which is that the consequences of keeping or not keeping the Torah laws are inescapable, that what happens to one is in the end the inevitable result of one's own behaviour. Also clearly stated is that this is a scientific law which was defined and stated using the language of religion to get the message across to listeners in such a way that they could understand at least the effects of this 'cause-and-effect relationship'. The relationship is stated in precise terms.

We are told that the cause-and-effect relationship applies to all without exception and at all times, wherever one may be, regardless of type of government, form of religion or social system or country. It applies whether you like it or not, agree or disagree. Freedom and independence of mind and person and the quality of life depend on one's behaviour.

Keeping or not keeping the Torah laws has consequences which cannot be avoided. The consequences are outlined both ways and we are told that the process is reversible. {1}

The Torah lists and describes the actual results of behaviour both ways, clearly and powerfully illustrating intermediate stages between the two ends of the scale. The results of observing the Law are described and so are those of disregarding the Law.

The process is reversible. Increasingly disregarding the Law results in greater suffering and oppression, increasingly behaving according to the Law results in greater freedom and a better life.

The relationship is stated in a way which enables people to benefit from the effects of their behaviour, even if they do not understand the underlying interrelation.

If we want freedom, independence, good life of high quality, then we have to follow these laws. If we do not, then we lose freedom, independence, good life and the country in which we live. This Cause-and-Effect Relationship is a fundamental scientific law. The consequences of our behaviour cannot be avoided but we can change the course of events by behaving differently.

It so happens that the relationship was stated in the Torah for the first time but this does not change the general validity of the relationship. Statistically speaking, whole communities prosper or suffer (are 'persecuted') as a consequence of their individual and thus collective behaviour.

Not knowing the law does not prevent consequences of one's behaviour.

Jewish Belief and Practice at the Present Time

Unaware of the Effects of their Behaviour

The social laws of the Torah are now but vaguely understood and commonly disregarded. Few are aware of their existence as a practical social system.

What is remarkable is that at the present time the Jewish people are unaware of the need to keep the laws, of the need to implement the social system and laws of behaviour which would guarantee their survival and security and a high standard of living in the land of Israel at the present time.

How come?

Two Thousand Years Ago

According to Torah law the role of those who are rich is seen to be that of administering money on behalf of the community and not that of enriching themselves at the expense of the community. People are entitled to support from the community not just when hungry or starving but so as to maintain their independence and improve their security.

Those who were wealthy simply did not wish to provide funds (to those who needed them) without charging interest and in the knowledge that the 'loan' would be cancelled after some years if it could not be repaid by those who remained in need.

As the community failed to ensure that those who were wealthy obeyed and followed the laws, they (the rich and powerful) had the laws changed on their own behalf to suit themselves. {2, 3, 4}

So about two thousand years ago, just before and during the formative years of Christianity, the Jewish establishment of that time argued against the social system of the Torah and succeeded in having the core laws, which prevented them from exploiting people, bypassed and the whole social system abrogated, in effect annulled. {3, 4, 5}

They did so by having their religious 'experts' argue against these laws over a considerable period of time and in this way succeeded in bypassing the social legislation.

But the changes the establishment of the time was making were so drastic that the process and the changes were recorded in what is now known as the Talmud because 'the law was becoming like two laws'. Even so, the establishment of the day attempted to hide what was actually being said by abstract arguments and sheer volume of words and succeeded to the extent that the memory of what they had done faded away into the background.

While this process took place and while the establishment changed Jewish religious belief and practice there were some who would not agree and recorded what was happening and how it was being done. Others, unable to change the course of events, formed communities who attempted to follow the fair and just social legislation. And this seems to have been how Christianity began in the first place. {5}

Basic Causes of Antisemitism

So we see that there are two apparently separate and distinct reasons for antisemitism *. On the one hand we have that persecution is at least instigated, or encouraged by condoning, by those who wish to oppress so as to exploit. On the other we have the fact that Jews behave in ways which by themselves cause the persecution, apparently unaware at present that persecution could arise as the direct and inevitable consequence of their own behaviour.

The fact is that it is because Jews as a people have not observed and at the present time do not observe the social laws of the Torah that they quite inevitably suffer from persecution, from antisemitism *.

On the one hand the Jew is persecuted by oppressors because of the laws of justice and equality he believes in as a matter of God-given law. On the other hand he suffers the direct consequences of not practicing, of not putting into effect, the very same laws he is being persecuted for.

Remedies and Cure

Obliterating the observance of the social laws will not prevent persecution from oppressors. On the other hand the dire consequences of not putting into effect the social system of the Torah are quite inevitable. Twice already were Jews driven out of Israel because the social system of the Torah was bypassed and rejected {2} and the third time is at present coming closer year by year.

Hence the Jew if he wishes to avoid antisemitism * has to find out about and put into effect the social system of the Torah under modern conditions. {7}

To the extent to which this is done will the knowledge spread that Jews are persecuted by oppressors and dictators because Jews are on the side of freedom and independence, that Jews are in the forefront of this struggle.

A New Factor has Entered into the Equation

This is the end of the twentieth century and a new factor has entered the equation. {6, 7}

Up to now it did not really matter whether a few people suffered, whether the odd village was wiped out in a war fought for the benefit of another establishment, whether a whole country and its people were devastated. Of course, it did matter but what I mean is that it did not mean the end of humanity. The point is that as a result of the impact of technology and increasing speed of transport and communication it is possible for the first time in the history of human beings on this planet for just one or only a very few socially irresponsible persons to do something or to introduce changes which could destroy us all as human beings or else make this planet uninhabitable for human beings.

I showed ten years ago in 'Social Responsibility, Profits and Social Accountability' {6} that we were experiencing a sequence of accidents and catastrophes which were occurring more and more frequently and were affecting more and more people.

Since then most people have become aware of this. But I also showed what could be done about this trend of events.

So now we do not have a choice. If we do not now observe and put into effect the social system of the Torah and its code of behaviour then the planet will become uninhabitable for human beings.

Notes

<1> The Torah, that is the five books of Moses (Also called Pentateuch; Part of Old Testament).

References

{ 1} See chapter 2.1:
'Struggle for Freedom: The Social Cause-and-Effect Relationship'
Manfred Davidmann

{ 2} See chapter 2.2:
'History Speaks: Monarchy, Exile and Maccabees'
Manfred Davidmann

{ 3} See chapter 2.3:
'At the Time of Jesus, This is What Actually Happened in Israel: The Truth about Hillel and his Times'
Manfred Davidmann

{ 4} See chapter 2.4:
'One Law for All: Freedom Now, Freedom for Ever'
Manfred Davidmann

{ 5} 'Origin of Christianity and Judaism: What Actually Happened, What Jesus Actually Taught and Later Changes'
Manfred Davidmann
www.solhaam.org

{ 6} In 'Messianic Struggle: The Worldwide Struggle for a
      Good and Secure Life for All, Here and Now'
      Manfred Davidmann
      ISBN 978-0-85192-059-7
      see chapter 2: 'Social Responsibility, Profits and
      Social Accountability'

{ 7} In 'Judaism: Basis – Past – Present – Future, Part 2'
      Manfred Davidmann
      ISBN 978-0-85192-061-0
      see chapter 7: 'The Way Ahead: Policies for a Better
      Future'

* Changed by editor to: "antisemitism" (like in title, summary, subtitle)
  (Was: "anti – semitism")

Chapter 5

The Right to the Land of Israel

Summary

Manfred Davidmann proves that the right to the land in which one lives,
that is the strength and success of a people, depends on how people
behave towards each other. And this applies to all.

The author shows that the history of the Jewish people provides a clear and convincing example.

Jewish people have been attacked and persecuted over 3,400 years because the Torah states the behaviour which gives strength, which provides a good life of high quality, which ensures independence and freedom from oppression and exploitation.

Jewish people survived because this knowledge about behaviour is essential for the survival of human ways of living on this planet. Now in Israel for the third time they should be establishing a way of living together based on equality, freedom and independence, a good life of high quality for each one, providing an example to be followed by other people.

The Torah clearly states that all must be free and equal, that no one may oppress or exploit another. Manfred Davidmann points out that the Torah records as a scientific law that the consequences of one's behaviour are inescapable. But Jews twice lost their country, were driven out of Israel, because they were unaware of the inevitability with which their own establishment was causing their downfall.

The same process is taking place today. The people are weakening to the point where expulsion and later persecution already appear possible and almost likely. The only way to change the pattern of events and reverse the trend is to change behaviour. The Jewish people need to ensure that the social laws and social system of the Torah are applied, and this means putting pressure on the secular and religious establishment to do so. It is the people who need to put pressure on their establishment to achieve this.

Manfred Davidmann points out that nowadays a new factor has entered into the equation. The impact of technology, of increasing speed of transport and communication, the accelerating speed of change, make it essential and urgent that the social laws and social system of the Torah be followed and applied. Otherwise the planet will become uninhabitable for human beings.

Contract and Promise

Promised Land

Jews have always maintained that Israel is the promised land, that this land called Israel was promised to Jews by God and thus is theirs, that it is their land. This is then taken to mean that there Jews may live just like other people, do as they please, have a state just like any other state.

It is perhaps because this property, this land in which milk and honey flows, has been singled out in such a special way by God, that so many try to benefit from the good life surely granted to all its inhabitants, that so many have struggled and are struggling to own and control this most desirable of all properties.

Persians, Babylonians, Seleucids and Egyptians all had a go as did Macedonians, Romans, Ottomans and Arabs. Christianity and Islam struggled to possess it for many years. Last but not least the Hebrews, the Jews of today, twice gained the country God had promised them only to be driven out later. Returning each time, they have now returned once again and re-established for the third time their rule over the country.

One can understand that such a wonderful gift from God should be in such demand - but how come the land changed hands so frequently, how come the bailiffs came so often and so regularly?

Covenant

Perhaps it is simplistic to consider that God would enter into a one-sided and unconditional commitment, saying "There it is. It is yours to do with as you please" and then turn his back on subsequent proceedings.

There is the matter of the 'Covenant'. It is this which makes Jews the 'chosen' people. At Mount Sinai, Jews in effect agreed the Covenant, that contract between God and the Jewish people by which Jews agreed to accept and observe God's commandments as a matter of law and to be held accountable for the extent to which they did so. On the other hand, God promised that if they observed God's commandments then they and their descendants would live secure lives of high quality in the promised land.

Interesting is that Jews are entitled to stay in Israel and use the land but only to the extent to which the laws are followed and observed. So it appears that the bailiffs have come in so often in the past to expel the land's occupants because they did not observe the essential laws, because they ignored the small print of the agreement, of the contract.

Contract

The contract document, namely the Torah, was written down at the time, has not been changed, is public knowledge.

It lays down in precise terms a comprehensive social system and rules of behaviour which form the basis of, and ensure, a quality of life and a standard of living which have still not been achieved. It also states clearly the rewards for observing and the dire consequences of ignoring or breaking the laws of the Torah.

We are told that the consequences of one's behaviour are inevitable since they are determined by a scientific and inescapable cause-and-effect relationship {1}.

So how did it come about that the Jewish people were expelled twice from the country God promised them with their grip on the country weakening at the present time?

Without a shadow of a doubt the Jewish people lost the country in the past because they did not fulfil their part of the bargain, because they broke the terms of the Covenant. In other words, they behaved in such a way as to weaken themselves as individuals and as a people to the point where their defeat and expulsion into poverty and persecution were inescapable as a consequence of their behaviour and in accordance with the Cause-and-effect relationship.

In the language of religion, the land of Israel does not belong to anyone other than God. Those who live in it may use and benefit from the land but only as long as they follow God's laws. If they do not, then in due course the land is repossessed and transferred to someone else. Ignorance is no excuse. Those who stop following the law lose their entitlement to use it and are in due course driven out and persecuted. History of the Jewish people in Israel proved this again and again. {2}

Hence the right to the land of Israel and the future prosperity of its inhabitants and of the Jewish people depend on following the social laws and the social system of the Torah.

Ignorance is no excuse.

We have to know about these laws and follow them in the light of conditions existing at the present time {5}, if we wish to stay in Israel and prosper.

Social Laws and the Social System of the Torah.
The Social Cause-and-Effect Relationship.

(The whole of this chapter has been taken verbatim from reference {8}: Causes of Antisemitism)

The Law Defines Human Rights

The Torah's social laws and social system <1> include a statement of scientific social laws of behaviour, of human rights, of social and community organisation.

It is the social laws of the Torah which in effect state that all are equal, that no person may exploit another or oppress so as to exploit. All have the right to be free and independent masters of their own fate and there has to be a system of social security which guarantees not just freedom from need but also protection against loss of material and spiritual independence. In effect, oppression can be and has to be resisted, struggled against and opposed.

The essential social provisions of Torah law are clear and to the point. This is what the Torah lays down as a matter of law {1}:

1. The community has to provide ('lend') money to those who need it, free of interest.
2. All such loans, if outstanding, are to be cancelled every seventh year.
3. The country's wealth, and this applies particularly to productive capital such as land, belongs equally to all and needs to be shared out.
4. Inhabitants are also entitled to have a sabbatical year every seventh year. During this sabbatical year they are entitled to be freed from work at the expense of the community.

Every person is entitled as a matter of right to social security. This means that people are entitled to be supported by the community not only when they fall on hard times but also to maintain their independence as independent breadwinners for their families. For example, the community has to provide backup funds to those who need them and they have to be provided as and when required.

To prevent people being exploited through their need these funds have to be provided without charging interest and such 'loans' are cancelled every seventh year if the borrower has been unable to repay them.

It is the inhabitants who keep the social laws, who keep Torah law, who are entitled to these rights.

Consequences of One's Behaviour (Social Cause-and-Effect Relationship)

So far we have had a look at the social laws and system of the Torah. But the Torah also clearly states the consequences of keeping or rejecting the social laws and social system of the Torah. {1}

In the language of religion the Torah states a scientific law, the Social Cause-and-effect Relationship {1}, which is that the consequences of keeping or not keeping the Torah laws are inescapable, that what happens to one is in the end the inevitable result of one's own behaviour. Also clearly stated is that this is a scientific law which was defined and stated using the language of religion to get the message across to listeners in such a way that they could understand at least the effects of this 'cause-and-effect relationship'. The relationship is stated in precise terms.

We are told that the cause-and-effect relationship applies to all without exception and at all times, wherever one may be, regardless of type of government, form of religion or social system or country. It applies whether you like it or not, agree or disagree. Freedom and independence of mind and person and the quality of life depend on one's behaviour.

Keeping or not keeping the Torah laws has consequences which cannot be avoided. The consequences are outlined both ways and we are told that the process is reversible. {1}

The Torah lists and describes the actual results of behaviour both ways, clearly and powerfully illustrating intermediate stages between the two ends of the scale. The results of observing the Law are described and so are those of disregarding the Law.

The process is reversible. Increasingly disregarding the Law results in greater suffering and oppression, increasingly behaving according to the Law results in greater freedom and a better life.

The relationship is stated in a way which enables people to benefit from the effects of their behaviour, even if they do not understand the underlying interrelation.

If we want freedom, independence, good life of high quality, then we have to follow these laws. If we do not, then we lose freedom, independence, good life and the country in which we live. This Cause-and-effect Relationship is a scientific law. The consequences of our behaviour cannot be avoided but we can change the course of events by behaving differently.

It so happens that the relationship was stated in the Torah for the first time but this does not change the general validity of the relationship. Statistically speaking, whole communities prosper or suffer (are 'persecuted') as a consequence of their individual and thus collective behaviour.

Not knowing the law does not prevent consequences of one's behaviour.

Jewish Belief and Practice at the Present Time.

Unaware of the Effects of their Behaviour

The social laws of the Torah are now but vaguely understood and commonly disregarded. Few are aware of their existence as a practical social system.

What is remarkable is that at the present time the Jewish people are unaware of the need to keep the laws, of the need to implement the social system and laws of behaviour which would guarantee their survival and security and a high standard of living in the land of Israel at the present time.

How come?

Two Thousand Years Ago

According to Torah law the role of those who are rich is seen to be that of administering money on behalf of the community and not that of enriching themselves at the expense of the community. People are entitled to support from the community not just when hungry or starving but so as to maintain their independence and improve their security.

Those who were wealthy simply did not wish to provide funds (to those who needed them) without charging interest and in the knowledge that the 'loan' would be cancelled after some years if it could not be repaid by those who remained in need.

As the community failed to ensure that those who were wealthy obeyed and followed the laws, they (the rich and powerful) had the laws changed on their own behalf to suit themselves. {2, 3, 4}

So about two thousand years ago, just before and during the formative years of Christianity, the Jewish establishment of that time argued against the social system of the Torah and succeeded in having the core laws, which prevented them from exploiting people, bypassed and the whole social system abrogated, in effect annulled. {3, 4, 5}

They did so by having their religious 'experts' argue against these laws over a considerable period of time and in this way they succeeded in bypassing the social legislation.

But the changes the establishment of the time was making were so drastic that 'the law was becoming like two laws'. These changes and what was happening were recorded in what is now known as the Talmud. Even so, the establishment of the day attempted to hide what was actually being said by abstract arguments and sheer volume of words and succeeded to the extent that the memory of what they had done faded away into the background.

While this process took place and while the establishment changed Jewish religious belief and practice there were some who would not agree and recorded what was happening and how it was being done. Others, unable to change the course of events, formed communities who attempted to follow the fair and just social legislation. {5}

The Right to the Land

What is outstandingly important is that the Cause-and-effect relationship applies to all people and at all times, and history bears this out. {1}

Indeed it is Scripture which clearly lists the kind of behaviour which caused Jews to be driven out from Israel on previous occasions.

History clearly and convincingly illustrates the working of the relationship through successive periods of exile and return to Erez Israel. The events speak for themselves. There is no need to keep repeating the same mistakes. {11}

Laws of Government {1, 2}

The laws of government in the Torah lay down in effect that it is the establishment which should serve the people and not the people serving the establishment.

The leadership, the establishment, may not enrich themselves, may not form enforcing organisations or systems, may not have a better quality of life than that of the community.

Leadership Role of the Establishment

The Jewish religion teaches that all are equal and that one may neither exploit nor be exploited, and sets out a social system for ensuring that these laws are applied, for ensuring that Jewish rulers and establishments serve their people.

The social system guarantees everyone's personal and material independence with the community supporting those who are in need, supporting those whose independence is threatened or those who wish to establish their own material independence, say by setting up their own enterprise.

The role of the establishment is to lead you in the struggle for a better and more secure life of better quality, struggling with you and for you and living as you do and at your standard of living.

However, it is much easier to tell the rich to share their wealth than actually convince them to do so. But history has proved beyond any doubt that the consequences of one's behaviour are as stated. The reason some of our lives resemble hell rather than heaven is because we have been unable to ensure that all are equal, because we have allowed some of us to oppress and exploit the others.

Lessons from History

The Monarchy

During the period of the monarchy, that is during the period of Saul, David and Solomon, we see central military authority being more effective in an emergency and see the military leader subsequently taking over the administration, taking over the government. This is followed by increasing centralisation of power and the formation of an establishment (secular and religious) which serves the source of power and is used to oppress the people. Military personnel are used to give and obey orders but the skills involved are completely different from those expected from an effective manager. In general, while authoritarian organisations are effective in an emergency they are generally ineffective and wasteful at other times. What we see is increasing centralisation of power, increasing corruption and oppression, increasing enslavement of the people with consequent social stress and subsequent destruction. {2}

Struggle of the Maccabees {2}

To begin with, the Maccabees * were united and struggled against brutal foreign oppression. They struggled for Torah, freedom and the people. Against them were foreign invaders who believed in slavery and who were trying to impose their way of life through imposing their beliefs.

After three generations the situation had changed and we now see very clearly increasing internal confrontation, a struggle between people and Torah on the one hand against oppressive rulers and their oppressing establishment on the other.

Following the popular rebellion for Judaism, for Jewish law and thus for freedom, the rulers formed a dynasty and a supporting establishment, had tasted power and meant to have it. Hence they battled for power with each other, allied themselves with foreign powers against each other. In so doing they divided the people and weakened all.

The oppression of Jew by Jew, of the Jewish people by their own rulers and establishment, and the resulting struggle between them defeated both. It ended Maccabean rule, lost the land which had been gained, resulted in enormous hardship to the people. It resulted in the handing over of the country and its people to Herod and the subsequent introduction by Herod of 'hellenisation'. This meant the introduction and popularisation of a foreign ideology, supporting and based on slavery. It was indeed this which the Maccabees had revolted against.

The Jewish leadership, the Jewish establishment, supported centralised power, the oppressive ruling authority and its influence, since the ideas which were being imported helped them to oppress their own people. In so doing they disregarded the welfare of the people, disregarded Jewish law, disregarded the intent and purpose of Jewish law.

Outstanding is that the people were unable to restrain their leaders. The result was total destruction of people and country, and the dispersion of the Jewish people.

Church, State and Religion

Consider the subtle relations between church and state. They are important because the Church is interested in and cares for people while the state looks after the material problems of life.

But then there are different kinds of states and different kinds of churches.

Some states consist of governments which serve the rulers by oppressing the people so that they can be exploited and such states stifle opposition and protest. Here those at the top and experts who in reality serve the rulers, tell people what they should do and have to do.

Other states consist of governments where those who govern serve the people and are accountable to them, where decisions are made at the lowest possible level by referendum with experts explaining the consequences both ways when a decision has to be made.

Some churches serve the rulers and then these theological 'experts' in effect condition the people into gladly serving the rulers, into gladly allowing themselves to be exploited, the general approach then being 'gladly accept the tough life you are leading, the reward will come in a next life'.

Other churches preach that it is the will of God that all people are equal, that no person may exploit another, that it is the role of the establishment to serve the people.

The modern Jew is being taught, is being misled into thinking, that the Cause-and-effect Relationship has merely religious significance. This is intended to convey that whether or not one follows these laws is purely a matter between oneself and God alone, that God can be persuaded to forgive and forget, that the consequences of one's actions can be avoided. Hence the synagogues overflow at the New Year and on the Day of Atonement, that is on the day of judgement and on the day the verdict is decided.

Instead, what Jews should and have to be taught is that the social laws and the social system of the Torah have to be applied in our daily lives and that neglecting to do this results inevitably in loss of country and persecution.

The relations between church and state are subtle and important and particularly so when considering the Jewish religion and Israel.

Holding the Establishment Accountable

The interests of the so-called establishment have apparently remained unchanged. Today's establishment seems to see its position of authority, patronage and influence over the community threatened by Jewish social legislation.

Actively competing with each other for adherents and for funds, the establishments of the different Jewish sects maintain that their own form of belief and practice is right and that every one else is wrong. So they do not wish to acknowledge that any part of what they teach may need amending, could possibly be wrong.

Further, this is the end of the twentieth century and the people are educated. Hence unable once again to merely argue away the religious social legislation in the face of an educated people, wishing to avoid public controversy, knowledge about the overriding importance of the social laws of the Torah is not being passed on to the population.

It was because the people could not ensure observance of the laws by their establishment that the country was lost on each occasion in the past {2}. What determined the outcome in each case was that the people did not hold their establishment accountable for what the establishment was doing.

If the people remain unaware of what happened in the past because the knowledge about the overriding importance of the social laws of the Torah is being kept from them, then the people are unable to pressurise the establishment into adhering to the social system and social laws of the Torah. In that case the loss of the country and later persecution of Jews is inevitable.

If you are poor, if life is tough and harsh, if survival depends on obeying the orders of secular or religious hierarchies, if you are oppressed and/or exploited, then have another look. The only way to improve the quality of life is to struggle so as to put into effect and live according to the social laws and system of the Torah.

The Jewish religion teaches that it is the will of God that all people are equal, that no person may exploit another, that it is the role of the establishment to serve the people and not that of the people to serve the establishment. It teaches as a matter of law that all are equal and may neither exploit nor be exploited.

It takes a good deal of stamina to tell one's students or congregation that what was taught or preached only yesterday needs updating in the light of new knowledge, or to take time off from day-to-day activities to keep up-to-date. But we live in times of change, in times of accelerating change, and updating one's knowledge has by itself become a necessary day-to-day activity without which the expert cannot remain 'expert' for very long. And this applies to both secular and religious experts.

A New Factor has Entered into the Equation

This is the end of the twentieth century and a new factor has entered the equation. {6, 7}

Up to now it did not really matter whether a few people suffered, whether the odd village was wiped out in a war fought for the benefit of another establishment, whether a whole country and its people were devastated. Of course, it did matter but what I mean is that it did not mean the end of humanity. The point is that as a result of the impact of technology and increasing speed of transport and communication it is possible for the first time in the history of human beings on this planet for just one or only a very few socially irresponsible persons to do something or to introduce changes which could destroy us all as human beings or else make this planet uninhabitable for human beings.

I showed ten years ago in 'Social Responsibility, Profits and Social Accountability' {6} that we were experiencing a sequence of accidents and catastrophes which were occurring more and more frequently and were affecting more and more people.

Since then most people have become aware of this. But I also showed what could be done about this trend of events.

So now we do not have a choice. If we do not now observe and put into effect the social system of the Torah and its code of behaviour then the planet will become uninhabitable for human beings.

Conclusions

In everyday language and in the language of science we know that people are affected and changed by their own behaviour and that communities stand or fall according to their actions, as a result of the behaviour of the community as a whole. Oppress and exploit and your community will get weaker and weaker and fail in the end. Follow a pattern of social behaviour and establish a social system which are based on social fairness and justice and you will gain strength and prosper and this will continue while you are doing so.

You know as well as I do that the developed world has a high standard of living which resulted from the application of a humane system of behaviour, generally referred to as democracy. Underdeveloped countries with authoritarian governments, on the other hand, have extremely low standards of living and this is not improving relative to that of developed countries, the differentials continuing to increase.

And what we have seen here that it is up to us whether or not we follow the Torah's social laws and apply its social system in our daily lives. We know what the inevitable consequences will be, either way {1, 9}. The dire consequences of not putting into effect the social system of the Torah are quite inevitable.

Twice already were Jews driven out of Israel because the social system of the Torah was bypassed and rejected {2} and the third time is coming closer year by year.

The right to the land of Israel depends on following the social laws. The people have to be told about the relevance of the social laws under present conditions {5}.

Notes

<1> The Torah, that is the five books of Moses
(Also called Pentateuch; Part of Old Testament).

References

{1} See chapter 2.1:
'Struggle for Freedom: The Social Cause-and-Effect Relationship'
Manfred Davidmann

{2} See chapter 2.2:
'History Speaks: Monarchy, Exile and Maccabees'
Manfred Davidmann

{3} See chapter 2.3:
,At the Time of Jesus, This is What Actually Happened
in Israel: The Truth about Hillel and his Times'
Manfred Davidmann

{4} See chapter 2.4:
,One Law for All: Freedom Now, Freedom for Ever'
Manfred Davidmann

{5} In 'Judaism: Basis – Past – Present – Future, Part 2'
Manfred Davidmann
ISBN 978-0-85192-061-0
see chapter 7: 'The Way Ahead: Policies for a Better Future'

{6} In 'Messianic Struggle: The Worldwide Struggle for a Good and
Secure Life for All, Here and Now'
Manfred Davidmann
ISBN 978-0-85192-059-7
see chapter 2: 'Social Responsibility, Profits and Social
Accountability'

{7} In ,The Human Mind and How it Works: Groups Minds in Action:
     How the Human Group Mind Shapes the Quality of Our Life and
     Living'
     Manfred Davidmann
     ISBN 978-0-85192-055-9
     see chapter 9: 'The Will to Work: What People Struggle to Achieve'

{8} See chapter 4:
     ,Causes of Antisemitism'
     Manfred Davidmann

{9} See chapter 3:
     'Jewish Belief and Practice'
     Manfred Davidmann
     (See Part 3: 'Social Cause-and-Effect Relationship in the Torah')

* Changed by editor to: "Maccabees"
   (Was: "maccabees")

Chapter 6

About the Author

Manfred Davidmann is an internationally well-known and respected scientist and consultant, and author of a number of books and reports which have had considerable impact. His work usually breaks new ground and opens up new understanding and is written in meaningful and easily understood language. Outstanding is that his work is generally accepted as factual, objective and unbiased.

His works have made known and publicised the human rights, the social laws and social system, and the intense worldwide struggle to achieve them, to achieve freedom, liberty, independence and a good and secure life, here and now in this life.

Here some of his works are described under the following headings

General Management (Middle, Senior and Top Level)

Community Conflicts and Confrontations

The Worldwide Struggle for a Better Life

Brain, Mind and Group Minds. Mental Health and Corresponding Social Organisations, of Individuals, People and Communities

Government and Religion, Church and State

Cooperatives and Cooperation

General Management (Middle, Senior and Top Level)

As said already, Manfred Davidmann is an internationally well-known and respected scientist and consultant, and author of a number of books and reports which have had considerable impact. His work usually breaks new ground and opens up new understanding and is written in meaningful and easily understood language. Outstanding is that his work is generally accepted as factual, objective and unbiased.

He brings to his tasks a rare combination of practical experience, knowledge and understanding backed by years spent training middle and top-level managers. Expert knowledge is expressed in clear and meaningful language.

What Manfred Davidmann has done in his work on the general management of enterprises and communities is to lay the foundation for, and develop, 'management science'. He developed and defined the scope and content of General Management, in these reports:

Directing and Managing Change

Organising

Motivation

Style of Management and Leadership

Role of Managers under Different Styles of Management

Work and Pay, Incomes and Differentials: Employer, Employee and Community

Using Words to Communicate Effectively

'Directing and Managing Change' (1979, 2006)
includes
adapting to change, deciding what needs to be done;
planning ahead, getting results, evaluating progress
and performance;
and appraisal interviews and target-setting meetings.

'Using Words to Communicate Effectively' (1998, 2006)
shows how to communicate more effectively, covering aspects of thinking, writing, speaking and listening as well as formal and informal communications. Consists of guidelines found useful by practising middle and senior managers and by university students.

'Organising' (1981, 2006)
is a comprehensive review showing how to arrange matters so that people can work together successfully and well. It is about achieving effective co-operation and teamwork, particularly in large organisations where many experts have to work together in teams to enable aims and objectives to be achieved.

The most confused and intractable organisational problems tend to be about functional relationships and coordinating. Concerning these, the report's descriptions, definitions, specifications and examples, are outstanding.

'Motivation Summary' (1982, 1998)
In **'Motivation Summary'**, Manfred Davidmann summarises different motivation theories, draws on his earlier work including evidence from his U.K. study, and utilises material used by him for lecturing to degree-level students and for training experienced middle and senior managers.

'Style of Management and Leadership' (1981, 2006)
Manfred Davidmann's work **'Style of Management and Leadership'** is a landmark in management and community science and methodology. Over 770,000 copies have been downloaded from his website, worldwide, so far (April 2011).

'Role of Managers under Different Styles of Management' (1982, 1998) is a short summary of the role of managers under authoritarian and participative styles of management. It also covers decision making and the basic characteristics of each style.

The term 'Participation', meaning by this 'participation in decision-making', was first coined, and defined, by Manfred Davidmann when he published his analysis and recommendations about the style of management, in 1981. His works on style of management and on participation in decision-making in management, leadership and government, are widely known, studied and applied, and sprouted a whole literature ranging from the scientific to misleading politically-motivated misrepresentations.

It was Manfred Davidmann who in 1981 formulated, clearly stated and then published ('Style of Management and Leadership', 1981) his principle that the real political struggle was not between political 'left' and 'right', but was for participation in decision-making, for the right to make the decisions.

Manfred Davidmann's concept of participative government and management, of participation in decision-making, has become a household word, in daily use when referring to government and management styles, worldwide. His concepts are applied all the way from village government and community projects to national policies and elections, are applied by cooperatives, companies and global corporations alike.

Clearly defined and described in 'Style of Management and Leadership' is the whole scale of style of management and organising, from fully authoritarian to fully participative. It applies to community organisations, commercial enterprises, political parties, whole countries. The social assumptions underlying each of the styles are given, as are problems they create, the symptoms by which they can be recognised, and the ways people work together or against each other within them.

The extent to which authority is balanced between top and bottom, and the corresponding style of management, are also discussed. This work pulls the diverse world-wide events in labour relations and in government/people confrontation into a meaningful, clear and highly significant picture of interrelated events fitting into a consistent pattern.

Community Conflicts and Confrontations

How local and national governments are managing our affairs is of crucial importance to every citizen. Government has to make ends meet, has to bring about a rising standard of secure living, social security and an increasing quality of life for its citizens.

"There can be ups and downs but", says Manfred Davidmann, "failure to make ends meet is just as directly and surely the result of bad leadership and management as it is in any commercial enterprise." This is a severe criticism also of the kind of experts and consultants used, and of the way they are used. "The quality of one's experts and whether and how their expertise is used, and applied, are of decisive importance."

Manfred Davidmann's report 'Work and Pay, Incomes and Differentials: Employer, Employee and Community' (1981, 2007) is a concise all-embracing review and analysis of the whole subject, in clear and easily understood language. What makes this report so special is that it covers incomes and differentials from the point of view of the owner or employer, from that of the individual and his family and from that of the community, discussing their interests and requirements.

When talking about pay, incomes and differentials we are dealing with matters which are at the centre of confrontation and conflict and around which rage controversy and strife. We are dealing with matters which determine how one man stands in relation to another, with something which depends on negotiation and bargaining between those who employ and those who are employed. The result is that almost all one sees about pay and differentials is biased towards one side or the other and both points of view are then equally misleading.

But Manfred Davidmann here provides the underlying knowledge and understanding for scientific determination and prediction of rates of pay, remuneration and differentials, of remuneration scales and of national patterns of pay and differentials.

These correlations and methods represent a major breakthrough and rates of pay, incomes and differentials can be assessed with a high degree of reliability. Now pay bargaining can include agreeing basic guide-lines of the kind described here as governing pay increases.

Illustrated are National Remuneration Scales which record the remuneration pattern for a group or profession and the position of every individual in it, showing also how income depends on age and degree of success. Illustrated also is the National Remuneration Pattern which is a precise pictorial record of the differentials within a country, from top to bottom, from young to old. Both are used to assess changes in pay, remuneration and differentials for individuals, groups and professions.

However, it is easier to tell the rich to share their wealth with the poor than to persuade them to actually do so. And companies, corporations and governments, owners, managers, experts and politicians, too often work for personal gain instead of serving employees, customers or citizens, exploiting instead of serving their community.

Just consider the following examples of corporate and individual antisocial practices.

One of the most controversial operations of multinationals, transfer pricing, has been clearly described and defined by Manfred Davidmann in his report '**Multinational Operations: Transfer Pricing and Taxation**' (1991, 2006).

The report showed that multinational companies were minimising their liability for corporation tax by transfer pricing, that is by making book entries which transfer profits to the country with the lowest corporation tax.

Say a multinational has increased its profits in such ways. As the government's expenses have not changed it must make up this shortfall elsewhere. From its other tax payers, say from its citizens. So its citizens pay more tax, the government can now spend the same amount as before, the multinational's profits have increased.

This tax avoidance is legal and governments have not legislated to prevent this practice.

The multinational, and this means the owners and directors of the multinational, are thus in effect taxing the country's citizens, its population, in this way increasing the multinational's profits and thus their own incomes and wealth.

A matter far removed from earning reasonable profits from providing needed quality goods and services at reasonable prices in open competition with other corporations.

Fifteen years ago, Manfred Davidmann coined the phrase 'Exporting Employment and Importing Unemployment', and pointed to, and warned about, the social and economic consequences of what is now often euphemistically called 'outsourcing' or 'globalisation'.

In his report '**Exporting and Importing of Employment and Unemployment**' (1996, 2002) he pointed out that imports were being priced at what the market will bear, or just under, and that if the enormous profit margins were left uncontrolled, these would then cause production to move from high-wage to low-wage countries. The consequence is a lowering of the standard of living in high-wage countries to that in low-wage countries, instead of a raising of the standard of living in low-wage countries to that in high wage countries.

"Unemployment has reached an unacceptable level" says Manfred Davidmann. It is a principle of economics that social costs have to be paid by those causing them. But manufacturers and suppliers tend to increase their profits by passing on to the community the social costs of their operations, costs such as disposal of packaging and waste, or of polluting.

"The social costs of unemployment have to be paid by the enterprise which caused the unemployment in the first place" says Manfred Davidmann. "Social costs need to be allowed for when making decisions, need to be charged to the enterprise or organisation which is causing them. And this applies equally well to the social costs of redundancy and unemployment when transferring operations to countries with lower wages or fewer environmental safeguards."

It was Manfred Davidmann who twenty years ago demolished the then-current economic myths about 'Price Inflation' and 'Wage Inflation', and about inflation and unemployment.

In "**Inflation, Balance of Payments and Currency Exchange Rates**" (1981, 2006), Manfred Davidmann explores how national and international accounts and accounting reflect the quality of management in national and local government, reflect multinational operations such as devaluation pricing, profits maximisation, transfer pricing, importing from low-wage countries, transferring work to low-wage countries. And he reviews different ways of balancing income and expenditure, causes of inflation, and tax avoidance.

In this report Manfred Davidmann reviews a country's ways out of a payments crisis and details the consequences of increasing interest rates, greater borrowing, selling assets or printing more money.

To give just a few examples, he:

>Shows how rising interest rates follow from balance of payments deficits.

>Shows how interest rates determine share prices and thus the extent to which pension funds are in surplus or underfunded.

>Shows how inflation affects currency exchange rates, trade and competing abroad.

Clear and meaningful language is backed by easily understood illustrations. And easy-to-follow diagrams illustrate the relationships.

The two coefficients of inequality between different countries, which Manfred Davidmann put forward in 1981 in this inflation report, are objective and effective measures of inequality and differentials.

The first he called 'Inequality between Countries'. The second, namely 'Relative Inequality between Countries', is numerically the same as the ratio between the GNP/person of the countries being compared. These measures of inequality are now in general use.

The Worldwide Struggle for a Better Life

In 'Motivation Summary' (1982, 1998), Manfred Davidmann summarises different motivation theories, draws on his earlier work including evidence from the U.K. study, and utilises material used by him for lecturing to degree-level students and for training experienced middle and senior managers.

This chapter provides an objective, comprehensive and clear definition of 'motivation', of the factors which motivate and of what people are striving to achieve.

"Motivated behaviour is purposeful, directed towards some end" says Manfred Davidmann. "The driving force is need. The direction is towards perceived reward and away from perceived punishment."

And in the workplace one aims to achieve either job satisfaction or money rewards or both. "Motivation towards better performance depends on the satisfaction of needs for responsibility, achievement, recognition and growth."

One works to achieve that which one needs and which one does not have. "Attaining goals leads to feelings of self-respect, strength and confidence", and "persistent lack of rewards leads to a view of society as being hostile and unrewarding".

Manfred Davidmann's fundamental work on motivation, 'The Will to Work: What People Struggle to Achieve' (1981, 2006), includes a detailed step-by-step listing of what people are struggling to achieve, their needs and wants, their achievements and objectives. It is a unique analysis of the worldwide struggle for a better life at all levels of life and development, in all countries.

What we see in the working environment is each person, family or community struggling to advance at their own level of development.

Manfred Davidmann here clearly defines and describes motivation, its basis and 'motivating'.

252

Starting by considering motivation from the point of view of the employer (productivity, remuneration, job satisfaction), this leads to considering what people want and what they struggle to achieve.

A key part of this chapter is community orientated, including a detailed step-by-step listing of what people are struggling to achieve, their needs and wants, their achievements and objectives.

It is a unique analysis of the worldwide struggle for a better life at all levels of life and development, in all countries. What we see in the working environment is each person, family or community struggling to advance at their own level of development.

This progression shows underdeveloped and developed people as they are, human beings at different stages of an identical struggle for a better life against those who wish to profit from their condition.

And you can assess how far the country/community you are living in has advanced in this struggle for independence and a good life for all, or where you are yourself on this scale.

Highlights are Figure 1 (Motivation of Directors) and Figure 3 (People's Needs and Wants, Achievements and Objectives: The Struggle for Independence and a Good Life).

In "**Family, Sex and the Individual**" (1998, 2011), Manfred Davidmann exposes the causes of what seems to be a progressive breaking down of family life and of social strength.

Clearly described and defined is the role of the family under modern conditions, and the differences between the behaviour of human beings and that of the primitive animals from which human beings evolved. He illustrated the underlying basis of teamwork within the family, stating the various roles and responsibilities and functional relationships of its members for effective teamwork within the family.

He was the first to clearly describe and show, thirteen years ago, the effects of increasing life spans on the family, on its members and on their responsibilities.

We now live much longer and the time spent full-time at home looking after the family places women at a disadvantage when returning to work outside the family after the children have been brought up. So women need to be supported when returning to work.

And Manfred Davidmann showed that the family compensates women for the life-long effects of their contribution towards the upbringing of the children. It is the role of the spouse, of the husband, to continue to provide for the family. A life-long contribution from him which means she does not lose out for the rest of her life because she stayed at home to look after the children, the husband's input into the family balancing her input of bringing up the children and looking after the family's members.

This work also investigates the impact of casual sexual relations and its effects on individuals, family and community, on the social strength of individuals and communities.

And it examines and relates dominance and confrontation within the family to that in the working environment and considers oppression and exploitation within and outside the family.

Human rights are based on controlling primitive dominating behaviour, on concern, care and affection for our young and our families, for people and for our communities. Human rights express themselves in co-operation and teamwork between men and women to achieve a good life of high quality.

It is in democracies that a high standard of living has been achieved. In democracies people can struggle openly for a better life but we see that what has been gained has to be defended and extended.

This work is an unprecedented and comprehensive overview, states new insights, proves basic underlying causes.

The main report **What People are Struggling Against: How Society is Organised for Controlling and Exploiting People** (1998, 2002), brings together key conclusions from four studies undertaken by Manfred Davidmann to obtain a better understanding of why people have to struggle throughout their adult lives, in all countries and organisations, at all levels, to maintain and improve their standard of living and quality of life. We know what people are struggling to achieve and so this study was undertaken to explore why people have to struggle by looking at what they are struggling against.

This work looks at the way 'Economics' is being used to misinform and mislead the general public, and looks at the role and vested interests of experts. It describes how companies (corporations) accumulate their capital and reserves from moneys taken from customers and how people's massive savings are placed under the control of others. And shows how taxpayers' moneys are used in different ways to enlarge the profits of companies.

It discusses and illustrates the internal struggles taking place in political parties and all other organisations, for achieving greater democracy and against those wishing to overpower democratic processes of decision-making.

In '**Democracy, Socialism and Communism: The Worldwide Struggle for a Better Life**' (2008) Manfred Davidmann outlined the battlefield in these terms:

Participative (democratic) organisation rests on the population electing representatives, on the basis of each person having one vote. Representatives are responsible to, and accountable to, the population for putting into effect policies decided by the population.

What underlies participative organisation (democracy) is decision-making by the people at the level of the people.

What needs to be stressed is that in a participative (democratic) organisation policies are decided by a well-informed population at the level of the population and that policies then become binding on management or government. It was Manfred Davidmann who formulated, clearly stated and then published ('Style of Management and Leadership', 1981) his principle that the real political struggle was not between political 'left' and 'right', but was for participation in decision-making, for the right to make the decisions.

Representatives, governments or government officials do not have the authority or right to reduce or sign away the participative (democratic) rights of the electors, of the population.

The real struggle is not between political left and right, but is a struggle for participation, that is for the right of the population to be well-informed and to make the decisions which then become binding on management or government, as outlined by Manfred Davidmann in '**Multinational Summits and Agreements, Top-level Decision-making and Democracy**' (2002).

Brain, Mind and Group Minds. Mental Health and Corresponding Social Organisations, of Individuals, People and Communities.

In '**How the Human Brain Developed and How the Human Mind Works**' (1998, 2006), Manfred Davidmann explains how the human brain evolved and functions, how the human mind works, and how brain and mind interact. This fundamental work provides fascinating insights clearly expressed in meaningful language, including a much clearer appreciation of the different functions of the two halves of the brain, and of the different kinds of sleep and memory.

The work showed how brain and mind determine what people do and how they do it, what people aim to achieve and how in the struggle for a better life we adapt to the world in which we live.

It proved that images penetrate deeply into the ancient and primitive parts of the human brain and how certain images can be "brutalising society, seemingly legalising, making acceptable, inconsiderate and unfeeling behaviour towards other people."

Relating the functioning of the brain to behavior, this report showed how human behavior is affected by the primitive instincts of our reptilian ancestors. It seems that instinctive behavior has to be controlled, and is modified according to the environment in which we find ourselves, in every generation, and that the mammalian and human parts of the brain play a major part in this.

Manfred Davidmann considers that humane behavior is based on feelings of care and affection for the young and for the family, and then for other people and the community. From this emerges a sense of social responsibility: People matter and are important, and need to be treated well.

A key finding of Manfred Davidmann's report is that the right hemisphere of the human brain is able to communicate by using images with the brain's older and more primitive component organs which have no verbal skills. And this enables us to communicate intentionally (that is "consciously") with our autonomic nervous system and by visualizing control of body functions and to affect our body's immune system. Clinical trials have shown remarkable success in areas such as the treatment of cancer and heart disease.

The day-night-day sleep pattern, the "DEEP sleep"/"REM sleep" sequence, and how the different halves of the brain communicate by means of images with the older parts of the brain, are correlated and illustrated. Manfred Davidmann makes the point that the brain paralyzes the body to enable dreaming to take place, that dreaming performs an essential function, and he explains the role and meaning of dreams and dreaming.

Manfred Davidmann considers that humane behavior is based on feelings of care and affection for the young and for the family, and then for other people and the community. From this emerges a sense of social responsibility: People matter and are important, and need to be treated well.

As a result of the work in this report, there emerged a much clearer appreciation of what happens during the course of a night's sleep, and clear explanations of the role of dreaming and the meaning of dreams.

The report explores the functioning and role of the two halves of the human brain and the relationship between them. It is the right half which usually communicates with the primitive parts of the human brain and this is related to the functioning of the autonomic nervous system and the immune system.

When Manfred Davidmann first announced his Group Mind Theory in 1973, this theory and his concepts and terms such as 'group minds', were completely new and unheard of. The second edition was published in 1998 and made available on the internet in 1999.

His "human group minds and how they function", that is the Group Mind Science he originated, are now widely quoted and discussed, have sprouted a whole literature about group minds ranging from publications of scientific institutions and in reference books, to unscientific misleading look-alikes about human minds.

In 'The Human Group Mind and How It Works' (1973, 1978), Manfred Davidmann outlines, describes, uncovers and proves the subconscious existence and workings of group minds by the extraordinary way in which they affect and determine what individuals and communities do. This is shown to explain how human communities and society are organised and function, countrywide and worldwide, and consequent confrontations and struggles from dictatorship to democracy. We are here looking at what motivates and drives human beings, seeing how the mind shapes the way in which we live, suffer, struggle and achieve.

Included are comprehensive but concise reviews of mental health and mental illness. There are sections which discuss how conflict arises within the mind, and the mind theories of Freud and of Jung are reviewed.

Manfred Davidmann's Group Mind Science is proved by the way in which it explains and predicts not only the mental problems of individuals but also society's social problems.

It predicts and explains the way in which society is organised as well as human activities and organisation, explains dominance, co-operation, non-conformity and conflict as well as why people are struggling and what they are struggling against.

The subconscious existence and workings of group minds become apparent by the extraordinary way in which they affect and determine what individuals and communities do. The chapters of this book which deal with how we live and struggle, with the way our communities and societies are organised and function, describe how our minds shape our lives, communities and society, and uncover the workings of group minds.

Manfred Davidmann's Group Mind Science represents substantial beneficial healing powers. Following the work of Freud and Jung, it is regarded as scientifically proved, as meaningful, objective and practical, as applying worldwide to all human beings in all societies and cultures and at all stages of development.

Manfred Davidmann's Group Mind Science is based on deep knowledge and understanding of the real world, and proved by the way in which it explains and predicts human activities and organisation as well as the mental problems of individuals and society's social problems. Its insights enable us to solve such problems effectively.

The work about 'The Human Group Mind', on how human minds work and operate, on human group minds, consists of four consecutive parts, as follows:

'The Human Group Mind and How It Works' (1973, 1998)
The 'Group Mind' science is outlined and described. There are sections which discuss how conflict arises within the mind, mental health and illness, dominance, creativity and hearing voices.

Shows how our minds shape our lives, communities and society.

'Manipulated Communities and Populations' (1973, 1998)
The workings of group minds is shown to explain how human communities and society are organised and the consequent confrontations and struggles from dictatorship to democracy.

Discusses how mass media are forming and manipulating public opinions and illustrates how writers and artists have been sensing and expressing the underlying subconscious reality.

'Manipulated Individuals' (1973, 1998)
Shows how emotional unreasoning behaviour is being reinforced to make it easier to mislead and exploit.

Reviews available information on incidence and causes of psychosomatic illnesses.

'Freedom, Liberty and Good Life: Overcoming Corrupt Manipulations' (1973, 2001)
The Group Mind science of the way in which human minds work is proved by the way in which it explains and predicts human activities and organisation as well as mental problems of individuals and society's social problems. Its insights enable us to solve such problems effectively.

When individuals, communities and populations are manipulated, then behaviour is all-important. This report shows how we can overcome corrupt manipulations, how behaviour determines our standard of living and the quality of our lives, and describes the kind of behaviour and social organisation on which depend liberty, freedom and a good and secure life for all.

Government and Religion, Church and State

Manfred Davidmann's The God-given Human Rights, Social Laws and Social System (2003) is a comprehensive statement of the God-given human rights and obligations which underlie freedom, liberty, independence and well-being. They underlie and determine a good life of high quality. People at all stages of development are struggling to achieve these rights and benefits, all over the planet.

Directly relevant to today's social and economic problems, these rights and obligations determine the quality of life in areas such as social and economic security, social responsibility and accountability, ownership and decision-making, government and management, humane behaviour, teamwork and trustful cooperation.

> These human rights, these social rules and this social system, are the very foundation of the three main religions of Judaism, Christianity and Islam.

> Manfred Davidmann discovered that what these religions have in common is that in each case a ruling elite succeeded in bypassing or overturning the religion's essential God-given benevolent social provisions and human rights, in this way exposing their communities and whole populations to oppression and exploitation.

What Manfred Davidmann has done with his works on the Pentateuch and the Bible, on religion and church-state relations, is to expose and correct the misinterpretations and mistranslations of the past. His works are major breakthroughs, constituting essential information for understanding the meaning and significance of the Pentateuch and the Bible.

The Pentateuch records and details the Social Cause-and-Effect Relationship, a fundamental scientific law which is stated as such and which was discovered by Manfred Davidmann. In his **'Struggle for Freedom: The Social Cause-and-Effect Relationship'** (1978, 2002) he shows that this law states that the consequences of keeping or not keeping the social laws are inescapable, that what happens to one is in the end the inevitable result of one's own behavior. It is stated to enable people to benefit from knowing the effects of their behaviour.

Ignorance of these rules of behavior is no excuse and the relationship applies to all. History and social science confirm it, the prophets knew and understood it and predicted accordingly. Jesus confirmed it; the Koran records Prophet Mohammed repeatedly confirming the Pentateuch, referring to it both as a guide and as a warning.

Whole communities prosper or suffer as a consequence of their collective behavior. Manfred Davidmann says, "The consequences of our behavior cannot be avoided but we can change the course of events by changing our behavior."

He states "A new factor has entered the equation. It is now possible for the first time in the history of human beings on this planet for just one or only a few socially irresponsible persons to do something or to introduce changes which could destroy us all or else make this planet uninhabitable for human beings."

The Ten Commandments are so important and are so well known because it is behaviour in accordance with these laws which is the basis for people trusting each other and so for people co-operating and working well with each other. They are listed in '**Struggle for Freedom: The Social Cause-and-Effect Relationship**' (1978, 2002) both in biblical language and in plain English.

It is the Ten Commandments as a whole which underlie freedom, independence and strength to oppose and resist oppression. Wherever there is any spiritual and material freedom today it exists because people followed these laws (rules) of behaviour and it exists to the extent to which they do so. In other words, following the provisions of the law results in freedom and ensures it, ensures strength and security.

History shows that in the past the people have been betrayed again and again, by non-observant leaderships no matter whether right or left and by so-called orthodox or fundamentalist leaderships who weakened the application of the law so as to be able to oppress the people in order to exploit them. It was those who did not follow the law who in the past grasped power and then weakened and defeated the hope for achieving freedom and a good life for the people and thus in due course for all humanity.

It is equally certain that the same battle is being fought today and it is just as certain that on the one hand is the opportunity to gain freedom while on the other hand our defeat can only result in mankind rapidly destroying itself.

To free ourselves from mental conditioning and brainwashing we have to follow the Ten Commandments and apply the social laws and the social system of the Pentateuch.

In **'Democracy, Socialism and Communism: The Worldwide Struggle for a Better Life'** (2008), Manfred Davidmann exposes what people are struggling against, the secretive manipulations of bureaucracy, oppressors and exploiters.

He shows that underlying Judaism, Christianity and Islam are the same fundamental benevolent and egalitarian social laws and social system which also underlie Democracy, Socialism and Communism (See **'The God-given Human Rights, Social Laws and Social System'** (2003) above). He traces them to their origin and proves from contemporary written records that in each case the ruling and religious hierarchies (bureaucracies) soon bypassed or annulled the 'God-given' social laws and social system, replacing them with 'man-made', ruler- and hierarchy-serving obedience-demanding protest-silencing indoctrination.

It is these revisionist versions which are being taught and believed today and here we see clearly the causes of present controversies and conflicts between church and state, between beliefs and practice, in these religions.

This work also covers dominance and confrontation within the family and in the working environment, how men and women relate to each other, and the role of the family. The family is decisive in determining the quality of life; it is a source of strength and support in a time of need.

It shows how the media are being used for 'social engineering', a kind of brainwashing aimed at turning the struggle of the working population into 'self-defeating' directions, into 'scoring own goals'.

Manfred Davidmann's groundbreaking discoveries about Judaism, Christianity and Islam, published over twenty-five years, are acknowledged as major advances. And in his report "**Judaism, Christianity and Islam**" (2004), we see for the first time the complete sequence of consecutive events.

Manfred Davidmann has shown that underlying Judaism, Christianity and Islam are the Pentateuch's benevolent and egalitarian social laws and social system which include laws protecting the people by restraining the behaviour of their rulers. Those in positions of trust, responsibility or authority must not oppress people and the laws forbid personal gain from the misuse of wealth or position.

He not only proves the meaning and intent of Genesis, the first volume of the Pentateuch, but also exposes the mistranslations and political misrepresentations of the past. For example he established the meaning of the names of God which had been 'lost'.

Manfred Davidmann's work **'The Meaning of Genesis: Creation, Evolution and the Origin of Evil'** (2000) proves that there is no conflict or contradiction between Darwin's theory of evolution by natural selection and what is written in Genesis. Conflicts have arisen because some parts of Genesis have been mistranslated or misinterpreted.

The 'Creationism' hypothesis apparently assumes that the resulting erroneous text correctly states God's deeds. Following the publication of Manfred Davidmann's work, and of the publicity it generated, the 'Creationism' hypothesis was abandoned as untenable. But a similar hypothesis was then put forward called 'Intelligent Design' which apparently assumes that the same erroneous text could correctly state the deeds of some other supernatural being.

What Manfred Davidmann proves in **'The Meaning of Genesis: Creation, Evolution and the Origin of Evil'** (2000) is that Genesis clearly states the evolution from reptilian to mammalian instincts, feelings and behaviour and the evolution and behaviour of human beings from humanoids (animals resembling humans) through Homo erectus (early man) to Homo sapiens (human beings, ourselves).

For example, the allegory telling about Adam and Eve in the Garden of Eden describes the evolution of Homo sapiens (human beings, ourselves) from Homo erectus. Genesis records that childbirth became more difficult as a result of the increased brain size (evolution of neocortex) which enabled Homo sapiens to know the difference between good and evil and to choose between them. Also stated is the necessary division of work between the male and the female, as equals in different roles, in protecting and bringing up their children, and much more.

What Manfred Davidmann has done with his works on the Pentateuch and the Bible, on religion and church-state relations, is to expose and correct the misinterpretations and mistranslations of the past. His works are major breakthroughs, constituting essential information for understanding the meaning and significance of the Pentateuch and the Bible.

For example, in **"Meaning and Significance of the Names of God in Genesis"** (2000), Manfred Davidmann proved the meaning and significance of the different names of God which had been lost.

In **"Meaning and Intent of Genesis: Essential Notes on Hebrew Grammar,"** (2000) he stated the fundamental rules which were ignored at time of translation because required background knowledge was not available, with consequent mistranslations.

And in **"Bible Translations, Versions, Codes and Hidden Information in Bible and Talmud"** (2001), he showed how changes made in the past obscured the intended meaning.

In his book 'ISLAM: Basis - Past - Present - Future', (2003, 2010) Manfred Davidmann assembles, evaluates and objectively records the events of the formative years which shaped Islam. He enables one to understand how Islam came to be and its present beliefs and practices, conflicts and confrontations.

Knowing about Prophet Mohammed's struggle for recognition of his mission and message, is of vital importance if one wishes to understand what Mohammed taught and the Koran. Just what upset the elite so thoroughly and persistently that it caused him and his followers to be harshly opposed and actively persecuted?

The events and struggles which took place after Mohammed's death, and how the Koran and Islam came to be, shaped Muslim belief and practice, formed Sunnism and Shiism, underlie today's conflicts and confrontations within Islam.

Cooperatives and Cooperation

When people are exploited and oppressed they co-operate with each other to escape from poverty, to overcome exploitation and oppression. As do people wishing to improve working conditions and the quality of their lives. They get together and form co-operatives.

Manfred Davidmann's book 'Co-operatives and Co-operation: Causes of Failure, Guidelines for Success' (1973-2006, 2011) is based on and includes a series of eight studies of co-operatives and mutual societies which were undertaken to determine causes of failure and reasons for success, to see how these enterprises were controlled and managed, to learn from their mistakes, to understand why members of established co-ops are dissatisfied with what they are getting from their co-ops.

As a matter of principle, all profits (surplus) made by a co-operative or mutual society belongs to its members as individuals. Any profit which is retained and added to reserves is the total of amounts which in effect were deducted from the profit share of each individual member.

Manfred Davidmann showed with these case studies that, for example, co-ops and mutual societies retain much of the profits and that their members then cease to be entitled to them.

    Component Case Studies

        Mutual Societies
            Trustee Savings Bank
            Credit Unions
            Building Societies

Consumer Co-ops
Co-operative Retail Services Ltd
Co-operative Wholesale Society Ltd
The Co-operative Bank PLC
Co-operative Insurance Society Ltd

Producer (Worker) Co-ops
John Lewis Partnership plc
Mondragon Co-operatives
Kibbutzim (Plural of 'kibbutz')

Manfred Davidmann

ISLAM: Basis – Past – Present- Future

Knowing about Prophet Mohammed's struggle for recognition of his mission and message, is of vital importance if one wishes to understand what Mohammed taught and the Koran. Just what upset the elite so thoroughly and persistently that it caused him and his followers to be harshly opposed and actively persecuted?

The events and struggles which took place after Mohammed's death, and how the Koran and Islam came to be, shaped Muslim belief and practice, formed Sunnism and Shiism, underlie today's conflicts and confrontations within Islam.

In this book Manfred Davidmann assembles, evaluates and objectively records the events of the formative years which shaped Islam. He enables one to understand how Islam came to be and its present beliefs and practices, conflicts and confrontations. Comprehensiveness of information, and depth of analysis, can be judged by the book's chapter headings:

Prophet Mohammed's Struggle for a Better Life for All

Text, Language, Dialect and Interpretation of the Koran

The Divine Right to Rule

Compiling the Koran: Hadiths (Traditions) State the Underlying Reality

Caliph Uthman's Rearrangement of the 'as revealed' Koran's Chapters

Prophet Mohammed's Word of Allah and the Voice of the Ruling Elite

Muslims and Jews

Church and State, Government and Religion

    Judaism, Christianity and Islam

    Religion, Government and Education

The book, and the earlier individual research reports which are included in it, contains not only Manfred Davidmann's clear and factual compilations about what actually happened after Mohammed's death, but also his comprehensive and detailed findings, definitions and conclusions about the '**Text, Language, Dialect and Interpretation of the Koran**' (2003), about how the Koran was compiled and about its contents. Published 2003, guided to some extent by some of the Koran's 'abbreviated letters'.

Manfred Davidmann

God and People:
The Social Laws and Social System Underlying
Judaism, Christianity, Islam and Democracy

This book is a collection of works by Manfred Davidmann about the God-given human rights, social laws and social system, and about the worldwide struggle to achieve them, to achieve freedom, liberty, independence and a good and secure life, here and now in this life.

Manfred Davidmann not only proves the meaning and intent of Genesis, the first volume of the Pentateuch, but also exposes the mistranslations and political misrepresentations of the past. For example he establishes the meaning of the names of God which 'had been lost'.

Clearly described and defined is the role of the family under modern conditions, and the differences between the behaviour of human beings and that of the primitive animals from which human beings evolved.

The main chapter headings are:

> The Real World in which We Live
>
> The God-given Human Rights, Social Laws and Social System
>
> Struggle for Freedom, Liberty and Independence: The Social Cause-and-Effect Relationship
>
> Family and Community: Family, Sex and the Individual
>
> The Meaning of Genesis

Manfred Davidmann is an internationally well-known and respected scientist and consultant, and author of a number of books and reports which have had considerable impact. His work usually breaks new ground and opens up new understanding and is written in meaningful and easily understood language. Outstanding is that his work is generally accepted as factual, objective and unbiased.

Manfred Davidmann

THE HUMAN MIND AND HOW IT WORKS:
Group Minds in Action: How the Human Group Mind Shapes the Quality of Our Life and Living

Manfred Davidmann shows how the human brain evolved and functions, how the human mind works, and how brain and mind interact. This fundamental work provides fascinating insights clearly expressed in meaningful language, shows how brain and mind determine what people do and how they do it, what people aim to achieve and how in the struggle for a better life we adapt to the world in which we live.

The chapters of this book which deal with how our communities and societies are organised and function, describe how our group minds shape our lives, communities and society, explain the consequent confrontations and struggles from dictatorship to democracy.

Relating the functioning of the brain to behaviour, this work shows how human behavior is affected by the primitive instincts of our reptilian ancestors. There are sections which discuss how conflict arises within the mind, mental health and illness, dominance, creativity and hearing voices.

Comprehensiveness of information, and depth of analysis, can be judged by the book's chapter headings:

> The Human Brain and the Human Mind
> > How the Human Brain Developed and How the Human Mind Works
>
> The Human Group Mind
> > The Human Group Mind and How It Works
> > Manipulated Communities and Populations
> > Manipulated Individuals
> > Freedom, Liberty and Good Life: Overcoming Corrupt Manipulations
>
> What People Struggle to Achieve
> > Motivation Summary
> > What People are Struggling Against: How Society is Organised for Controlling and Exploiting People
> > The Will to Work: What People Struggle to Achieve
>
> Worldwide Struggle
> > Democracy, Socialism and Communism: The Worldwide Struggle for a Better Life

Manfred Davidmann

Cooperatives and Cooperation:
Causes of Failure, Guidelines for Success

When people are exploited and oppressed they cooperate with each other to escape from poverty, to overcome exploitation and oppression. As do people wishing to improve working conditions and the quality of their lives. They get together and form cooperatives.

Different forms of cooperatives tackle different kinds of problems. What they have in common is that they serve their members and the community, aiming to improve the quality of life for their members.

As a matter of principle, all profit (surplus) made by a cooperative or mutual society belongs to its members as individuals. Any profit which is retained and added to reserves is the total of amounts which in effect were deducted from the profit share of each individual member.

This book is based on a series of eight studies of cooperatives and mutual societies which were undertaken to determine causes of failure and reasons for success, to see how these enterprises were controlled and managed, to learn from their mistakes.

Its conclusions and recommendations are relevant and cover fundamental and practical problems of coops and mutual societies, of members, of direction, management and control.

Manfred Davidmann showed with these case studies that, for example, coops and mutual societies retain much of the profits and that their members then cease to be entitled to them.

> Component Case Studies
>> Mutual Societies
>>> Trustee Savings Bank
>>> Credit Unions
>>> Building Societies
>> Consumer Coops
>>> Cooperative Retail Services Ltd
>>> Cooperative Wholesale Society Ltd
>>>> The Cooperative Bank PLC
>>>> Cooperative Insurance Society Ltd
>> Producer (Worker) Coops
>>> John Lewis Partnership plc
>>> Mondragon Cooperatives
>>> Kibbutzim (Plural of 'kibbutz')

Manfred Davidmann

Management and Leadership:
Local, National, Multinational (Global),
Principles and Practice

The term 'Participation', meaning by this 'participation in decision-making', was first coined, and defined, by Manfred Davidmann when he published his analysis and recommendations about the style of management. His works on style of management and on participation in decision-making in management, leadership and government, are widely known, studied and applied.

Manfred Davidmann brings to his tasks a rare combination of practical experience, knowledge and understanding backed by years spent training middle and top-level managers. Expert knowledge is expressed in clear and meaningful language and easy-to-follow diagrams illustrate the relationships.

The main chapter headings are:

Style of Management and Leadership

Motivation

Directing and Managing Change

Organising

Work and Pay

Inflation, Balance of Payments and Currency Exchange Rates

Using Words to Communicate Effectively

How local and national governments are managing our affairs is of crucial importance to every citizen. Government has to make ends meet, has to bring about a rising standard of secure living, social security and an increasing quality of life for its citizens.

"There can be ups and downs but", says Manfred Davidmann, "failure to make ends meet is just as directly and surely the result of bad leadership and management as it is in any commercial enterprise."

Manfred Davidmann reviews ways of balancing income and expenditure, causes of inflation, and tax avoidance, reviews ways out of a payments crisis and details the consequences of increasing interest rates, greater borrowing, selling assets or printing more money.

One works to achieve that which one needs and which one does not have. "Attaining goals leads to feelings of self-respect, strength and confidence", and "persistent lack of rewards leads to a view of society as being hostile and unrewarding".

Manfred Davidmann

The Real World in Which We Live:
The Social Rules and Social System under Which We Suffer, Struggle, Survive and Prosper

This community orientated book brings together studies undertaken by Manfred Davidmann to obtain a better understanding of why people have to struggle throughout their adult lives, in all countries and organisations, at all levels, to maintain and improve their standard of living and quality of life. Manfred Davidmann says: "We know what people are struggling to achieve and so these studies explore why people have to struggle by looking at what they are   struggling against".

He discusses and illustrates the internal struggles taking place in political parties and all other organisations for achieving greater democracy and against those wishing to overpower democratic processes of decision-making.

And Manfred Davidmann here clearly defines and describes motivation, its basis and 'motivating'. He includes a detailed step-by-step listing of what people are struggling to achieve, their needs and wants, their achievements and objectives.

The depth of his analysis can be judged by the main chapter headings:

Ownership and Limited Liability

Community and Public Ownership

Ownership and Deciding Policy: Companies, Shareholders, Directors and Community

Multinational Summits and Agreements, Top-level Decision-making and Democracy

Exporting and Importing of Employment and Unemployment

Transfer Pricing and Taxation

Creating, Patenting and Marketing of New Forms of Life

What People are Struggling Against: How Society is Organised for Controlling and Exploiting People

Democracy Under Attack: Top-level Leadership and Decision-making

Taxing the Population for Private Profit

Corrupted Economics and Misguided (Misleading) Experts

Using Words to Communicate Effectively

The Will to Work: What People Struggle to Achieve

Manfred Davidmann says: "Decision-taking by leaderships has to be replaced by decision-making at the level of the people. The real struggle is not between political left and right, but is a struggle for participation (the right to make decisions)".

Manfred Davidmann

Messianic Struggle:
The Worldwide Struggle for a Good and Secure Life for All, Here and Now

Manfred Davidmann's fundamental works about management principles and leadership, community economics and needs, profit motivation and social costs, and participation in decision-making at all levels are major advances in human knowledge and key findings.

The author exposes humanity's hidden core confrontations, the source of oppression and enslavement, the role of biblical prophets and their warnings, how religious teachings were distorted, and he states the scientific benevolent social laws of behaviour and community organisation.

Following Manfred Davidmann's publications and recommendations, people are struggling now worldwide for a better life, for the right to make the decisions, for social security, for equality, freedom and independence, for socially responsible and humane behaviour, and the survival of humanity on this planet.

Comprehensiveness of information, and depth of analysis, can be judged by the book's chapter headings:

Social Responsibility, Profits and Social Accountability. Incidents, Disasters and Catastrophes. The Worldwide Struggle for Social Accountability. Community Aims and Community Leadership.

Work and Pay, Incomes and Differentials: Employer, Employee and Community

The Right to Strike

Reorganising the National Health Service: An Evaluation of the Griffiths Report

Community Economics: Principles

Social Responsibility and Accountability: Summary

The World at War! Multinational (Global) Operations, and Government Of, By, and For the People: Democracy Under Attack: The Struggle for the Right to take the Decisions, and for Social Accountability

The choice is yours: Unemployment, Charitable Social Security and Today's Religious Teachings or High Standard of Living, Satisfying Work and a Good Life, as God-given rights

Creationism and Intelligent Design, Evolution, Education or Indoctrination

The Way Ahead: Policies for a Better Future

The Global (Worldwide) Struggle for a Better Life and The Root of all Evil, the Source of All Good, and the Messianic Struggle

Faith and Trust in God, No Matter by What Name called